Children of 2020
Creating a Better Tomorrow

Valora Washington and JD Andrews, editors

Council for Professional Recognition
Washington, DC

National Association for the Education of Young Children
Washington, DC

Photo Credits

Front cover photos. Copyright © by: CAYL Institute (Community Advocates for Young Learners), Cambridge, Massachusetts (top row, second photo from right, and bottom row, middle photo); Harry Cutting Photography (top row, far left photo, center photo, and far right photo); Ellen B. Senisi (bottom row, far left and far right photos, and at the bottom, the large photo of adults); and Barbara Willer (top row, second photo from left).

Back cover photo. Copyright © by CAYL Institute.

Inside pages. Copyright © by: CAYL Institute (pages 15, 26, 29, 33, 39, 42, 45, 49, 50, 58, 65, 70, 75, 77, 87, 99, 100, 108, 112, 117, 126, 134, 139, and 150); Isabel Rios Leonard at Centro de Referencia Latinoamericano para la Educación Preescolar (pages 92 and 93); iStockphoto.com (pages 98, 101, and 161); Jonathan Meyers of JAM Photography (page 11); pics.am (page 8); Rosemount Center, Washington, DC (page 120); Julie Sarama and Douglas H. Clements (pages 82, 83, and 84); Ellen B. Senisi (page 1); World Bank Children's Center (page 22).

Children of 2020: Creating a Better Tomorrow

Copyright © 2010 by the Council for Professional Recognition, Washington, DC
All rights reserved. Printed in the United States of America.

Published by:

Council for Professional Recognition
2460 16th Street NW, Washington, DC 20009-3547

202-265-9090 | 800-424-4310 | www.cdacouncil.org

Kathy Ruby, *Publications Manager*

Marilyn M. Smith, *Program Associate*

Copublisher:

National Association for the Education of Young Children
1313 L Street NW, Suite 500, Washington, DC 20005-4101

202-232-8777 | 800-424-2460 | www.naeyc.org

Carol Copple, *Director of Publications and Initiatives in Educational Practice*

First printing: April 2010

Library of Congress Control Number: 2010926401

ISBN: 978-0-9820805-4-2

Council Item #2020
NAEYC Item #306

About the Editors

Valora Washington and JD Andrews work to create change in the crossroads of three intersecting fields: leadership development, organizational development, and early care and education. Dozens of emergent leaders have participated in fellowships that they have created, independently and collaboratively. Both are natives of the Midwest (Ohio and Indiana), and each holds a degree from Indiana University.

Valora Washington, PhD

Valora Washington is president of the Board of the Council for Professional Recognition and president of the CAYL Institute in Cambridge, Massachusetts. She directs several leadership programs in the field of early care and education. Also, she has cocreated several institutions, such as Michigan's Children, a statewide advocacy group, and the Early Childhood Funders Collaborative. She has served on numerous boards and commissions, including roles as co-chair of the Massachusetts Governor's School Readiness Commission, board chair for Voices for America's Children, secretary of the National Association for the Education of Young Children (NAEYC), and cochair of the National Head Start Association Commission on 2010. Valora is co-author or co-editor of over 50 publications, including *Children of 2010, Ready or Not: Early Care and Education Faces New Challenges*, and *Keeping the Promise: A Study of the Massachusetts Child Care Voucher System.*

vwashington@cayl.org

www.cayl.org

JD Andrews, PhD

JD Andrews is chairman of the Council for Professional Recognition, which he helped establish in 1985. The council administers the Child Development Associate (CDA) National Credential Program and publishes materials to support professional-development activities. He is also recognized for his outstanding leadership at the National Association for the Education of Young Children (1973–1999), where he helped a small, volunteer-supported, annual meeting become one of the largest education conferences in the nation. During his tenure, NAEYC grew to 100,000 members from 20,000. A visionary who identifies paths not obvious to others, JD has leadership roles with numerous boards and committees of corporations and organizations. Over many decades, he has been actively involved in the civil rights movement, working primarily in the South, and was a major participant in planning the 1963 March on Washington.

jdandrews@cdacouncil.org

www.cdacouncil.org

Dedication

We dedicate this volume in honor of the 25th anniversary of the Council
for Professional Recognition. The Council's premier program,
the Child Development Associate credential, has been
awarded to over 250,000 early care and education
staff since 1975.

Children of 2020 explores the potential and opportunities for the next ten years
and invites readers to advance the field through "smart improvisation."
The importance of excellence, equity, and leadership in our multicultural
democracy is emphasized. National leaders present up-to date analyses of
progress and challenges in 22 topic areas related to the vision, knowledge base,
and strategies for young children. Useful "improv workshops" throughout
the book offer pointers and discussion questions to encourage readers to
take personal responsibility and action on behalf of the children of 2020.
This book is recommended for readers who want to update their knowledge
base and explore successful new strategies in many topic areas
from eminent thought leaders in the field.

CONTENTS

Act II: Knowledge — Information to Guide Future Practices

Act III: Strategies — Facilitating Outcomes for the Children of 2020

Act IV: Denouement — Taking Personal Responsibility for the Children of 2020

Acknowledgments

We, the co-editors of *Children of 2010*, created this sequel, *Children of 2020*, because throughout the past decade, we continued to hear about the multiple ways readers used the original book published by NAEYC in 1998. As we approached the year 2010 and evaluated the content of *Children of 2010* alongside the current state of our nation's children, we knew a follow-up volume was in order. The prediction of the era of plurality in our nation by 2010 is indeed a reality, but many challenges remain; our nation is far from assuring equity and quality to all children in key areas, including education, health care, and community services. *Children of 2020* is recognition that the work for equity and quality in early care and education must continue, and in fact, must adapt to a 21st century context.

In preparing this sequel to *Children of 2010*, we first and foremost express appreciation to the authors. We asked them to synthesize their most current information and forward-looking thoughts about what we all must do now to create a better tomorrow for the children of 2020. Any doubts we had about exploring the unknown future were quickly eliminated by the eager response of the invited authors. They enthusiastically accepted our challenge to update our vision, knowledge base, and strategies, as well as to create a volume of hope and constructive ideas to guide our collective leadership. We thank the authors for recognizing that creating a better tomorrow depends on the actions we take today. In this vein, we specifically acknowledge the family of Asa Hilliard, who graciously worked with us to include excerpts from one of the last essays he wrote before his untimely death.

Many people shared and supported our dream to focus on the children of 2020. Among these we recognize, with gratitude, Jim Kendrick, who helped conceptualize both *Children of 2010* and *Children of 2020*; Carol Copple, an expert editor and friend from the National Association for the Education of Young Children; and Ron Silverman, our gifted copy editor.

Several staff members from the Council for Professional Recognition played key roles in the production of the book. We acknowledge Kathy Ruby for design and production, Myra Hailesalassie for coordination and communication among the authors, and Karolina Jasinska and Walker Lambert for their expert research.

Valora's organization, The CAYL Institute (Community Advocates for Young Learners) of Cambridge, Massachusetts, is a significant and valuable partner in this project. Many of the photos in this volume come from CAYL's work with early care and education leaders and programs, including elementary school principals. Winnie Hagan is the primary photographer. Evelyn Nellum offered helpful ideas about the design. Jessica D'Amico provided essential office support, and the teamwork of Marie Enochty, Jordan Faigan, Brenda Gadson, and Jennifer Trapp enabled Valora to give the time needed to work on this book. Finally, support from the Barr Foundation, the Nellie Mae Educational Foundation, and the Schott Foundation for Public Education played vital roles.

And most of all, we thank Marilyn M. Smith of the executive staff of the Council for Professional Recognition. Given her incredible work ethic, her role in both *Children of 2010* and *Children of 2020* cannot be overstated. A joy to work with, Marilyn offers unparalleled insight and wisdom drawn from her deep knowledge of the field and its leaders; her ability to focus on big concepts while giving careful attention to details; and her commitment to young children as well as to the people who work with children in early care and education settings.

To you the reader: our wish is that you gain new information, ideas, insights, and skills from the material you are about to read. We would enjoy hearing your thoughts about this work.

Sincerely,

Valora Washington and JD Andrews, co-editors

Introduction

Creating tomorrow by what you do today

We, early care and education professionals, are enablers of the American Dream. Our contributions to the lives of young children are increasingly important to the future of democracy in the United States for three reasons:

- We are typically children's first out-of-home educators — the first "social system" to identify children's strengths and potential as contributors to our "common wealth." Quality care and development during the early years is the base on which all subsequent education reform must rest.

- Our programs are often the first place where children become keenly aware of and experience interactions with people from many different cultures, languages, religions, and family backgrounds. How we handle this privilege is important in our rapidly diversifying nation.

- The process and daily routines of early care and education lays a foundation for children's emergent ideas of freedom and democracy: how and whether children are provided choices, are listened to, and are supported in our environments confirms for each child his or her own value.

There is no doubt: we enable the American Dream. For these reasons, and many others, our vision, knowledge, and strategies for working with young children and their families must be clear, purposeful, and aligned.

Our nation is undergoing an astounding transition to an economy where knowledge is at the core and competition is global. Change is inevitable, and the education of our young must keep pace with these changes. In a global economy, inequity weakens our national potential and shackles the individual at risk of being shut out from the American Dream. Given the increasingly global economic and geopolitical interdependencies in which our children will live, healthy early development for every child is a legacy that our children — and we as a society and democracy — desperately need.

The research is clear: we create tomorrow by what we do today.

Early care and education enables the American Dream

There are many perspectives about the American Dream, but at the core is the conviction that all of us — including our children — have an inalienable right to opportunity: learn and develop, gain a solid education, work diligently in school and career, achieve, and pursue a happy and fulfilling life. For many, this encompasses a promise of our children "moving up," advancing beyond the attainment of parents and grandparents. It is a bold vision that promises opportunity to all regardless of race, class, or income.

The audacity of the American Dream has been a cohesive force that has united our nation, inspired achievement in the face of great obstacles, and radiated hope throughout the world. Yet, for our shared vision to be viable in the 21st century, we must acknowledge and accommodate significant change. In 1998, we wrote: "What is unique about the 21st century is that, eventually, no single racial or ethnic group will constitute a majority of the U.S. population. This means that democracy will require an unprecedented level of cooperation, communication, and teamwork among people who are different."[1] In 2010, we further acknowledge that the future of democracy depends on our ability to make the dream accessible to all, regardless of different backgrounds and unique needs.

We in the field of early care and education, working with others, must take action if we are to transform the American Dream into a vibrant reality that enables democracy to flourish in a remarkably diverse nation. Too often, the reality has fallen painfully short of the promise. The dreams for millions of children in the United States are diminished because of gaps in access to a nurturing environment, quality education, health care, and community services. In a most un-American way, the shortfalls in access to opportunity disproportionately hurt the country's historic minorities, negating the basic premise of the United States that all of us are equal.

The American Dream

The American Dream is a national ethos of the United States of America in which democratic ideals are perceived as a promise of prosperity for its people. In the American Dream, first expressed by James Truslow Adams in 1931, citizens of every rank feel that they can achieve a "better, richer, and happier life." The idea of the American Dream is rooted in the second sentence of the Declaration of Independence which states that "all men are created equal" and that they have "certain inalienable Rights" including "Life, Liberty and the pursuit of Happiness."

The "American Dream" has been credited with helping to build a cohesive American experience but has also been blamed for overinflated expectations. The presence of the American Dream has not historically helped the majority of minority race and lower class American citizens to gain a greater degree of social equality and influence. Instead, the American wealth structure has often been observed to sustain class differences in which well-positioned groups continue to be advantaged. . . .

The meaning of the "American Dream" has evolved over the course of American history. While historically traced to the New World mystique — the availability of land and the continuing American expansion — the ethos today simply indicates the ability, through participation in the resonant society and culture of the United States, to bring prosperity to oneself.

America has been viewed . . . as a land in which one's prospects in life are defined by one's talents and energy rather than by one's family wealth or political connections.

According to the dream, this includes the opportunity for one's children to grow up and receive an American education and its consequent career opportunities. It is the opportunity to make individual choices without the restrictions of class, caste, religion, race, or ethnic group.

Abridged from *Wikipedia*
en.wikipedia.org/wiki/American_dream
Accessed February 16, 2010

From 2010 to 2020

This book is a follow up to *Children of 2010,* which was developed in 1998 and published by the National Association for the Education of Young Children. *Children of 2010* was a means for thinking collaboratively and for defining a framework that would promote a better life for children. Demographic changes were then foreseeable, and we pointed out that by 2010, children of color would represent the majority of young people in such populous states as California, Florida, New York, and Texas. At the time, Los Angeles alone had over 100 ethnic groups, and residents spoke 70 languages. The book's focus was on making democracy and the American Dream work for an era of plurality in which, ultimately, no single group would constitute a majority of the U.S. population.

Children of 2010 was based on a series of dialogues conducted by a small group of national leaders who were working to create a better future for children, youth, and families. It advanced the idea of diversity and the idea of civic engagement to promote better outcomes for all children by addressing strategic issues: demographic forecasts, trends in populations and languages, the media, movements to change society, and visions for children and for the country as a whole.

Whereas *Children of 2010* was a call for vision and dialog, this book, *Children of 2020,* is a call to action. The focus of our efforts is on children from birth through age 8 years. We know that these are the formative years, the developmental foundation for lifelong learning, the first steps to future opportunities, and the emerging steps of each individual dream.

Shifting the Paradigm

Learning begins at birth, if not before, and the quality of the developmental environment matters greatly. Indeed, our nation cannot realize its commitment to the American Dream unless education becomes a civil right — and unless we dramatically improve outcomes for all children

---

The Urgency of Shifting Demographics

Breaking through resistance and creating strategies that better equip teachers, home visitors, and other human-service professionals to commit to work from a culturally informed perspective is difficult because it requires adults to challenge their own values and beliefs. Yet, there is an urgent need for progress when considering the shifting demographics of our country. Unspoken beliefs that undermine or disrespect the cultural values and beliefs that children and families bring into our programs can impact parental engagement and a child's developing self-concept because adults tend to act on what they believe.

For example, teachers who believe that all children must learn English, even at the expense of losing their home language, may be less likely to truly embrace and value implementing practices that involve utilizing home-language expressions as a part of interacting regularly with children and their parents. Some go so far as to reject bilingualism for nonnative English-speaking children even as they seek bilingual learning experiences for their own children.

Tammy Mann,
From Chapter 9

---

during their early years. The American Dream for all children will require a paradigm shift from student remediation to child development. Now, many of our public efforts and budgets are targeted to fixing problems after they occur. The public tends to focus on pupil outcomes in the later years — such as high school graduation rates, academic progression, readiness for postsecondary education, and dropout rates among specific population groupings. This focus endures although research has repeatedly revealed that it is more cost effective and less damaging to children to provide quality care and learning during the early years rather than pay for remediation during later years.

We believe that a paradigm shift is possible — that we as a nation can provide healthy environments for young children, rather than spend the great sums of money we do now for repetition of grades, health care for preventable ailments, juvenile-justice programs, and unemployable youth with limited education and skills.

Millions of solutions exist

Children of 2020 challenges you as readers to take action to change the paradigm. Helping children start and stay on a successful trajectory from an early age will enable the later years to be ones of educational and personal achievement, rather than remediation, catch-up, and problem-solving.

Children of 2020 has been developed from the perspective of the early care and education field in the United States, and much of the book is devoted to articles by some of the field's most eminent thought leaders. Yet the overall content is relevant to parents, personnel in allied professions such as health and social services, civic leaders, and business people as well. Our goals are to inspire you to think about your *vision* for children and families, to expand your *knowledge* about the research underlying our professional practice, and to encourage you to adapt new *strategies* that make you more effective in your own program or community.

As this book is being written, the United States is in the midst of game-changing economic challenges that limit the financial investment that localities, states, and the federal government believe they can devote to the young. We assert, however, that quality care and education are too important to wait for a "big bang" of new spending or sweeping initiatives. Moreover, there is no single big solution that we're trying to promote. Rather, our goal is more ambitious, more difficult, and hopefully much more enduring: asking and encouraging you to recommit to act on millions of little solutions, appropriate ones for each child, each program, and each community. Overall, this is a matter of serving all young children better by strengthening care, education, and development; working smarter and more collaboratively; improving quality; and focusing the entire community and its resources to move toward better outcomes for every child.

Children of 2020 is written to support you to lead breakthrough improvements as a result of increased knowledge about research and strategies that could be applied to your situation. In addition, although public will seems to be mounting, we must step up our collective action to turn public will into the willpower that increased and sustainable budgets represent. Establishing a publicly acknowledged commitment to each child's foundational years is a breakthrough as significant to the 21st century as putting a person on the moon was for the 20th century.

Terms We Use

Consistent with analysis by Stacie Goffin and Valora Washington, the editors of *Children of 2020* use the term "early care and education" (ECE) to refer to those programs that directly seek to support and enhance children's early development and learning, regardless of the program's sponsorship. We view the term as inclusive, encompassing early care and education as well as the related work performed by colleagues in social services and physical and mental health.

You, the reader, will notice that contributors to this volume use many terms to describe the early care and education field, reflecting what Goffin and Washington describe as the field's challenges around its purpose, identity, and responsibilities. It is the editors' hope that, by 2020, there will be greater consensus within the field — a consensus that will promote better outcomes for children as well as clearer communication and collaboration among us.

Progress and possibilities

Significant advances in early care and education over the past decade give us hope and confidence about achieving much better outcomes for children in the future. Clearer visions about diversity, new knowledge, and effective program strategies have greatly advanced the field of early care and education. Remarkable progress has been made despite the decade's painful events, which included terrorist attacks, wars, and an uncertain economy. Here is a brief look at some of our accomplishments:[2]

- Cultural diversity and demographic change evolved from a topic of dialogue in 1998 to a fact of life in 2010. Today diversity is more visible among professionals, school administrators, and other leaders; children typically have much greater access to positive, diverse images and role models through the media and educational materials. Certainly this trend should and will continue, as most people realize, if not accept, that diversity as mainstream.

- National recognition has grown for the contribution of early learning to children's school and lifelong success. This is partly because groundbreaking, well-publicized research has expanded our knowledge about how young children develop and learn.

- More public schools are recognizing the importance of the early years and the need for a continuum of care and education from birth through the elementary school years.

- Enrollment in early learning programs has increased dramatically, in part because of the acknowledgement that high-quality early learning environments are instrumental in helping to reduce academic achievement gaps.

- More services are available to support earlier identification of special needs and provide appropriate follow-up.

- The importance of professional development in advancing the field and supporting child development is gaining attention. Many in our profession have made significant progress in getting additional training, credentials, and knowledge. There have been documented improvements in the quality of programs available to young children, though much remains to be done. Much of the advancement has come as a result of voluntary national standards, state content and program standards, professional-development systems, and state financial incentives.

- Promising strategies to improve quality and outcomes are being introduced at a rapid pace, as governors and state legislatures have made publicly funded prekindergarten a reality in 38 states and Washington, DC.

- Economic analysis has demonstrated that early learning programs are wise investments that help individuals and ultimately save taxpayers money. This fact has become a powerful advocacy tool.

- Business and policy leaders increasingly embrace the importance of high-quality programs to develop future generations of healthy, curious, achieving children; to expand the availability of future human capital; and to advance global competitiveness.

While these advancements are significant, we have much to do if, in 2020, we want to celebrate the attainment of quality early care and education as a civil right for all children. Imagine looking into the eyes of those future children, and think of all that we need to change as preparation during the next 10 years — while hopefully improving life for the children we nurture in the intervening years.

Action for 2020

We hope this book inspires you to action, recognizing that a paradigm shift ultimately involves the entire community: parents as well as professionals in child care, health, public schools, and other fields, not just early care and education programs. Indeed, there is an urgent need for broader understanding of the comprehensive nature of the support required for young children, to complement the current emphasis on academic readiness. An action agenda must encompass work resulting in deeper public recognition of ideas such as:

- The remarkable learning potential of infants and toddlers.

- The value of play in child development and learning.

- Outdoor activities to increase socialization and learning.

- Family culture as a dimension of success in school settings.

- Racial identity as a factor in development.

- The importance of social-emotional development.

- The imperative to invest in adult learning, collaboration, and learning communities.

Many promising innovations already exist in these important areas, and *Children of 2020* presents some of the most exciting of these: the growth of state prekindergarten programs, initiatives to coordinate or integrate learning from age 3 through grade 3, research about dual-language learners, findings about the remarkable mathematical abilities of toddlers, the importance of culturally affirmative learning environments, and cooperation among professionals within communities.

Each of us must realize that it is within our power to make a difference for children by

Why 2020?

Children from every year are important, of course, but we have focused on the children of 2020 for this book. This is an acknowledgement that there is much to do to make our communities, early care, and education as they ought to be for all of our children. It also emphasizes the fact that the trend toward ethnic and racial diversity will continue in the future.

We envision that many, many changes must take place over the coming years, leading to the long-term goal of helping all children have access to the American Dream. Along the journey to 2020, we will do everything possible to improve the quality of opportunity of children in years present.

challenging our pet assumptions, learning more, renewing our vision and commitment, and implementing needed change in cooperation with our colleagues. You have the power to develop a unique vision for 2020, achieve quality improvements, and build community commitment.

We do not underestimate the difficulty of bringing about change — that's why we continue to emphasize the importance of collegial dialog, learning communities, collaborative planning, and collective action. We encourage adaptive leadership as both a skill and a point of view.[3]

The articles in this book demonstrate that professionals in many, many communities are already taking the initiative to improve outcomes now and in the future. We are asking you, the reader, to reflect on their experiences and consider adaptations that are suitable for you.

Together we can do it. Together, because of what we do today, we can create the tomorrow we envision.

> ### *Smart Improv*
>
> *Improv* is improvisation, where actors make up the script. Educators do it all the time to meet the unique needs of individual children.
>
> We emphasize improv in this book because real progress will require all of us to break with tradition — to discard the old scripts that have fallen short of achieving quality outcomes for our children.
>
> We have combined improv with *smart*, because we are advocating an approach to innovation based on research, validated innovation, collaboration, consultation, and professional assistance.
>
> *Smart improv* is an action-oriented approach to tailoring better policies, programs, and daily practices to serve children — one community at a time and one child at a time.
>
> Smart improv means we can take the initiative now, as individuals and communities.

An Improv in Four Acts

Children of 2020 has an action-oriented focus. It asks you readers to act individually and collectively to improve the quality of outcomes for all our children. Because of this, we have organized the book like a theater play in four acts, with a focus on "smart improvisation" around your vision, leadership, and strategies. It is likely that you already use the idea of "smart improvisation" as you explore solutions for the unique needs of each child and classroom, or each program and community.

Children of 2020 is structured as smart improv to emphasize the leadership role you must play to achieve your vision for children, and to actually use the knowledge summarized in this text. Your work with children and families is an improvisation because all communities and children are different; your work with children and families is smart because it is rooted in a strong knowledge base. You and other readers will apply smart improv, adapting each act and the outcomes to your own program or community. The four acts outline a step-by-step action strategy:

- **Act I: Vision — Imagining the World for Children of 2020.** Reaching for a world as it ought to be for children is both an independent and collective task. We begin with visions of where key thought leaders see us heading to improve the lives of children. You will be asked to get involved by discussing visions appropriate to your individual situation or to your program or community, where there will be multiple visions.

- **Act II: Knowledge — Information to Guide Future Practices.** Here the book aims to extend your knowledge base through presentations of important syntheses of current research findings. In addition, it is important to gain up-to-date knowledge about your own community with its diverse families and children. You get involved by learning, putting the research into practice, and exploring areas for which more information would be useful to you.

- **Act III: Strategies — Facilitating Outcomes for the Children of 2020.** We provide some examples of important strategies that others are using to create change. Which of these strategies are relevant or useful for you? You will be asked to tailor your strategies to your own situation, based on the previous acts about vision and knowledge.

- **Act IV: Denouement — Taking Personal Responsibility for the Children of 2020.** This is about outcomes. You, the readers, will ultimately be responsible for the quality outcomes needed for 2020. In the final act, we present guidelines to help you design your own successful improvisation to the four-act play.

We're asking you, the reader, to apply your creativity to the four-act smart improv. You and your colleagues are and will be the actors for your community, and you will improvise an action script appropriate for your community. This book will serve as a guide for each act. Each act has three sections:

- *Commentary* — providing coaching suggestions about how you can prepare individually and collaboratively to achieve smart improv in your community.

- *Articles by leaders in the early care and education field* — helping prepare you as an actor by providing a broad perspective on emerging ideas and innovative practices.

- *Improv workshop* — providing pointers and discussion questions that will guide you in carrying out intelligent actions that meet the needs of children in your own community.

This book is a starting point. Smart improv is required now, because there may be children in your community with urgent, unmet needs. Smart improv is required as we progress toward 2020, because we create tomorrow based on what we do today. You and your colleagues will think of new ideas, and you may try out better approaches that we haven't even thought of yet. Your input is required. Now join us in using smart improv as an action tool for 2020. Just imagine how your drama might unfold.

It can be a long and bumpy road, growing from baby to adulthood. I hope the grownups do a good job getting ready for us.

Improv Workshop

Translating Ideas into Intelligent Action

The purpose of the improv workshops that follow each act is to sharpen your focus on specific challenges in your community that cry out for leadership from you and your colleagues. The articles that await you in *Children of 2020* are replete with ideas about vision, knowledge about development and learning, and strategies that get good results. All will help you and your team enhance your capacity to make constructive changes in your work and community.

As you prepare to read this book, we suggest that you consider forming a learning team with whom you can discuss and act upon the ideas in the book. Collaboration among you will spark new ideas and can build a support group for introducing better strategies and practices. In addition, explore as a group the characteristics of your community and the needs of young children.

Here are some topics for individual reflection and group discussion:

1. Over the past 10 years, what do you see as the most significant areas of progress in the early care and education field?

2. How do issues of diversity such as race, culture, language, and social class impact your work? How have these issues changed over the past 10 years? When you look ahead to 2020, what do you think diversity issues will look like?

3. Think broadly about the setting in which you will perform your smart improv. In 1990, 2010, and 2020, how has the care and education of young children been transformed in your community? Here are a few areas to think about:

    a. Prevalence of early care and education staff who hold credentials such as the Child Development Associate or two- and four-year college degrees.

    b. Proportion of prekindergarten children in public schools.

    c. Diversity of the child population.

    d. Number of accredited programs.

    e. Extent of local and state media coverage.

    f. Involvement by leaders outside of the field of early care and education, including faith communities, medical or legal personnel, government agencies, businesses and civic organizations.

4. Consider the degree to which the following statement applies to your community: "The dreams for millions of children in the United States are diminished because of gaps in access to a nurturing environment, quality education, health care, and community services."

    a. Estimate the percentage of children in your community who lack access to these essential opportunities during their formative years (birth through age 8).

    b. Identify the socioeconomic and ethnic/racial identity of the children most in need.

5. Name specific organizations in your community that could work with you and your colleagues to address these concerns. ▶

Act I: Vision
Imagining the World for the Children of 2020

Commentary

The American Dream begins with a vision, as does smart improvisation in the early care and education field. What should the world be like for the children of 2020?

Vision matters. Different visions suggest different pathways for the future. Different visions demand different skills and knowledge for their accomplishment. And, different visions suggest different expectations about what, when, why, how, and from whom children should learn.

Vision statements serve many valuable roles: they keep our eyes on the prize and remind us of why it is important to consistently give our best effort; they guide our choices and decisions about policies and strategies; and they serve as the benchmark to evaluate if we are making progress toward our goals.

Reaching for a world as it ought to be for children is both an independent and collective task. A vision is an aspiration and a decision

to move in a particular direction. Successful implementation of any vision will require more coordinated collective effort within the field of early care and education. However, it is important to recognize that vision is also held within each individual. For change to occur there must be individuals who own and share clear beliefs about what all children deserve and who are willing to act on those beliefs.

Various sectors, curricula, and programs in our field infer different visions. Recognizing this fact, *Children of 2020* presents visions from six diverse perspectives. Here you will read vision statements expressed by an elementary school principal, higher education leaders, a prominent national organization, an executive from the world of philanthropy, and content specialists.

I Still Have a Dream

And so even though we face the difficulties of today and tomorrow, I still have a dream. It is a dream deeply rooted in the American dream.

—Martin Luther King,
August 28, 1963

As you read, ask yourself questions such as:

- Is there a core, defining intent that unites these vision statements?

- To what ages of children do these visions refer?

- How do these ideas conform to my view of the field of early care and education?

These six vision statements are offered in Act I as a stimulus for preparing your own vision. In the improv workshop that follows the six vision statements, we will challenge you and your colleagues to develop, or refine, your own personal vision statement about the opportunities you believe all children deserve and the specific parts of this vision that you commit to adopt as your long-term professional goals.

The following thoughts provide a flavor of what is to come from our six commentaries, but read each vision statement carefully and make notes for creating your own vision statement.

PREVIEW OF VISION
Thoughts from Act I

Full-Service Community Schools *Detris Adelabu, Tina M. Durand, and Jackie Jenkins-Scott, Wheelock College*	Schools must become the village center, the community hub, for children and families — letting go of traditional boundaries that have often disconnected schools from the broader community.
Hopes, Dreams, Intentions *Luis A. Hernandez, Early Childhood Education Specialist*	What do we want our children to learn from us? It may be common-sense life lessons: do great work in school, play well with others, etc. I would also want good, noble, joyful children — an inspiration to all those around them.
Two-Generational Approach *Hedy N. Chang, Independent Consultant*	Keeping the American Dream alive is not easy. It will require a wide array of stakeholders. Early childhood professionals should not underestimate the lasting impact they can make when they take steps to ensure families are equipped to help their children succeed in school.
PreK-Third Grade: A Paradigm Shift *Ruby Takanishi, Foundation for Child Development*	Early educators must work with the K–12 education system as partners in shaping a seamless learning experience for children from birth to at least third grade or beyond. There must be reciprocal give and take — both sides have much to learn from each other.
The Leadership Role of Elementary School Principals *Jeffrey A. Wolff, Clyde F. Brown Elementary School, Millis, Massachusetts*	Universal preschool within public education is my vision for the children of 2020. The future of education in America depends on a strong PreK–3 program. Elementary school principals must step up to the plate and make it happen for young children.
Realizing the Dream for America's Children *Marian Wright Edelman and Cathy Grace, Children's Defense Fund*	Dreaming is not folly. It is often the only way things come to pass. But dreaming alone is not enough — a map to follow for those who act on the dream is essential, as is the army of soldiers needed to build and see the dream through to completion — until every child is safe and healthy and educated

After reading the vision statements in full, continue with the Act I improv workshop. ▶

Full-Service Community Schools

Detris Adelabu, Tina M. Durand, and Jackie Jenkins-Scott[4]

What kind of a world do we want for our children, both now and in the future? How do we determine which practices and policies are in the best interest of children? Although decisions about children's development, care, supervision, and education have been foremost concerns of families throughout the last century, these questions take on added urgency and complexity in the new millennium. The world, it seems, is truly in motion, and the economic, technological, sociocultural, and political changes related to globalization are unprecedented. Although the United States has always been a nation of immigrants, the number of immigrants living in U.S. households has risen by 16% in recent years, and one in five children is either an immigrant or the child of immigrants.[5] Insofar as the circumstances, needs, beliefs, and practices of diverse families differ, it is important that educators, social-service providers, and policymakers be attuned to these changes as they make decisions that influence the current and future well-being of children.

A consideration of what is in the best interest of children raises the following questions: Who defines "best"? Best for which children and families? Under which set of circumstances or particular contexts? Although the answer to these questions might often be "It depends," perhaps it can be said with some certainty that creating environments for children that are safe, peaceful, happy, and supportive, where children are healthy and can grow and thrive to their full human potential, should be a vision that has universal appeal and applicability. Indeed, this

is the vision embodied in the UN Convention on the Rights of the Child, adopted in 1989 as the first international instrument (although not ratified by the United States) that articulates the aforementioned goals for children within the context of children's human rights.

A vision for the children of 2020 requires a multifaceted lens — one that does not view the institutions responsible for the care, education, and health of children (for example, families, schools, and hospitals) as bounded and distinct, but interconnected and interdependent. Using the concept of social capital to refer to the relationships and interactions between children and the adults in their world, sociologist James Coleman[6] commented on the importance of strong networks of support for children. In the next generation, he called for a reinvestment in community in the form of collaborative effort between the many adults in children's lives. In a society that is stratified along racial and class-based lines, where access to resources is inequitable and the relative isolation of the nuclear family structure predominates, social reinvestment has never been more challenging, yet more necessary and important.

In the United States, as in many nations, early care and education settings play a pivotal role in nurturing, socializing, and teaching many children the skills needed to succeed in formal schooling and become productive members of society. W. E. B. Du Bois powerfully argued that "of all the civil rights for which the world has struggled and fought for 5,000 years, the right to learn is undoubtedly the most fundamental."[7]

Unfortunately, this issue continues to be the most important one facing children of 2020. Indeed, a child's right to learn must be at the top of our agenda as we work to create an education system that serves all children.

What is the pathway to achieve this vision by 2020? Critically examining notions of education and its central place in the community. Although the most effective means of bringing about positive change in society remains a quality education, schools alone cannot be responsible for solving the historical and societal woes that have led to America's failure to educate all of its children.

As early as 1916, John Dewey stated that every child deserves an excellent education, one that focuses on the whole individual, including his or her social, personal, and academic development.[8] Nearly 100 years later, we fail to provide this most inalienable right to all children, raising the question: what is taking us so long? While this question seems simple, the answer requires a critical dialogue about historical, social, political, and economic factors that, by virtue of our complacency, have led to a system that does not support the belief that all children can learn and that all children deserve a quality education. We are decades beyond legal religious and ethnic school segregation, yet there are still too many segregated schools and too many children in school settings where there are assumptions that certain children cannot and will not achieve.

Our vision for children of 2020 is to move beyond deficit models of education and to reinvent schools based on the fundamental belief that all children can learn and achieve, that it is our responsibility to help children grow and thrive. The education system of 2020 must be dynamic, flexible, and multifaceted. Early childhood curricula must be grounded in a solid understanding of children's development (for example, the self-regulatory capacities of a 3-year-old are far less developed than those of a 10-year-old) yet must be open and responsive to the enormous variability that characterizes development across the lifespan. In the classroom, this variability emerges in countless ways, such as in children's

> **Perhaps the greatest and most important challenge the field of early care and education will face in the new millennium is how to respond to student and family diversity.**

individual styles of learning and processing information, uses of language, levels of activity, and social interaction patterns. Schools must pay special attention to children who are learning English as a second language yet continue to provide validation, instruction, and support for children's heritage languages.

Across all grade levels, effective pedagogy requires a skillful combination of explicit instruction, sensitive and warm interactions, responsive feedback, and opportunities for inquiry-based learning, rather than a polarization of approaches characterized as either child-centered or teacher-centered.[9] Schools must have uniformly high expectations for all students yet be responsive to the focus on accountability among politicians, policymakers, and scholars with creativity, persistence, confidence, and insight. At the state, district, and individual school levels, teachers must be supported in using more-robust means of assessing children's growth and learning that are sensitive to the social context and resources that exist in their communities. The unequivocal message to all stakeholders must be that accountability should not be monolithic in concept or high-stakes in implementation, especially at the early childhood level.[10] Schools must facilitate the process-oriented, critical-thinking, and technological skills that children will need to be successful citizens in the far-reaching, rapidly changing global economy.

Schools must let go of traditional boundaries that have often disconnected them from the broader community. While school learning is vital to children's achievement, in addition to the home environment, children also learn through engagement with community-based organizations, including churches, shops, pizzerias, salons, clinics, and civic, social, and public-service agencies. To meet the needs of the whole child, schools must be re-created as organizations that partner with many groups and residents who make up the school community. In essence, we need to work to create and support full-service community schools.[11]

Such schools (for example, the Harlem Children's Zone[12] and the Comer School Development Program[13]) recognize that it still takes a village to raise a child, and it takes a community to provide each child with a quality education. The children of 2020 must be provided more opportunity to engage with the community through experiences such as volunteerism and service-based community learning. According to M. Fine, et al., "knowledge is alive, rooted in social relations, and most powerful when produced collaboratively through community-based social action."[14] Full-service community schools also build strong family-school partnerships. These schools incorporate high levels of family communication, marked by mutual respect and sharing of knowledge, and in turn report improved student achievement.[15] The challenge to strong family-school partnerships in many schools has been in sharing decision-making and school governance, and in finding ways for all families to connect to the school community. Reinventing traditional public schools as full-service community schools can help to fill

the chasm that exists between many schools and families.

Perhaps the greatest and most important challenge the field of early care and education will face in the new millennium is how to respond to student and family diversity. According to He and Hobbs,[16] by the year 2030, ethnic minority children age 5 and younger will outnumber their non-Hispanic white counterparts by half a million.[17] Whether they are the children of newly arrived immigrants or of groups with multiple generations of residence in the United States, ethnic minority children represent the future of the changing racial/ethnic landscape in this country. Although it may be said with some degree of certainty that all families want their children to be successful in school, complexities of culture, family background, language, values, and attitudes frame and influence the way families view education and their role in supporting it.

One of the most significant challenges the U.S. education system must face is the preparation of teachers (the majority of whom are white and middle-class) to work effectively with ethnic minority children in ways that are respectful, meaningful, and empowering.[18] To do this, education must move beyond a simple tolerance and respect for diversity to an appreciation, a celebration, and an incorporation of diversity; this paradigm shift has the potential to empower children to be more empathic, responsive, and motivated. Diversity is not defined in simple terms, but refers to the myriad experiences and attributes that contribute to each person's uniqueness, regardless of cultural or ethnic heritage or community, such as social class, gender, occupational status, income, sexual orientation, ability, disability, religion, and education.

To truly celebrate and incorporate diversity in early childhood settings, early childhood teachers and caregivers must engage in a careful examination of their own biases and assumptions about children and families from racial/ethnic and sociocultural contexts other than their own, and be willing to consider differences not as deficiencies but as potential sources of strength. As cultural psychologist Barbara Rogoff notes,[19] we need to "suspend" our judgments about the beliefs and practices of those who believe or do things differently long enough to consider the meanings and functions different practices may have for a particular family. In short, providing care and education in which all children can thrive requires moving diversity out of the margins of the curriculum, only to be addressed when it is time to showcase the unique traditions and practices of "another" cultural group, and infusing principles of diversity, equity, and social justice into our teaching and our interactions with children and families.[20]

There are enormous rewards to engaging in the difficult work of becoming more cross-culturally competent, both professionally and personally. These rewards may be evident in an increased ability to assist a family in bridging two disparate cultures. It may exist in being able to see a child who presents as "difficult" in a new light — a light that recasts a supposedly "difficult" behavior not as something this child is doing to be disruptive, but as a positive, adaptive strength. It can exist in the understanding that a child might be responding in the only way he or she knows based on experience, and that you have the potential to introduce new ways of responding that will enhance school experiences. It may exist in the acquisition of new knowledge. It may exist in increased self-awareness and a wider perspective, enabling each of us to be more successful in a global society.

We must also greatly improve society's perceptions of teachers as competent individuals, capable of educating all of America's children. A recent story illustrates this point: A young woman planned to become a teacher if her job as a buyer for a high-end department store did not work out. She had heard about a one-year, alternative teacher-preparation program that would have her in the classroom after one semester. In her mind, it had taken four years of college to become a buyer and would take only a year to become a teacher. Similar stories are all too common and highlight the need to shift societal perceptions of the teaching profession. While we know there are excellent alternative teacher-preparation programs aimed at filling a shortage of qualified teachers in many communities, societal perceptions of these programs can diminish the professional identity of teachers. Contributing to the diminishing professional identity of birth–12 educators is the lack of universal curricular standards for teacher-preparation programs. Although regional and national accreditation bodies exist in the field, there are no universal curricular standards. Teacher-preparation program requirements vary among institutions and from state to state. A teacher deemed qualified/certified to teach in one state may not meet certification standards in another state. By varying our expectations and standards in teacher-preparation programs, we create teachers who in turn pass on varied expectations of and standards for a quality education to America's children.

It is also important that we view teachers (as well as school administrators and other adults who interact with children) as primary learners in the school community, open to new teaching and learning experiences, and to intimately engaging with all children and their families. Critical to the concept of teachers as primary learners is the adoption of a view of teaching as dynamic, not just at the level of the classroom but also at the level of the individual student. Over time, teachers who view themselves as primary learners in the school community grow to understand how learning might occur for the individual child at each shift in development. They also work to acquire the skills necessary to individualize instruction and to shift their expectations of individual student achievement. The focus shifts from "What is wrong with Johnny, why can't he read?" to "What can I as a teacher do differently to support Johnny as he learns to read?" To engage at this level in educating America's children, it is important that teachers are provided mentoring and ongoing professional development to support their pathway to becoming experienced educators.

If birth–12 schools are to be considered communities, then institutions of higher education must be residents in the neighborhood. As community residents, institutions of higher education become a part of the day-to-day experiences of birth–12 educators. Their residency will enable them to gain knowledge useful to building college curricula, restructuring teacher education, mentoring preservice teachers, and offering professional development to educators in ways that are more relevant to the reality of what happens in schools. The entire school community must also receive the training and support that will allow it to effectively work with children across ethnic, cultural, socioeconomic, gender, achievement, sexual-orientation, religious, and all other demographic classifications. Teacher-preparation programs can no longer isolate discussions of diversity to a particular course or class period. If we are going to be about the business of educating all of America's children, then all of America's children should be reflected in the everyday teaching and learning experiences that occur in teacher preparation. Teacher-preparation programs must produce technologically literate educators who can effectively integrate technology in ways that help students gain a deeper meaning of course content.

In summary, to live up to our vision, we must:

- Recognize a quality education as a natural, essential, and inalienable right for all children.

- Reconceptualize/re-create public schools as communities.

- Reestablish the professional identity of birth–12 educators.

- Move beyond tolerance of diversity to celebrating and incorporating diversity.

- Engage educators in reflective examination of their attitudes around diversity issues.

- Strengthen state and federal policy guiding standards for teacher preparation.

- Establish teachers, administrators, and school employees as primary learners in the school community.

- Strengthen birth–12 and higher-education partnerships.

- Conceptualize teacher-education programs that support the role of schools as communities.

How do we take our proposals to scale?

A promising vision for children of 2020 is the prospect of using knowledge gained from full-service community schools to design schools that support the development of the whole child. We know that full-service community schools engage families, improve student achievement, and strengthen communities. In essence, they live up to the goals that we have for public education. We also envision federal and state policies that mandate a quality education for all children as a natural, essential, and inalienable right, and we envision universal curricular standards, grounded in knowledge of how children learn and develop, to guide curricular decisions in teacher-preparation programs. Shared high standards and expectations across teacher-preparation programs will grow to become shared high standards and expectations at the level of the student. To get there, it is important that we document and replicate effective strategies that promote student achievement while simultaneously avoiding a cookie-cutter approach to reinventing public education. While all teacher-preparation programs and academic learning environments should not look the same, we must have at our core the understanding that:

- Relationships matter.
- Education transcends the boundaries of schools.
- Expectations matter.
- Diversity matters.
- People learn differently.
- Quality counts.
- Communities are critical to the educational process and success.
- Policy matters.

We envision a society where all children know they are loved and respected, and where they are supported to reach their full human potential — physically, spiritually, emotionally, and intellectually. But as with any vision, there must be a call to action and a community response. We, as villagers, must relentlessly act to create learning communities that effectively educate and enhance the life opportunities of all children. ▶

> *Hope for the children of 2020:*
>
> *That all children live in a world free of violence, where they know they are loved and respected, and supported to reach their full human potential — physically, spiritually, emotionally, and intellectually.*

About the Authors

Detris Adelabu, *Chair and Associate Professor, Human Development, Wheelock College*

Tina M. Durand, *Assistant Professor, Human Development, Wheelock College*
tdurand@wheelock.edu

Jackie Jenkins-Scott, *President, Wheelock College*
Jjenkins-scott@wheelock.edu

Professional focus

Adelabu studies African American adolescents' school achievement, examining perceptions of the future, school climate, and ethnic identity.

Durand's interests are ecological factors associated with early school experiences of Latino children and families.

Jenkins-Scott is the 13th president of Wheelock College, a private college with a public mission to improve the lives of children and families.

Hopes, Dreams, Intentions

Luis A. Hernandez

Is there a way to predict the future for a new generation, the children of 2020? Trying to imagine that future is an incredible and impossible task. Every family dreams of the very best for its children. Those dreams represent our collective hope for a new generation. And as professionals who work with our youngest children, it is our responsibility to provide in philosophy and practice the tools that will allow those families, as well as communities, to realize their dreams. It is our professional duty to provide the best now and in the future.

If we were to paint a picture of a future generation, that canvas would have a color palette drawn from the current spectrum of our hopes and dreams — a generation that is multicultural, free-spirited, diverse, free of racism, bilingual, sensitive to the planet, good to one another, educated, violence free, healthy, safe, full of spirit, and loving. These are colorful terms, drawn from a contemporary world to provide the hues for a better future, the dream for a new generation. The desire is for those colors to remain vibrant, real, and permanent. For the class of 2020, let's provide a legacy and foundation of what is right, good, and just.

As professionals, we have the responsibility to put into motion the circumstances that create positive environments and conditions for the best in early care and learning. This collective responsibility represents a call to action. Together we must create a blueprint of dynamic practices in which children can flourish to their full potential, be it today or tomorrow. The task begins with creating the future now. We understand the many roadblocks to this work. But with wisdom and infectious enthusiasm, the profession can surmount barriers on the road to quality care and education. Our parents dreamed of reaching the moon, and, as a people, we landed on the moon. To succeed, a vision, even with risks, requires knowledge, skills, research, talent, innovation, and hard work. Each step in the progress of early childhood education relies on continuous improvement of ideas, thoughts, and practices. That process impacts children now and in that unpredictable future.

Ideals are powerful intentions that lead to the many lessons learned along the way. Ideals evolve to meet changes in family needs, public policies, current research, professional recognition, and effort. Many challenges remain in the world of early childhood education, despite our successes and ample evidence of progress. Yes, ratios are better, health and safety rules are in place, professional development is readily available, resources and materials abound, and accreditation is the norm. And yet we continue to diligently work to improve every aspect of our field: professional recognition, salary equity, safe and healthy environments for children, appropriate practices for every stage of child development. Each step forward that we take, each success, is an example of the hard work needed to achieve an ideal of what can be better for children.

While we continue to struggle with issues close to our backyard, the world continues to come closer to our fences. We begin to see the children of the world in our classrooms, and they expand our view of their world. We begin to look beyond our borders. A global perspective requires the effort to understand and support children who lack the basics: shelter, sanitation, food — so much of what is taken for granted in our lives. Those children, together with our children, will be the generation of 2020.

As the planet becomes smaller, the plight and rights of all children become the cause for all those working with children and families everywhere. This represents the bedrock of our calling, the basis for those ethical standards that will transform early care and education. It is a resolve to build a world of meaningful equality for children and families. This action is based on the philosophies, principles, research, and practices that are the essence of our profession. For all children now and in 2020, we can provide rich developmental and learning experiences based on the joy and excitement of their young years. And as teachers, we should all exercise expanded professional talents with deeper purpose, passion, and values.

Where we've been

In thinking of the 2020 generation, personal journeys and the histories of our own families provide insight to where we have been and where we may be heading. In my own family, none of my grandparents ever flew on an airplane. My parents flew no more than six times in their lives. Today, I fly every week to work in locations hundreds of miles from home. My grandparents walked to their farms. My parents rode the subway everyday to their jobs in factories and restaurants. Neither of those generations could have imagined the world we live in today, a world shaped by technology, by airplanes, the Internet, and cellular phones. But think about what they taught us, the lessons they shared that still shape our lives, the values they imparted that still have meaning in a world they couldn't imagine and wouldn't recognize.

We know that the world our children inhabit will be different from our own, but we can still ask: What do we want our children to learn from us? Is there a particular richness or some practical wisdom that our children can capture from us? It may be commonsense life lessons: do great work in school, play well with others, be cheerful and helpful, be respectful and kind, be competent and caring. I would also want good, noble, joyful children who were an inspiration to all those around them. Human values carried from generation to generation exist without the trap of nostalgia for "good old-fashioned days and ways." All our advice and good intentions will only go so far in reaching for the best. Just look how well we listened to our elders growing up!

As with all previous generations, the generation of 2020 will be different. How different? We can't say. But we can predict one key difference. In all likelihood, the majority of parents in the 2020 generation will have grown up in some type of group care themselves: preschools, nurseries, and child care programs. The parents of the next generation are today's young people in high school or college, or serving in the armed forces, or working in a fast-food restaurant. Their frame of reference regarding early childhood and education in general will shape their children's attitudes toward teachers and programs. As it is now, teacher and family relationships and regular communication will still be important. And we want to make sure that by 2020, the care of children will be of the highest quality in terms of incredible relationships, fostering development and learning.

Our field of early childhood education constitutes a significant shift in human history, an evolution from parents as primary caregivers to a system of children being cared for by people outside their immediate families. Many of us come from a time where our mothers and other relatives took care of the children. Organized group care is still a human endeavor in its infancy. The mothers and fathers of 2020 will still need to build trusting relationships with complete strangers, with the person who will become their child's favorite teacher. We can shape how the next generation builds these relationships, how tomorrow's parents view education, by delivering a quality experience today. It will be the parents of the 2020 children who, with their own positive memories of their child care experiences, will infuse their children with the excitement of finger painting, walks in the neighborhood, listening to stories, making new friends, and having great teachers.

What might be important

There are some items of importance that we want the children of 2020 to take along to the future; some are the same things that our parents and teachers gave us. Foremost, be and act naturally as universal children: play extensively, explore all possibilities, interact with others, and build skills to be proud of. Sometimes the process will include the guidance of adults, but much of the process will emerge from the talents, skills, and abilities of the natural child. The balance of organized practices and play should complement the child's sense of curiosity and discovery, competence and tenacity in creating, having an active social life, and negotiating ways to cooperate. The message rings true for today and for 2020.

And each child in 2020 will come from an individual living family tree, unique in its structure and dynamics. Family life will be the basis of a child's development and learning, as it was in the past, and as it is today. The ingredients of family life and its impact on the individual child will form the backbone for values, beliefs, character, and joy. These important pieces of family life must be factors used by early educators as they design program services, curriculum practices, and communication venues. Genuine relationships between early educators and families build trust and respect, and they validate the life of the child in all its possibilities.

Effective work in the areas of child development and early learning recognizes that attention to individual children and their families is the key to best practices. As we engage and support

> **We need to ensure that the focus on academics and the push for achievement doesn't crowd out unexpected experiences that ignite the power of multiple skills, or deny children the opportunity to explore, to play in surprising ways, or to have joy shape their day.**

children and parents, our best professional standards are challenged, stretched, and enhanced, be it now or in 2020. The field of early childhood education sparkles with the interactions, practices, and relationships of children with their families, children with their teachers, and parents and teachers. Memories are a testimony of lasting relationships, in the way we still remember our earliest teachers. The children of 2020 will also have memories of adults who made a difference with their approaches to play, motivation for learning, and the opportunities to be.

Where we might be

As the children of 2020 propel us toward a future, a few messages will tend to prevail: Be a person of love! Develop your character! Be free! Get an education! Be you! Such slogans are easy to promote; they have been used on us, and we continue the pattern. The challenge for any next generation is to keep those messages vital and relevant. It will also be the responsibility of adults to persistently model the ideals we cherish. Want more loving children in 2020? Love them now. Want children with outstanding morals and values? Be ethical yourself. Want children to relish education? Be a person who loves learning. Want children to be free and wonderful individuals? Be that yourself.

Recently I was in a group of visitors to a rural primary school in Ireland, and the children entertained us. With parents proudly sitting in the audience, the children sang traditional and top 10 tunes, they played musical instruments, a few danced country jigs, and others had solo recitals. All of us in the audience were mesmerized by individual talents as well as the tremendous group effort. The children lived on farms where their parents raised sheep or cows or pigs, and they all attended a small country school. We saw a snapshot of children who helped around the farm, enjoyed their schoolwork, and participated joyfully in the musical performance with their families. The humble community effort was a fountain of pride and achievement for adults and children alike.

We were inspired by the performance but saddened by the thought of how rare this experience may be. As a society we have allowed ourselves to become focused on academics, assessments, tests and more tests, the achieve-

ment push, the fear of failure. We have surrendered, compromised, and diminished many basic fundamentals of our work because of policy pressures toward accountability "outcomes" of what is dictated to be academically important. We're violating essential early childhood education principles, and young children are missing out on dancing and cheated of the opportunity to sing.

Memories of that classroom visit in Ireland can provide the motivational force we need to improve and better the circumstances for the children of 2010 and 2020, by striving for a better balance in children's lives, with singing, dancing, music, watering gardens, sharing toys, reading, writing, knowing numbers. We need to ensure that the focus on academics and the push for achievement doesn't crowd out unexpected experiences that ignite the power of multiple skills, or deny children the opportunity to explore, to play in surprising ways, or to have joy shape their day. We also must enlist parents as proud partners in what the children and teachers of 2020 can create: a colorful community canvas of active learners. Be it in Ireland or a center down the street, the potential and abilities of children and their families are there to be discovered.

Almost being there

As teachers and leaders in early childhood, we can shape the world that the children of 2020 and their parents will inhabit. The next decade will require leadership that recognizes the fact of dynamic and constant change; our early childhood practices must provide stability for families today while changing to meet the relevant needs of tomorrow. The time between now and 2020 is not that great. Many of us today will be in classrooms with the children of 2020. We will read stories that still mesmerize, we will discover a bird's nest up a tree on a morning walk with the children, and we may still kick balls in the playground. Different and constant may be the core theme in our work with children. Perhaps the old adage "The more things change, the more they stay the same" has nimble implications in working with young children.

Almost being there and curious of the coming times, professionals will continue to polish their own skills, keeping in mind that their work is transformational today or tomorrow. Who would want to visit a doctor who has not refreshed his or her skills in the last 10 years? The same applies to us. We must continue to update, revise, and expand our teaching and care practices. It is our responsibility to bring wisdom to the next generation, based on past experiences and future desires. As teachers of the 2020 class, we represent a tremendous resource for each child coming through that door. We will need our own fountain of energy and resourcefulness to engage children in ever-new ways. A classroom community is built; it is a place for exploration and discovery, with the warmth of friendship and care.

Hopes, dreams, and intentions must become active commitments in order to continuously transform early childhood education now and in 2020. We must have the good sense to try to be the very best of an incredible profession. The excellence of our professional work beckons and welcomes new children and their families every year. Our passion must be for formidable teaching practices, sharp observations, the magic of

teachable moments, and the joy of rich conversations and interactions with the children. ▶

Hope for
the children of 2020:

For children across all borders to have joy and meaning in their lives through peace, educational opportunities, and family unity.

About the Author

Luis A. Hernandez, *Early Childhood Education Specialist* Luiswku@aol.com

Professional focus

Hernandez's professional work focuses on language development, early literacy, and dual-language learning; leadership and professional development; cultural dynamics and changing demographics; and early childhood education management issues and topics.

Two-Generational Approach

3

Hedy N. Chang

My vision for 2020 is that young children of all ethnic, class, and linguistic backgrounds have the opportunity to realize the American Dream, that is, the chance to prosper, even if you begin with very little, as long as you hold a job and work hard. For many families, especially parents mired in low-wage, dead-end jobs, the American Dream is not achieved in a single generation but realized when they see their children graduate from high school, attend college, and find their place among America's middle class.

This shared desire to see our children succeed is a form of common ground that binds together members of U.S. society across any perceived differences. It is the hope that draws new families to the United States and the promise that keeps those who have lived here for generations willing to invest in building a strong nation. For many parents, it is the belief that inspires them to wake up every morning, to send their children to school, and to do what it takes to go to work every day — even in the most arduous conditions.

Our country is at a crossroads: we can preserve the American Dream for future generations, or we can create a permanent underclass. In today's global economy, obtaining a decent job typically requires a college degree. Yet vast numbers of students in the United States do not even obtain a high school diploma. More than one-third of all students (and nearly half of all Latino and African American students) currently fail to graduate on time from high school; most eventually drop out.

Although we often think of dropping out as affecting students in high school or perhaps middle school, in reality, the crisis begins far earlier. Studies show that by the end of third grade, less than half of all children in the United States are reading proficiently so they can "read to learn" in their other subjects.[21] The majority (73%) of children who enter fourth grade at a first- or second-grade reading level never catch up. Chronic absence (missing a month or more of school) is an even earlier indicator of academic risk. Children of all socioeconomic backgrounds do worse academically in first grade if they were chronically absent in kindergarten. Among poor children, chronic absence in kindergarten predicts the lowest levels of educational achievement at the end of fifth grade. Nationwide, chronic absence affects nearly 10% of kindergartners and first-graders. In some communities, chronic early absence affects 25% of all K–3 students.[22]

Despite these challenging statistics, our country has the opportunity to change this troubling trajectory if we are willing to embrace and support two-generational approaches to families moving out of poverty. A two-generational approach involves simultaneously helping families to promote the educational success of their children, starting in the early years, and advancing greater economic security among low-income families. Early childhood educators have an especially important role to play because they influence whether children have a chance to get on the path to high school and college graduation.

Helping families promote the educational success of their children, starting in the early years

A two-generation approach starts by recognizing the critical role parents play as their children's first and lifelong teachers. While classroom teachers can have a tremendous impact on a child's life, parents (broadly defined to refer to the adults with ongoing responsibility for raising a child) typically have the greatest influence as they provide guidance throughout their children's growing-up years. Programs are shortsighted when they focus only on working with a child, rather than also recognizing the value of engaging and investing in the capacity of parents to ensure their child's well-being.

Early childhood educators play an especially important role. Preschool or kindergarten is often the first time many parents experience sharing responsibility for raising their child with an adult who is not a family member. A positive experience can lay the foundation for later parent involvement by helping parents gain the confidence and skills needed to continue to be involved. Three factors significantly influence whether parents become engaged.[23] The first is whether parents believe they should play an active role in their children's education and have a positive sense of self-efficacy for helping their children learn. The second is whether the school welcomes and invites their involvement. The third is whether parents' life context (socioeconomic situation, knowledge, skills, and time) supports involvement.

While parent engagement is essential for all children, it does not always happen. Such engagement is generally highest among middle-class parents who feel they should be actively involved and are much more likely to believe they can make a difference, especially since most were themselves successful in school. Engaging all families is possible, however, when schools deliberately demonstrate they respect and value all children and their parents, especially those who have been most marginalized,

and promote a wide variety of opportunities for participation. It often requires helping teachers who may come from different class, ethnic, and linguistic backgrounds develop personal and trusting relationships with parents across differences and build upon the practices of the home to support learning in the classroom.

Educators of young children should also keep in mind that they are in a position to shape how parents understand what it means to be engaged in their children's education. Too often, especially in tight budget times, the emphasis of parent engagement is encouraging families to add to the resources available by helping with fundraising, volunteering in the classroom, or donating supplies. While these activities are valuable, they do not represent what is, in my view, most essential, and they can further alienate low-income and working-poor families who often lack the resources to make such contributions.

Early childhood educators could instead embrace the 3A Framework developed in a partnership between the America's Promise Alliance and The Annie E. Casey Foundation. It proposes focusing parent engagement on three concepts critical to short- and long-term educational success:

- *Attendance Every Day:* Ensure children go to school regularly.

- *Achievement Every Year:* Monitor and help children make satisfactory progress each year.

- *Attainment Over Time:* Set high expectations for children and plan for attaining.[24]

Early childhood educators can encourage parents to take an active role in promoting these concepts. They can, for example, help parents understand that preschool and kindergarten are not just nice experiences to help socialize a child to a group experience but are critical to a child's long-term academic success. They can use positive incentives to encourage regular attendance among all children and families, and reach out and connect families to available social or economic supports if they are having difficulty

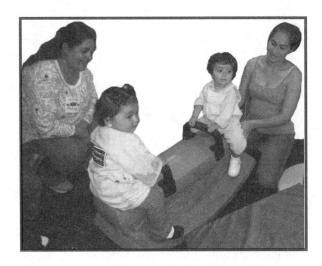

getting their children to school. At the same time, early childhood educators can familiarize parents what their children are expected to learn each year given their age, and what they can do if their children do not appear to be developing as anticipated. They can also work with parents to introduce children to positive adult role models from their community and help all children believe they can be anything they want to be. Early childhood professionals can take advantage of their ability to connect with parents at a key transition point. Giving parenting advice is tricky business because it can easily be construed as veiled criticism. As children enter formal schooling, however, parents may be more open to advice about how to handle a new phase in their family's life.

Advancing greater economic security among low-income families

While virtually all families want their children to succeed in school, the ability of parents to support their child's well-being is deeply affected by their economic conditions. Whether children enter school ready to learn depends upon whether their parents have the patience, resources, and time to nurture their social and emotional development through, for example, reading every day, or helping a child understand the consequences of inappropriate actions. Finding the right balance between work and time with family is a challenge for nearly every par-

ent. It is especially tough for those working long hours at multiple jobs and constantly worried about being able to adequately cloth, shelter, and feed their families.

Rather than simply accept poverty as a given, early childhood programs and educators can help families gain access to economic supports even though this may be, for many, a new area of work. By identifying and partnering with community agencies with expertise in workforce development and financial services, early childhood programs can:

- Encourage greater utilization of available economic supports, such as earned income tax credits and free tax preparation, food stamps, and public health insurance.

- Connect families to financial education and asset-building resources that help them plan for the financial future and avoid predatory lending.

Many families, especially those with limited ability to use English or low levels of literacy, may not utilize the economic supports available to them, even though they can significantly increase family income or reduce expenses by several thousand dollars. Reasons vary, from lack of awareness, to invasive and cumbersome paperwork requirements, to fears of social stigma and inconvenient access.

And families struggling to make ends meet often turn to credit cards, payday loans, and other forms of predatory lending. Unfortunately, these actions typically worsen the financial crisis and leave families without resources to weather an unexpected emergency or invest in a better future for themselves and their children. Recognizing these challenges, especially in today's economy, a growing number of resources are available in communities offering access to financial education, credit counseling, and innovative savings programs.

Early childhood educators can make a difference when they promote awareness of these economic resources and connect families to agencies that can help them secure these benefits. They can even offer their own facilities as sites for benefits assistance, financial-management classes, and free tax preparation offered by other agencies.[25] Because financial issues are often highly sensitive, families may be more receptive to such resources when they are introduced by someone they trust (such as their early childhood educator) rather than a stranger. A key first step to making these partnerships work is providing early childhood workers with professional development so they are familiar with these economic supports, why they are important, and how they can be accessed. Ironically, many child care workers could themselves benefit from this information. Given the poor benefits and pay for many jobs in the early childhood field, many workers face the same financial challenges as the families they serve.

While families of all backgrounds share the same American Dream, the paths taken to achieve this common goal will not always be the same. To be most effective, two-generation strategies need to be tailored to the strengths and challenges of particular populations and communities. For example, what helps a newly arrived immigrant parent who speaks little or no English is likely to differ significantly from what works for an American-born teen parent. Bicultural leaders who can help to navigate across differences in culture and language are often invaluable for designing programs, policies, and practices that avoid cultural missteps and meaningfully reach out to families from other cultures and languages. In many communities, early childhood educators may, in fact, be some of these important community leaders. Because child care has traditionally had relatively low barriers to entry, its workers are generally more reflective of the communities served than the professionals in many other fields. In order to

work in the child care field, many have had to learn to become both bicultural and bilingual, and as a result they can help to design and implement strategies that work and engage the families most in need of support.

Keeping the American Dream alive is not easy, especially given the challenging economic times in which we live. It will require a wide array of stakeholders, from policymakers to community members, across the United States to adopt and support two-generational approaches to moving families out of poverty. Early childhood professionals and programs, however, should not underestimate the lasting impact they can have when they take steps to ensure families are equipped to help their children succeed in school, starting as early as possible, and access resources that can assist them in making ends meet and planning for their financial future. ▶

Hope for the children of 2020:

That children from all ethnic and linguistic backgrounds have an equal opportunity to succeed in school and prosper.

About the Author

Hedy N. Chang, *Independent Consultant*
hnchang@earthlink.net

Professional focus

Chang's focus is on two-generational approaches to moving families out of poverty.

PreK–Third Grade: A Paradigm Shift

Ruby Takanishi

In the next 10 years, we must take a giant step to assure that all young children in the United States have the opportunity to experience high-quality prekindergarten (preK) as a regular part of a transformed American education system that starts with programs at 3 years of age and never ends. In the year 2020, all American children will be engaged with a new primary education system that provides a coherent and sequenced set of learning experiences that is the foundation for later educational success.

We have the research now, and we will have more in the next decade, that documents the enormous learning capacity of young children. Our responsibility is to design educational experiences that take this capacity as a starting point and support children to achieve their full potential every day of their lives. Unless we meet this responsibility, we will continue to relegate millions of children to lives of frustration and hopelessness that are associated with inadequate educational attainment.

This vision will require a paradigm shift in how early education defines itself today. The portrayal of K–12 education as a skill-and-drill, mentally deadening experience that robs children of their childhood must change. The narrow focus on social and emotional development must end. The idea that children cannot learn, at their level of development, concepts about mathematics and science, about art and about reading, is archaic and inconsistent with current research about child development. Such thinking limits children's potential, and, most importantly, it limits their opportunities to lead a good life. All children can be educated in ways that are consistent with their development and with respect for their individuality.

Right now, in 2010, we fall far short of achieving this vision for the majority of America's children. A child today is less likely to graduate from high school than his or her parents were. The college graduation rates in the United States are below the levels of the 1970s. This is nothing less than a national crisis.

Unless we make a commitment to changing our ideas about what is good education for children from the beginning, and have high aspirations for their futures, we will do them and our country a great disservice. Children who are not well-educated tend not to be healthy adults. They are less able to provide for themselves and for their children. Most importantly, they have difficulty contributing to their own children's educational success. Their underachievement challenges the values of our democratic form of government, which relies on the intelligence and wise decision-making abilities of its citizens.

> **" Early educators must abandon their position that they are the only ones who know the right way to work with young children. "**

Why we must act now

It is now widely accepted that public investments in quality preK programs can contribute to narrowing the gap between children as they enter kindergarten. Starting early is virtually a mantra. What is still the subject of debate is whether quality preK alone can sustain the gains made from early learning programs.

There is growing consensus that gains made in good preK programs must be sustained by quality education during the K–3 years at the minimum. Low-income children who attend elementary schools with inexperienced teachers and principals are particularly prone to loss of their preK gains. Research also shows that low-income children are vulnerable when they experience several grades of poor teaching, and that when they experience several years of good teachers, they thrive.

Thus, states and school districts throughout the country are implementing PreK–3 initiatives to connect more closely their preK programs with the early grades of elementary education. The more mature implementers have achievement data to support the efficiency of this approach, especially for children living in low-income families.

Third grade achievement is increasingly recognized as a crucial turning point in children's educational trajectories. Children who are not proficient in reading and mathematics by the end of third grade are unlikely to catch up. Many will become discouraged and drop out of school, emotionally at first and physically when they are able to walk out the door.

There are encouraging signs that states are taking a birth-to-postgraduate-education coordinated-alignment approach to education reform. Governors are establishing councils and other initiatives. In reality, only a few states have a clear plan for and implementation of a birth-to-postsecondary-education strategy. In the next ten years, the most important education reform that the federal government can encourage and that states can undertake is moving toward a PreK–3 primary education system as the foundation for all later educational achievement.

A preK–3 primary education system is not a magic bullet; nothing really is, given the complex factors that influence children's lives. But such a system is a crucial and necessary part of narrowing the disturbing achievement gap in America. No solution to the gap in struggling schools can be effective without a preK–3 system as the basic building block.

Pathways: Five priorities for achieving the vision

To achieve the vision of a transformed primary education system that spans from preK into third grade, I offer five priorities for moving forward.

First, we must reframe primary education for the 21st century as starting with excellent preK education for 3- and 4-year-olds, followed by equally excellent full-day kindergarten, and excellent educational experiences at least into third grade.

Second, we must reframe what is shared responsibility or accountability for children's learning by the end of third grade as involving three major partners: preK/early learning programs, K–3 education, and families. All must work together so children are ready for the challenges of middle school, high school, and college. No one party is responsible for how children learn.

Third, we must work on aligning common standards, curricula, and assessment from preK to third grade. The educational experience of children should be well-rounded, including the arts and social competence, as well as reading, writing, mathematics, and dual-language learning... The benefits to both native English-language speakers and children who are learning English as a second language are cognitive and social, and can have long-term economic payoffs in a global society. Crafting national, voluntary standards that begin with preK, are informed by the developmental requirements of young children, and continue into postsecondary education is critical to guide learning and assessment.

Fourth, we must seriously invest in preparing and supporting educators during this period, through preservice and in-service professional development. All teachers should have a preK–3 teaching credential and should be supported by teaching assistants who have a minimum of an Associate of Arts degree or are working toward an education degree as student teachers. A preK–3 teaching credential could also contribute to the necessary horizontal alignment of learning with grades and vertical alignment across grades. Teacher quality should be as highly demanded as it is for the K–12 education system. Once teachers are in the classrooms, resources to support their continuing development are paramount.

Fifth, we must rethink family engagement in children's learning. First, we must focus on enhancing the literacy skills of parents, especially when they have not been adequately educated. Second, we must engage parents closely in what their children are learning in the classroom so there is an alignment between what children learn and what parents do to support that learning over the years.

What early educators can do: cultural change

To create a preK–3 primary education system that reaches everyone, early educators must reach out to and also respond to K–12 educators who recognize the value of early learning and of early educators. These educators seek to partner respectfully with early educators to create seamless learning continuums from early learning programs, whether in public schools or elsewhere, through joint professional-development-and-assessment feedback loops that assure that children learn in a developmentally informed sequence from one year to the next. Every year counts, and every year that is a quality educational experience counts significantly for children's performance.

What is involved is the hard work of cultural contact and cultural change. Early education and K–12 education are now largely separate cultures with their own values and ways of operating. The two cultures are institutionalized by different funding streams, requirements, assessments, and accountability systems. There are typically separate standards for young children's learning, although some change is now occurring to align standards for early learning and K–12 education. Except in a few states, information about preK children is not part of state longitudinal education data systems. All of this must change, and change is not easy.

Early educators must abandon their position that they are the only ones who know the right way to work with young children. They must work with the K–12 education system as partners in shaping a seamless learning experience for children from birth to at least third grade. There must be reciprocal give and take; both sides have much to learn from each other.

K–12 educators must also change their ways, including how they see early educators. As the preparation of educators (principals and superintendents, as well as teachers) becomes more deeply developmentally informed, early educators will find common ground with other educators from K–12 and beyond. A long-term effort at the National Council for the Accreditation of Teacher Education focuses on how schools of education and other sites for preparation can better educate teachers about child and adolescent development.

Everyone's eyes must be on the prize: well-educated, well-prepared, ethical, and thoughtful lifelong learners. No one level of education has ownership over children's learning. At present, with a few exceptions, we have a situation of cultural conflict. But a preK–3 education system presents an opportunity to move from conflict to contact and eventually genuine cooperation. Children will surely benefit as the quality of their educational experiences improves.

No more lost generations

Because we have not provided opportunities for all young children to experience a high-quality early education, followed and sustained by a high-quality elementary education, we have lost too many generations of children to underachievement and diminished lives. This state of affairs is intolerable. David Gergen, a usually dispassionate observer, has called this "a national scandal."

During the Great Depression, Langston Hughes wrote a poem titled "Let America Be America Again." That America assures that all our children receive the best education we can provide in a society that values equality of opportunity. Educating each child well is the civil and human rights issue of our time. If we start in their early years, by 2020, each child will be engaged in a system of primary education that integrates the best of preK and K–3 education. Only then will we have a chance to make a difference in children's lives. ▶

Hope for the children of 2020:

That by 2020, the United States will have signed the UN Declaration on the Rights of Children and joined the rest of the world in according all our children the basic rights to education, health, and a good life.

About the Author

Ruby Takanishi, PhD, *President, Foundation for Child Development* communications@fcd-us.org

Professional focus

Takanishi's passion over the past 40 years has been to connect research with public policy to assure equal opportunity for every child to succeed in life.

The Leadership Role of Elementary School Principals

Jeffrey A. Wolff

As a society, we want the very best for our youngest members. Improvements in pre- and postnatal natal care have dramatically increased survival rates for infants and improved the health of young children.

Research has provided parents the tools to understand what is best for their children's health. We are better at early detection and treatment of serious childhood diseases. As a result, young children are healthier than ever before. In addition, advances in media technology have put more information into the hands of young children. Their knowledge base is greater than that of children 40 or 50 years ago. They have a greater awareness of the world around them.

However, society has not focused as much attention on the youngest learners within the educational system. I hope this will change over the next 10 years. We must invest in our future by focusing our resources where they will pay the greatest dividends. My experience as an elementary school principal, as well as my affiliation with the CAYL (Community Advocates for Young Learners) Institute in Cambridge, Massachusetts, has led me to conclude that we must reexamine our educational priorities and reallocate some of our public school resources to the early childhood years.

Young children in the year 2020 will need to attend public school by age 4. It must be mandatory, and it must be free. It must be a full-day program. Kindergarten must be mandatory, free, and full-day as well. Public and private preschools must work together to provide low-cost programs for 2- and 3-year-olds, especially in low-income areas. Private child care centers should be encouraged to locate near public elementary schools and work together. Public schools should try to provide onsite child care for their employees. School districts should be required to develop outreach programs to identify parents and children from birth to school age and bring them into local elementary schools.

Ideally, all elementary schools should offer education to children from age 3 to grade 3. I offer this recommendation because, in order to focus and align resources on one age group, staff members from the other age groups need to be near one another physically so they can work closely together as a team.

Elementary school principals must lead the way on these early childhood initiatives. Their leadership is crucial. As promoted by the CAYL Institute, principals must be "architects of change"[26] and advocates for children ages 3 to 7.

The rationale for this shift in the focus and funding of public education is clear. A sturdy home has a solid foundation that supports the whole structure. Engineers and architects spend countless hours designing an appropriate and safe foundation for a high-rise building. Highly qualified building inspectors examine every section of the foundation to make sure it can support the weight of the building.

The early years of a child's life are the foundation. They must be strong and able to support the child later in life. School districts try to allocate funding fairly among elementary, middle, and high schools. Sometimes high schools receive a greater share of the resources because activities for teen students such as sports and Advanced Placement classes are expensive. I believe that school funding should be allocated so that elementary schools receive a larger share of the pie. This may be costly, but it is absolutely necessary for the success of everyone. We should strengthen the literacy, numeracy, and social skills of children 3 to 7. This investment will pay huge dividends. Elementary school principals need to advocate for this reallocation. In the end, the investment in early childhood education will save money at the middle and high school levels.

The pathway to my vision can be compared to the best-selling book *Good to Great,* by Jim Collins.[27] Developing and promoting a vision is like building a successful company. *Good to Great* reviews what companies have done to become successful. One key component of such companies is that they "confront the brutal facts." In order to become great, companies need to identify their weaknesses.

One brutal fact of public education is the high overall cost of some reforms we have implemented and the inconsistent results this funding has produced. Federal legislation such as No Child Left Behind[28] has mandated curriculum accountability programs utilizing state-mandated testing. The testing is expensive, the funding to so-called underperforming schools is massive, and the after-school tutoring programs are expensive. Initiatives such as charter schools, performance pay for teachers, and drop-out prevention programs are also not the answers for lasting school reform. Business leaders are pushing for reform at the high-school level because they want better-prepared graduates to fill their technical positions and are looking for a five-year return on their investment. If they focused on early childhood education, their return on investment would be 15 years away, which is too long for many chief executive officers.

The brutal fact is that we spend millions of dollars to attempt to fix surface cracks in our educational system. We plug these leaks only to see others sprout. We can fix many of the problems found in our middle and high schools if we prevent them in elementary schools. In *Annual Growth, Catch-Up Growth,* Lynn Fielding, Nancy Kerr, and Paul Rosier write, "Irony is discovering that the most cost-effective way to diminish low student achievement in high school occurs between birth and age five."[29] Two more great comparisons in *Good to Great* are the "hedgehog concept" and the "flywheel." Collins writes:

> *"The good-to-great companies are more like hedgehogs — simple, dowdy creatures that know one big thing and stick to it. The comparison companies are more like foxes — crafty, cunning creatures that know many things yet lack consistency."*[30]

"Sustainable transformations follow a predictable pattern of build-up and breakthrough. Like pushing on a giant, heavy flywheel, it takes a lot of effort to get the thing moving at all, but with persistent pushing in a consistent direction over a long period of time, the flywheel builds momentum, eventually hitting a point of breakthrough."[31]

We need to be hedgehogs who focus on one thing — improving early childhood programs — rather than foxes who run around fixing surface cracks inconsistently. Today, we as elementary school principals start to slowly push on that big flywheel. Gradually, we will build momentum so we can reach breakthrough by 2020.

> ❝ **The window of opportunity is there, but we need to reallocate resources to the early childhood years.** ❞

There are several significant issues to consider.

First, the importance of working with young children in public schools must be recognized as having value within school systems. The field of early care and education has been slow to recognize its importance within the American educational system. Early in my career, a central administrator commented to me that, "The high school is the jewel of the district." This belief is not uncommon. The high school may be the largest building. It may house the administrative offices or some community services. Elections may be held there. Community events may take place there. However, the real "jewel" of any district is its youngest students. The inquisitiveness and enthusiasm of a 4-year-old should be what drives us to be better. We owe it to them.

The impact of failure to focus on the early years falls hardest on the poor. In *Annual Growth, Catch-Up Growth*, Fielding et al. write, "When public services like police protection or public education fail, the burden is disproportionately borne by the poor who cannot compensate with gated communities and private academies. The only hope for the poor is that we in public education deliver on our promise."[32]

Second, the public must recognize the value of working with young children in public schools.

When the public considers the necessity for school reform, its focus tends to be on issues related to secondary schools. For example, in a *Policy to Action Brief* of the Foundation of Child Development, "The Case for Investing in PreK–3rd Education: Challenging Myths about School Reform," Rima Shore[33] observes that most reform efforts target middle and high schools because most people feel that children in elementary schools are doing fine. Annual polls tell us that public opinion of elementary schools is very high, but high schools are rated much lower.

This perception is mistaken. Elementary schools have serious achievement gaps. I believe the positive public opinion of elementary schools is a result of low expectations for young children and their teachers. Parents are fooled by the cuteness of many visual displays found in the hallways of elementary schools. It lulls them into a false sense of security. It lets elementary schools off the hook. That's a big mistake.

A third issue is the misconception that a good preK program guarantees later achievement. Shore writes, "When schools link preK education with the elementary grades, creating a common organizational structure and coherent sets of academic and social goals, the gains that children make in high-quality PreK programs are more likely to persist."[34] The key is to couple quality preK with follow-up resources in grades K–3. It's a whole-school approach that emphasizes the need to place preK programs inside elementary schools rather than in separate early childhood centers. Collaboration of teachers between grades ensures success in the early childhood years. They need to live together in one building. They are a learning community with common goals. They are accountable to one another. The elementary school principals are the leaders of this community. They need to demand that preschool programs be housed at their schools. They must include preschool children in the fabric of the elementary schools. Administrative attention must focus on preschools, kindergartens, and early childhood programs.

This vision sounds good, but how do we make it happen? Several proposals can make this vision a reality for the children of 2020. I don't *think* these wonderful things will happen for young people, I *know* they will happen. There is too much solid research to deny the importance of learning from ages 3 to 7. The preK–3 approach is inevitable. Fixing surface cracks is too expensive. Remediate in the early years and you will solve the problems permanently.

The window of opportunity is there, but we need to reallocate resources to the early childhood years. One way to do that is to change the ages at which children attend public school. Currently, children attend school from 5 to 18. We could adjust this to ages 4 to 17. College students would graduate at 21, producing an extra year of employment and helping our economy. Or perhaps college graduates could perform a year of public service before employment. They could volunteer in our public schools. Another way to fund preK for all 4-year-olds would be through a national sales tax on the purchase of items over $50, a national lottery to benefit early childhood programs, or a tax on Internet services.

These funding options are important, but not crucial, to the success of my vision. The most critical component is the support of elementary school principals, who must sell the idea to parents, teachers, central administrators, the public, business leaders, and politicians. Researchers in education need to publish more studies on the benefits of early intervention.

In *Annual Growth, Catch-Up Growth*, Fielding *et al.* write:

> "Every year a new wave of kindergarten students hit the beaches of our schools. Every year 40 percent of these students are already one to three years behind, just like the last wave and just like the next wave. We are locked into immense catch-up programs for these students — adding new layers of instruction and resources from kindergarten through twelfth grade."[35]

We need to reach these children before age 5. Principals need to reach out to parents of preschoolers and bring them into our schools. Parents need training to help their children before they enter public school. We can't play catch-up with so many children. The parent-school-community partnership needs to be stronger. Elementary school principals need to begin pushing on that big flywheel. It may feel very heavy right now, but the more of us who push, the greater the momentum will be very soon. Universal preschool within public education is my vision for the children of 2020. The future of education in America depends on a strong preK–3 program. The focus, funding, and public support are desperately needed today to reach our goal. Elementary school principals must step up to the plate and make it happen for young children. ▶

About the Author

Jeffrey A. Wolff, *Principal, Clyde F. Brown Elementary School, Millis, MA*

jwolff@millisps.org

Professional focus

Wolff focuses on the leadership role of elementary school principals in early childhood education.

Hope for the children of 2020:

To change public education by reallocating resources. Elementary schools should receive greater funding to identify and remediate learning problems for children aged 3 to 7.

Realizing the Dream for America's Children

Marian Wright Edelman and Cathy Grace

America is going to hell if we don't use her vast resources to end poverty and make it possible for all of God's children to have the basic necessities of life.

—Martin Luther King, Jr[36]

In order to articulate clearly a vision for the future of children in our country, it is important to recall the past and use it as a yardstick to measure our progress toward realizing the hopes expressed decades earlier. Over forty years ago, Dr. Martin Luther King, Jr., died calling for a multiracial Poor People's Campaign to end poverty and establish economic justice for all in our rich nation. He was prophetic in his warning that we must combat the triple evils of "excessive materialism, militarism and racism,"[37] as they could be our undoing. If he were alive today, we know he would be leading the crusade to establish a level playing field for all of our young people.

In America today:[38]

- There are 39.8 million poor people, including 14.1 million poor children — 1 in 5. In 1968, there were 25.4 million poor people and 11 million poor children.

- Children are the poorest age group, with child poverty rates highest.

- Minorities make up 70% of the population in the 100 counties with the highest rates of child poverty.

- Basic health-care coverage for children is not affordable or accessible; over 8 million are uninsured, and millions more are underinsured.

- Disparities in child outcomes are evident as early as age 9 months and grow larger by 24 months. The disparities exist across cognitive, social, behavioral, and health outcomes. Children from more at-risk backgrounds based on income status, racial/ethnic minority groups, home language other than English, and low maternal education scored lower on a cognitive assessment than children from families with more-advantaged backgrounds.

- A child or teen is killed by a gun every 2 hours 45 minutes, almost nine children a day, 61 per week.

- Racial and economic disparities are fueling a cradle-to-prison pipeline crisis that has become the new American apartheid. Nationally, one in three African American and one in six Latino boys born in 2001 are at risk of imprisonment.

- We are the only nation other than Somalia that has not ratified the UN Convention on the Rights of the Child, which provides a comprehensive framework for action both at home and in our relationships with other countries, especially those that we seek to help through our overseas aid.

Yet, there is new promise for America with the election of a young, visionary, and courageous African American president. He symbolizes a time of transforming change and rekindled hope for all children and people in America and the world. In a world that is two-thirds poor and non-Caucasian, this election by a strong majority of voters signaled a day of which Dr. King and others dreamed. By electing Barack Obama president, the American people recognized the rich diversity of our human community and the need to lead by example.

This great leadership victory alone is not the change we need, but it is the chance to achieve if we all come together to build the movement needed to end preventable maternal and child mortality, high numbers of teen pregnancies, inadequate access to high-quality early care and education programs for young children in poverty, school dropouts, and inequities in the juvenile justice system.

Our vision for children in 2020 includes a four-point plan of action:

First, significantly reduce child poverty. We must reset our nation's priorities that have resulted in the greatest gap between rich and poor in our history. This can be done by investing in the future of every child from birth through college. Each of us is responsible for ensuring our nation's future; working together and putting children's healthy development at the center of our decision-making and action is our only course if we expect to remain the champion of human rights and civil rights to the rest of the world.

We must commit ourselves to ending indefensible and preventable child poverty by 2015 — the deadline set by the UN Millennium Development Goals for developing nations— and the racial disparities suffered by millions of African American, Latino, and Native American children who are disproportionately poor in the richest county on Earth. Every family should have an adequate income based primarily on work, and there should be a decent safety net for anyone unable to work.

The truth is that America can afford to do this but does not have the political will. Every child in this country could be lifted out of poverty for less than nine months of the tax cuts for the top 1% and what we spend on less than four months of the Iraq and Afghanistan wars. Federal stimulus funds provided to states to offset the effects of the deepest economic recession we have seen in over 70 years are helping services remain at basic levels, but planning for the future should not be clouded by the unprecedented challenges of today. Economically we will recover, but without due diligence we will make the same mistakes — ignoring our children in favor of greed, power, and politics. We don't have a money problem; we have a values and priorities problem. We need to decide who should have the first call on government resources: those who need the most or those who have the most.

We believe that if certain policies and legislation were written and rewritten with children and families at the heart of the matter, we would lift our 14 million poor children out of poverty and stop throwing away over $500 billion annually in lost productivity, more crime, and serious health conditions by keeping them poor. Tax relief for low- and moderate-income families, including a fully refundable child-tax credit, would lift 2.1 million children out of poverty. Expanding and making fully refundable the Earned Income Tax Credit would lift millions more children from poverty. By increasing the minimum wage

> **We don't have a money problem; we have a values and priorities problem.**

to half the average wage, 1.7 million people would exit poverty. Expanding federal child care support to families earning 200% or less of the federal poverty level would lift 2.7 million children and parents out of poverty, and raising food-stamp participation to 85% of eligible individuals would reduce the poverty of 1.4 million people.

Why, when the answer is clear, are we, as a country, so slow to act? Will more children be a poverty statistic in 2020, millions more in extreme poverty, or will we change policy and mindset so dramatically in 2010, or 2012, or even 2015 that America can say in 2020 we have significantly reduced poverty?

Second, ensure adequate health coverage for children. Senior citizens have Medicare, and children should be guaranteed similar health protection in all 50 states. It is our ardent hope that by 2020, all children will be covered by a comprehensive health-care plan with a national safety net and all medically necessary services. But as an interim step, we propose:

- Making health insurance coverage available to all pregnant women.

- Establishing a national eligibility floor for child health coverage of 300% of the poverty level (about $66,000 for a family of four), with little cost-sharing below this level to ensure that eligible children get health coverage and access to care when needed. Those with incomes above 300% of the federal policy level would be able to get such coverage at an affordable price.

- Simplifying and merging the two current child health care bureaucracies, Medicaid and the Child Health Insurance Program, so that the geography of where a child lives no longer determines eligibility.

- Increasing availability of mental-health services to young children so

that early interventions can take place and children are diverted from the possibility of entering the Cradle to Prison Pipeline® resulting in a life of crime and a financial drain on society.

- Reducing the number of teen pregnancies.

Even though teen births fall and rise over any given period, a baby is born to a teen mother every minute. The best contraception is hope and school success. Giving a teen the tools to get out of poverty and to envision a future different from perhaps that of her mother is both a health issue and an education issue. Viable community health clinics and school-nurse programs show promise for helping teens make good life choices. Again, funding for both should be regarded as a national health-care priority and translated to a state-level priority if we are serious about reducing teen pregnancies and births, and lifting children out of poverty.

Third, offer access to high-quality early care and education programs for children. Much has been written about the value of high-quality early care and education programs and the components that determine quality. No one can dispute that all children, from the minute of birth, benefit from personal, positive interactions with the adults in their lives. No one disputes that for low-income children, consistent attendance in a high-quality early care and education program provides greater gains in cognitive development than those of their peers from higher income families. Yet, low-income families continue to have to choose between keeping the lights on and having their children attend high-quality early care and education programs. Again, this is not a money problem but rather a values and priorities problem.

If we are serious about leveling the educational playing field for all of America's children, we must leverage funds and remove the artificial barrier of private-versus-public assistance to families who seek support in doing right by their children. In that new mindset of partnership, we propose that in 2020, all families who are seek-

significantly address the current funding deficits and reach every child regardless of family income. The income barrier to high-quality early care and education programs millions of children face today will be a memory shared by parents and grandparents of the young children of 2020. By 2020, the use of Title I funds for early care and education programs will be the rule rather than the exception. Compensation for teachers of young children that is comparable to their public school counterparts will be a reality, and the turnover rate in the profession significantly reduced. In 2020, those who teach young children will have the educational credentials to be teachers of distinction and not teachers of last resort.

Fourth, reform the juvenile justice system. While the number of juveniles in secure detention facilities has declined, an overreliance on costly detention and punishment rather than prevention and early intervention is funneling hundreds of thousands of children and youths into the prison pipeline at enormous personal and taxpayer cost.

One of the most successful examples of rehabilitating children in youth detention is the "Missouri Miracle," which reduced recidivism and brought significant cost savings to the state. This was accomplished through a full range of juvenile programs, from day treatment, to community-based facilities, to secure detention. In 2005, the national average cost for a youth in a community-based facility was about $41,000 a year; for secure care it was about $57,000 a year. Some states spend from $100,000 to $200,000 per year for a single bed in a youth correction facility.

In light of the tremendous cost to taxpayers and the undetermined personal cost to youths and their families, we envision a new method for correcting the life course of young people who are headed toward prison. In 2020, we will be providing options for all families to access social-service assistance in the form of mentors who use a research-based program to diffuse the potential destructive behaviors of youths and address families' roles in the problem. Our school systems will use money from

ing to better parent and educate their children will have access to high-quality home-visitation programs. Young children will participate in high-quality early care and education programs regardless of where families live or their income levels. The year 2020 will usher in the continuum of learning that has been talked about for so long and so many have tried to construct. Early care and education classrooms and home-based programs will unite with Head Start and prekindergarten programs in public and private schools to provide children an educational experience built on a research-based set of guidelines that is respectful of the child's developmental domains and culture. It will not be uncommon to visit classrooms in the Midwest or the Deep South that look and sound like those currently on the East or West coasts where a multitude of languages is spoken daily by teachers and children.

In 2020, federal funding for Head Start, Early Head Start, the Child Care and Development Fund program, and other educational programs for young children will be at levels that will the upcoming reauthorization of the Elementary and Secondary Education Act and other funds to eliminate from schools those things that lead children into the abyss of hopelessness and social dysfunction, especially dropping out of school. New school construction will emphasize the colocation of health services, social-services agencies, early care centers, and much more in order to make school sites community hubs that address family and child needs.

Prior to 2020, our country will acknowledge the brokenness of the juvenile justice system. Reform will occur, and by 2020 the system will be more focused on positive outcomes and less punitive. We will see a major needed paradigm shift to prevention and early intervention over costly and ineffective incarceration. Measures of the system's effectiveness will be based on low recidivism, and on youths completing high school and job-training programs, and not on the numbers of incarcerated juveniles or repeat youth offenders being locked up, as it is today. Community-based programs for youth supported through city, county, state, and federal budgets will be commonplace in 2020. These programs will be viable alternatives for children and youth who are tempted by the lure of gangs. Places of hope and reassurance will become the new gangs of 2020. The gangs of today, which serve as dysfunctional family units for many thousands of youths, will be replaced by a new family unit — a healthy one that teaches respect for self and others, and for the value of life, starting with their own.

Dreaming is not folly. It is often the only way things come to pass. But dreaming is not enough; what's also needed is a map for those who act on the dream to follow, as is an army of soldiers who will build and see the dream through to completion. And even when the job appears to be finished, it is not. More lessons will be learned and more needs revealed in making the dream a reality. So we must continue to dream, plan, act, and celebrate the work that is accomplished, and do it over and over again until every child is safe, and healthy, and educated. ▶

Hope for the children of 2020:

That the world will recognize the children's worth, the adults in their lives will value their innate curiosity and sense of wonder, and the systems designed to educate and keep them healthy will succeed. —Edelman

That Americans will come to value young children in the same way they value other national treasures. We all contribute to the preservation of our union; in the future it would be ideal if we could view the education and health concerns of young children in America as critical to its preservation. —Grace

About the Authors

Marian Wright Edelman, *President, The Children's Defense Fund*

Cathy Grace, EdD, *Director, Early Childhood Development Policy, The Children's Defense Fund*

Professional focus

Edelman's focus is supporting the rights of all children to be healthy, happy, and educated, so they will become productive adults.

Grace's professional interests have focused on low-income and rural young children and the quest to provide resources and develop policies that ensure their access to high-quality, comprehensive early care and education programs.

Improv Workshop

Translating Ideas into Intelligent Action

Workshop Agenda
- Reflections on vision articles
- Writing your vision
- Applying your vision

Reflections on the vision articles

As we read the six vision statements, we detect a *consistent tone of hope*. These authors are long-time educators and advocates who have weathered setbacks and disappointments, but their optimism continues to shine throughout their statements. They are acutely informed about the challenges and barriers, yet their response is to work not only harder, but *smarter*. They stay focused on the long term, knowing persistence is the only way to achieve breakthroughs for our children and our country's future. That is at the heart of *smart* improv: if one approach fails or a problem seems insurmountable, you keep searching for answers, exploring new knowledge, and trying out better ideas in pursuit of your vision. Another underlying theme of the six authors' visions is the *imperative of change*. But within the overall framework of change, you will find different approaches. Some authors focus on how early educators need to change, and others emphasize how society needs to change.

For example, the authors all agree that the traditional way the public education system (kindergarten through twelfth grade) is organized must expand — both upward and downward.

However, these authors have varying visions about the range of the desired extensions: stronger alignments are proposed for birth through third grade; preschool through third grade; ages 4 to 17; and prekindergarten through age 20.

Further, while authors share the goal of healthy development and high-quality education for all children, their visions convey how they have selected specific types of opportunities as the focus of their professional efforts. The authors' visions are shaped by the context in which they work, whether higher education or public schools, for example. This contextual focus reminds us of the strengths and challenges inherent in the early care and education field:

- Our work is often — and not surprisingly — driven by our identity with a particular sector of the broader field.

- There are multiple ways we must work to improve opportunities for children and their families.

- There are multiple dimensions *within* each opportunity. For example, whether in higher education or public schools, one must consider issues such as language, institutional settings, race, culture, and age focus.

- Many of us may not have "the big picture" of the field or the child in mind as we do our work.

"I'm counting on you! Will you help me achieve my American Dream?"

Do not underestimate the power of emboldening *your* dreams for the children of 2020, for their significance runs far deeper than vision statements and bullet-point lists of goals. In preparing for the improv workshop on vision, it helps to be self-aware — to understand what drives your dreams for the children of 2020. In addition, consider how individuals you know can be quite different from you. How would these differences affect their focus and dreams for children? How can the different visions fit together?

As a reader, you may have discovered additional themes and contrasts while reviewing the Vision articles in Act I. Take time to identify your own thoughts about the commonality and differences among the authors.

- Is there a core, defining intent that unites these vision statements?

- To what ages of children do these visions refer?

- How do these ideas conform to my view of the field of early care and education?

Writing your vision

Your vision should include the general direction of the change you seek as well your specific goals and priorities. How might you pursue your vision in your everyday professional activities? Also, your personal vision is a prerequisite to understanding and working with others to improve the quality of early care and education services. Equally important, clarity in your personal vision will provide you with a benchmark for comparing your thoughts with those of others who may have hopes and dreams that are different from yours.

- Make a list of the opportunities that should be available to all children and their families.

- Review the list and circle those items that are closely linked to your personal vision and/or specific areas where you are in a position to make a difference now.

- What are your hopes for the children of 2020?

- What would you see in 2020 that would be evidence that your hopes were achieved?

When you commit your vision to writing, it serves as a checkpoint to determine if your smart improv (discussions, decisions, and actions) is on track to achieve your goals.

Applying your vision

In smart improv, it is important to rehearse, even though your "script" will vary in everyday life. Here are several forms of practice:

- **Give a five-minute talk that summarizes your vision, your personal goals, and how you plan to connect these dreams in your ongoing actions.** Do this in a low-key, accepting setting, such as speaking to a friend or family member. This will give you practice in expressing your vision to others.

- **Make a list of the opportunities you will have this week, this month, and this year to act on your vision.** These should include the little actions you can apply on a daily basis, and perhaps one of your big priorities. Keep a tally; you will be surprised at how quickly all of the little action steps can add up to make a difference in the life of a child.

- **Brainstorm with others**. You can encourage each other in building your personal visions and putting them to work for the children of 2020. It is important that we also take time to view the hopes and priorities of others through their eyes. ▶

Act II: Knowledge
Information to Guide Future Practices

Commentary

The American Dream begins with a vision, but vision must be coupled with knowledge in order to create smart improvisation in the early care and education field. Different visions demand different skills and knowledge for their accomplishment. Is your knowledge base up-to-date?

Knowledge matters. Knowledge and assumptions are constantly changing, and professionals in all fields of endeavor have an obligation to stay current about emerging research and better practices.

You would be justifiably alarmed about being admitted to a hospital where the medical staff ignored new knowledge and continued to deliver surgery and treatment on the basis of methods common in the 1980s and 1990s. Undoubtedly, you would look for a better hospital — one where the medical personnel were seeking out new research findings, promising experimental developments, and improved practices.

All competent professionals practice a persistent habit of inquiry about their field in general, and about the specific situation in which they are working. Knowledge is at the heart of smart improv, and solid facts provide the foundation needed to achieve better outcomes for the children of 2020.

As you move toward your vision developed in Act I, you must seek current, validated information about how children develop and learn.

Keeping your knowledge base fresh can be a challenge because of the tendency to consider information about how children develop and learn as fixed, or static.

Recognizing this fact, for Act II of Children of 2020, we asked early care and education experts to synthesize what we have learned in eight key topical areas, describing new knowledge gained in the past decade and the implications of the information for our practices. Here you will read syntheses of new knowledge about learning and cognitive development, social-emotional development, racial identity, the role of culture, dual-language learners, mathematics, play, and life skills. The separation of knowledge into discrete topics was intentionally artificial, enabling easier communication and an emphasis on important new developments.

> ### *Knowledge as Building Blocks*
>
> Keep your work setting and children in mind while you work on Act II, because you will want to "harvest" the growing body of knowledge about children and learning. That is, you will be looking for ways to identify and apply validated information in the course of your everyday professional life.
>
> The articles for this act are topical, dealing with specific segments of learning and development. Segmenting the overall body of knowledge is for convenience in applying new information to your own everyday, specific situations.
>
> Please keep in mind that the knowledge areas are interrelated. In developing your smart improv, you will need to use the information as building blocks, combining ideas from several topics. Using multiple ideas together will help build powerful, comprehensive, integrated solutions for ECE in your community.

As you read, ask yourself questions such as:

- How do my vision, personal beliefs, and values interact with the information I am reading?
- How are these articles on discrete topics interrelated?
- Which of these ideas relate directly to my work? How can I learn more about this?
- What can I *do* with this information?

These knowledge syntheses are offered in Act II as information to stimulate action and professional development. In the improv workshop that follows the eight knowledge syntheses, we will challenge you and your colleagues to develop or refine and use your own knowledge base to strengthen opportunities for the children of 2020.

The following thoughts provide a flavor of what is to come from our eight commentaries, but read each knowledge synthesis carefully and make notes for creating your own knowledge-based improv.

PREVIEW OF KNOWLEDGE *Thoughts from Act II*	
Learning and Cognitive Development *Sue Bredekamp, Early Childhood Education Consultant*	For some time, early childhood education has been plagued by contentious either/or debates: teacher-directed or child-initiated; social-emotional or cognitive; play or academics. In each instance, the advisable, research-based approach is more accurately characterized as both/and.
Social-Emotional Development *Ann S. Epstein, HighScope Educational Research Foundation*	Research shows social and cognitive skills are linked. Academic readiness depends on social-emotional elements such as listening, task persistence, and flexible problem-solving. Young children who have emotionally secure and positive social experiences become able learners.

Culturally Responsive Perspective *Tammy Mann, Frederick Patterson Research Institute*	Awareness of one's own culture is the first step along the path toward a culturally informed point of view. Yet not enough attention has been paid to developing and implementing transformative professional-development experiences that equip early care and education professionals to practice from this perspective.
Racial Identity *Carol Brunson Day, National Black Child Development Institute*	Cultural/racial matching of teachers and students alone is not a panacea for education. More fundamental is the issue of having teachers who understand their students' cultures and incorporate them into their interactions together in class.
Language and Literacy for Bilingual and Monolingual Children *Linda M. Espinosa, University of Missouri-Columbia*	The increasing proportion of young children who are dual-language learners has major implications for the composition and preparation of the early childhood workforce. In order to realize the potential of early bilingualism, we will need highly skilled teachers who have achieved proficiency in bilingualism, multicultural perspectives, and effective teaching strategies.
The Mathematical Lives of Young Children *Julie Sarama and Douglas H. Clements, University at Buffalo, State University of New York*	The early years are a critical period for learning math. Children's early knowledge of math predicts not only later math achievement, but also their later reading achievement. Thus, it appears that math is a core component of cognition.
Play *David Elkind, Tufts University* *Learning and Life Skills*	The decade of 2000 to 2010 saw a great deal of attention paid to the play of young children. Research studies reinforce the importance of self-initiated play for social, emotional, and intellectual development.
Learning and Life Skills *Ellen Galinsky, Families and Work Institute*	We have focused on the content that young children need to learn, but we have paid much less attention to the life skills they need to have. These skills often make a critical difference in which children come to school ready to learn and which children are behind before they even enter kindergarten or first grade.

After reading the full articles about knowledge to help guide future ECE practices, continue with the Act II improv workshop. ▶

Learning and Cognitive Development

Sue Bredekamp

The last two decades have seen an explosion in research on child development and learning — both basic and applied — that has yet to have a significant impact on early education. Translating this research into practice could go a long way toward closing the persistent achievement gaps that exist for children from low-income backgrounds and dual-language learners, as well as preparing all the children of 2020 for the demands of the technological age in which they will live.

Findings from cognitive science in conjunction with brain research have contributed a great deal to our understanding of how children learn. In this commentary, I discuss three areas of ongoing study that have important implications for practice:

- Knowledge gained from the science of brain development.

- Research on domain-general processes that applies across developmental domains and subject-matter disciplines.

- Research on domain-specific processes that applies to specific content areas such as mathematics or literacy.[39]

Knowledge gained from brain research

Scientific study of the brain using the latest technologies has generated more widespread interest and popular dissemination than perhaps any other area of child-development research. Brain imagery provides powerful evidence of the critical importance of the early years. Seeing these images somehow convinces policymakers of what should have been obvious all along: that babies are learning from birth, and that early experience matters.

Despite the enthusiasm over brain research and its embrace by many early childhood educators who have cited it as proof that they have been right all along, to date the science of brain development provides limited guidance for specific practices. Nevertheless, comprehensive research reviews support several important conclusions:

- Because so much of the brain's most significant development occurs in utero, prenatal care and maternal health services such as that provided in Early Head Start should be a focus of national policy.

- Because neglect, abuse, and prolonged stress pose serious threats to healthy brain development, prevention and early intervention from birth are essential in light of the potentially lasting negative consequences.

- Because different parts of the brain are more responsive to experiences at different times, attention should be paid to windows of opportunity for particular types of learning, such as language, during the first five years of life.

- Because brains develop best in the context of loving relationships, play, opportunities to explore their world, and engaging things to learn about, children need high-quality, developmentally appropriate early childhood programs, like those typically promoted by child-development specialists.

- Because brain development is integrated and the areas within the brain become more connected as children get older, arbitrary distinctions between domains of development, such as social-emotional versus cognitive, and arguments over which is more important are irrelevant and unnecessarily distracting from more important goals for children.

By 2020, we will undoubtedly have a vastly larger body of knowledge on brain development that is likely to be more useful in guiding practices. However, there are inherent risks in this avenue of study. Brain research should be interpreted with caution because it can lead to the assumption that brain functioning is predetermined by heredity. In fact, brain research concludes the opposite: clearly, the physical changes that occur in children's brains during the early years cause changes in how children understand the world, while at the same time children's brains change as a result of enriching experiences and new learning.

Another possibility that early childhood educators must face is that future research may contradict their present concepts of good practice. If so, will the field then continue to embrace brain research?

Despite the newfound enthusiasm for brain research, we still know more about how the mind develops. Scientists have been studying learning much longer, and it is easier and less costly to do. A large body of research is now available that is more directly applicable to practice, which I discuss in the next sections.

Research on domain-general cognitive processes

During preschool and the primary grades, considerable growth and other kinds of change take place in the frontal lobes of the brain, which regulate cognitive processes that are essential for success in school and life. These processes include self-regulation, executive function, and symbolic representation, and they are affected significantly by early experiences.

These capacities underlie children's ability to succeed in school and later life. For example, children who cannot control their impulses are likely to struggle in the early grades, where focused attention is required to comprehend

reading and mathematics. Given their importance to all later functioning, these processes should be primary goals for young children. They should be incorporated into early learning standards, curricula, and assessment procedures. In addition, teachers should be prepared to use effective teaching strategies that promote development of these processes. These domain-general processes are the real basics of early education.

Self-regulation and executive function.

In a landmark report, *Neurons to Neighborhoods: The Science of Early Childhood Development,*[40] the National Research Council identified the process of moving from external to self-regulation as one of the primary tasks of the first five years of life. Self-regulation is the ability to monitor and adapt behaviors, emotions, and thinking to the demands of a situation. "Self-regulation" is the term most often used by psychologists who study social-emotional development, while cognitive psychologists use the term "executive function" to describe abilities that include effortful control, focused attention, planning (thinking ahead), reasoning, and monitoring cognitive processes. Lev Vygotsky believed that developing self-regulation is the primary task of the preschool years, providing the necessary foundation for the demands of formal schooling.

Self-regulated children can think before acting. They can stop doing something they would rather do (such as playing) and start doing something that is required (such as listening to a story or cleaning up). This is a big challenge for many preschoolers and a huge challenge for some. Although most children naturally improve in their self-regulatory abilities as their brains mature, some do not. In addition, there are observable differences in children's self-regulatory capacities beginning at birth. Therefore, one of the primary goals of preschool education should be for teachers to intentionally support the development of self-regulation.

A research-based preschool curriculum model, Tools of the Mind, is designed to

build these capacities in young children. Based on Vygotsky's sociocultural theory, the primary goal of Tools of the Mind[41] is building self-regulation along with the foundations of academic learning in early literacy and mathematics. Vygotsky believed that sociodramatic play is the leading activity that promotes the development of self-regulation during the preschool years and prepares children to learn on demand, the requirement of formal schooling. Tools of the Mind teachers help children engage in high–level, mature sociodramatic play, which involves a theme, roles, rules, props, and language interaction, and lasts 10 minutes or more. This type of play does not come naturally to children; it is the product of adults and older children pretending with children from an early age.

Today, most children spend more time with media or same-age peers in groups and do not necessarily have the kind of experiences that promote sociodramatic play. Therefore, Tools of the Mind teachers use specific strategies, including direct experiences, such as field trips, that provide fodder for rich play and language interaction. They also engage children in preparing written play plans, using scaffolded writing, that support self-regulation and early literacy skills. Empirical research demonstrates that children in Tools of the Mind classrooms, including those from low-income backgrounds and dual-language learners, perform significantly better on measures of executive function and on more traditional literacy and language measures.

The HighScope curriculum, which has a much longer tradition in the field, is another example of a model that promotes domain-general processes. The hallmark of the curriculum is the plan-do-review process. This strategy promotes planning (thinking ahead), decision-making, and problem-solving in young children. Moreover, the review aspect of the experience engages children in reflecting on and analyzing their experiences, which are metacognitive processes that build self-regulation and executive function as well. The HighScope curriculum is best known for the lasting positive effects of the Perry Preschool Project. Its greatest effects were in social and economic outcomes such as higher rates of high school graduation, productive employment, home ownership, and lower rates of criminal behavior. Most likely these outcomes are related to strengthening participants' self-regulation and executive function abilities at an early age.

Symbolic representation. An overly simplistic definition of symbolic representation is using one thing to stand for another. In reality, symbolic representation is highly complex. It underlies all of school learning, from understanding the alphabetic principle (that letter symbols are used to represent the sounds of spoken language) to comprehending the symbolic language of that most abstract of subjects, mathematics. This foundational capacity is so important to later learning and development that symbolic representation must also be a major goal of early childhood curriculum.

Teachers can promote symbolic representation in many ways. For example, play helps build symbolic representation. Even toddlers begin to develop representational abilities through pretend play. At first they use real objects or toys in their pretend play, such as when a toddler holds a toy phone to her ear. If adults encourage this type of play, children substitute other objects, such as when a preschooler pretends a block is a phone. Later, the child may simply hold a hand to her ear as though she is talking on the phone. Over time, children's symbolic representation abilities continue to expand along with their creative thinking and problem-solving. These experiences help children move from thought that is connected to physical action to using words and symbols to represent concepts mentally, which is essential for higher-level thinking.

Similarly, the visual arts promote symbolic representation. Children don't just create pretty pictures or models with clay and other materials (although that is an important part of art); they represent their interpretations of reality. For example, most third-graders accurately report that the Earth is round; however, when asked to draw a picture of it and where the people live, they may draw people standing on top of a flattened sphere or living inside it.

The world-renowned Reggio Emilia approach to early childhood education is sometimes misrepresented in the United States as an art program, when in fact what looks like art to many visitors are actually children's representations of their conceptual understanding. In Reggio Emilia, children use multiple means of representation to deepen their understandings. In figuring out how to represent a chair in clay, for example, they have to think about how to make it stand up, a different challenge than creating a two-dimensional drawing. Engaging children in activities such as pretend play, drawing, writing, and creating mathematical models (such

 Goldilocks sought comfort in solutions that were 'not too hard' or 'not too soft,' but 'just right.' Effective early childhood teaching occurs most often when teachers find that middle ground. 🙶

as using blocks to visually represent quantity) builds their capacity to later use abstract models such as maps and algorithms.

In addition to self-regulation, executive function, and symbolic representation, other domain-general processes, such as relationships and deliberate memory, should be goals of all early childhood programs. However, the curriculum must also address domain-specific processes that are particularly important for school success: reading and mathematics.

Domain-specific processes

Decades of research on early literacy and mathematics identifies the key skills and knowledge that predict later success in school and life. Although not as conclusive, research also provides guidance about effective teaching strategies in these domains. Given that there is considerable evidence, for example, that skills such as alphabet knowledge, phonological awareness, print awareness, early writing, and vocabulary lay the necessary foundation for learning to read, preschool programs have the responsibility to teach these skills. Above all, they have an obligation to use proven strategies to promote language development given its relationship to all other learning and the fact that language ability is so strongly related to the achievement gap in math as well as in reading.

The title of the National Research Council's 2009 report *Mathematics Learning in Early Childhood: Paths toward Excellence and Equity*[42] conveys its goal as well as its promise. Young children are capable of more sophisticated mathematics learning than previously assumed, and they are interested in and enjoy math. Unfortunately, the math achievement gap is already present in preschool and only widens as children go through school because later mathematics learning not only builds on earlier understanding, it depends on it. Here again, we have current knowledge to guide practice.

The early childhood curriculum needs to be content-rich; children need and want to learn.

Curriculum and teaching should include content and processes, some of which are specific to the subject area. For example, unitizing — finding or creating a mathematical unit — is a domain-specific skill that is important in learning number, geometry, spatial relations, and measurement. When children count, they have to use or identify a unit to be counted. For example, they can count people, or couples, or people's hands. When they measure length, they use a unit, whether it is their foot, their body, or a yardstick. When they create a pattern — such as two circles, three squares/two circles, three squares — they use and repeat a unit (*aa/bbb*). When they count by 2s, 5s, or 10s, the units are 2, 5, and 10.

Understanding and applying the concept of a unit is essential in mathematics. For example, to understand the base-ten place-value system, primary grade children must be able to recognize that 10 ones can form a single unit of 10. Children learn this abstract idea through many meaningful, concrete experiences, such as making patterns and counting. Similarly, unitizing applies to other subject areas such as reading and writing (words, phrases, sentences, paragraphs) or music. For this reason, unitizing is an example of a domain-specific process that should be a core idea in the early childhood curriculum.

Conclusions

For some time, early childhood education, not unlike all levels of education and the country as a whole, has been plagued by contentious either/or debates: teacher-directed or child-initiated; social-emotional or cognitive; play or academics. More than ever, research reveals the hollow nature of these arguments. In each instance, the advisable, research-based approach is more accurately characterized as both/and. For example, children need teacher-supported and child-initiated play experiences that promote both domain-general processes and domain-specific skills, knowledge, and processes.

A final conclusion from both research and years of experience and observation in the field is that early childhood education could benefit from embracing the Goldilocks solution. Goldilocks sought comfort in solutions that were "not too hard" or "not too soft," but "just right." Effective early childhood teaching occurs most often when teachers find that middle ground. For example, they shouldn't intrude on children's play (by doing too much), nor should they ignore it (doing too little); neither option leads to optimal development for children. Similarly, in the visual arts, they shouldn't focus too much on the product, nor should they leave children without the skills to produce progressively more personally satisfying art products. Teachers shouldn't think or solve problems for children, nor should they fail to teach children reasoning and problem-solving strategies.

All of the children of 2020 would benefit if early childhood educators applied more of the current knowledge gleaned from cognitive science and brain research. And the early childhood profession itself could benefit from rejecting either/or choices in favor of both/and solutions. Perhaps then, Goldilocks and the three bears can all sit down together and live happily ever after. ▶

About the Author

Sue Bredekamp, Early Childhood Education Consultant
joesueb@msn.com

Professional focus

Bredekamp is an early childhood education specialist who serves as a consultant on developmentally appropriate practice, curriculum, teaching, and professional development.

Hope for the children of 2020:

That every early childhood teacher will establish warm, positive relationships with children and reciprocal partnerships with families, embrace the realities of cultural and linguistic diversity, provide intellectually engaging curricula, and use effective teaching strategies to enhance children's learning and development.

Social-Emotional Development

Ann S. Epstein

Early childhood traditionally views development as a dynamic interplay of many factors. Yet in recent years, the spotlight on academics has dimmed our focus on social-emotional learning. Fortunately, alarms are being raised about this imbalance. Professionals, parents, and business and civic leaders worry about instilling compassion, tolerance, and ethics in tomorrow's citizens.

Four areas are especially vital to the individual well-being of the children of 2020 and the health of our society: demonstrating empathy, creating a moral code, negotiating social conflicts, and sharing in democracy.[43] There are two reasons to focus on these areas. First, scandals reported by the media have shaken our belief in the dependability of people and institutions. To prevent these wrongs, we can begin to establish a higher code of ethics in the formative years. Second, early childhood has important messages we are obligated to share. We don't have all the answers, but starting children on a path of healthy social and emotional development is a significant first step.

Following an overview of early social-emotional learning, this chapter addresses the four areas, summarizing what we know about children's development and how adults can scaffold their learning. Because supporting children's development also means attending to ourselves, a final section describes how teachers, families, and agencies can be role models to those we serve.

An overview of social-emotional learning

Emotional learning comprises the knowledge and skills to recognize and self-regulate feelings. Social learning involves principles and strategies to interact successfully with others. Dealing with one's emotional state is often a prerequisite to socializing well with others.

Social-emotional learning has four components:[44]

- **Emotional self-regulation and self-awareness** is responding to experiences with an appropriate range of immediate or delayed emotions. As children develop language and hold images (representations) in mind, they act with greater forethought and less impulsiveness. *Sklar and Lily both want Carrie to be their dog. Sklar says, "I can be a dog too, and Lily can be the owner for both dogs." Lily agrees and cuts long pieces of string to use as leashes.*

- **Social knowledge and understanding** is an awareness of social norms and customs. The shift from the "me" of toddlerhood to the "us" of preschool means becoming a community member. *Max helps Kayla put on her tennis shoes. "Now we can all go outside quicker," he tells the teacher.*

- **Social skills** are strategies for interacting with others, assisted by cognitive developments in perspective-taking and empathy. Emerging classification skills make preschoolers aware of how they are like and not like others. Adults can help them respect these differences. *Playing in the house area, Bret says to Kimi, "How did you get so tall? What did you eat?"*

- **Social dispositions** are enduring traits such as curiosity, humor, generosity, selfishness, and narrow-mindedness. Traits are shaped by innate temperamental differences, but environment influences how they are expressed, for example, as persistence versus stubbornness. *As Lute pulls the bus onto the blacktop, it gets stuck on a bike. He pulls several times, but the bus remains caught. He stoops to separate the vehicles, and steers the bus onto the blacktop.*

Research shows that social and cognitive skills are linked. Academic readiness depends on social-emotional elements such as listening, task persistence, and flexible problem-solving. Young children who have emotionally secure and positive social experiences become able learners. Early trauma puts children at risk for cognitive, perceptual-motor, affective, and social delays.

The recent attention to social-emotional learning is partly a backlash against the misconception that preschool's goal is to prepare children to read and do math upon kindergarten entry. Experts criticize this view and say that while traits such as curiosity, creativity, confidence, initiative, and persistence are not easy to define or measure, they, too, shape early learning. Consider how Jabiari discovers himself to be an independent and capable learner as he explores science:

At small-group time, after his teacher helps him plant seeds in a cup, Jabiari says, "I want to do another one by myself." As his teacher stands by, he tells her what he's doing step-by-step. Next week, when each child gets seeds for the outdoor garden, Jabiari says, "I know what to do." He digs a hole, puts in his seeds, and covers them up. "That's how it works," he says.

Achieving the right mix of academic and social skills is particularly critical for children at risk for behavioral and academic problems. Aggressive young children have trouble adjusting to school, are more likely to commit delinquent acts, and become liabilities rather than assets to society. That is why law-enforcement officials now tout the benefits of early childhood programs.

Renewed professional interest in social-emotional learning has been accompanied by increased press coverage. Being the center of attention is a mixed blessing. It highlights internal debates between one extreme that advocates letting children play with minimal adult intervention and the opposing view that promotes explicitly teaching a community's or society's values.

Public attention also demands we be accountable, which is good if we authentically assess how and what children learn. We must identify when development is healthy and when intervention is called for. We should also be cautious in defining "normal" so as not to (mis)label young children.

Finally, reintegrating social-emotional learning into the curriculum means discarding outdated ideas. There is a body of social-emotional knowledge children must master on a par with literacy and math skills. Moreover, children are more capable in this domain than previously thought.

In sum, the renewed interest in young children's social and emotional development is timely, but requires enlightened practitioners to keep up with the times. We need to be knowledgeable about this multidimensional domain and our multiple roles in supporting its early development.

Empathy

Today is Connor's first day at school. He stands at the side of the room. Jamaica leaves her friends in the house area and approaches him. She says, "You don't have any friends, so you can play with us." She leads him to the house area. "He can be the baby," she says, and hands him a blanket and a bottle. She pats Connor's arm and tucks the blanket around him.

What we know

Empathy is the ability to understand others' feelings by experiencing the same emotion oneself. Though young children are egocentric, research shows empathy begins as early as infancy.

At two months, babies look at and listen to one another. At six months, they monitor emotional expressions and react accordingly, approaching smiling caregivers or avoiding frowning ones. Toddlers turn toward sounds of distress, make appropriate facial expressions, and act prosocially to help, soothe, or share. By age 3, children are capable of perceptual perspective-taking, that is, picturing what others see or hear. Four-year-olds show conceptual perspective-taking, inferring thoughts, desires, and feelings, as Emily does in this anecdote: *Emily pats a child who cries when her mother leaves and says, "Your mommy will be back at outside time. When I'm sad, I draw my mommy a picture. Wanna make one for your mommy?"*

What we can do

Early experiences are critical in developing empathy. Adults can model awareness of and sensitivity to others, and build on the growing cognitive and social skills that underlie empathy:

Model caring behavior. Respond to children who are upset or angry. Individualize comfort based on what works for each child: stroking, a brief talk, or just standing nearby.

Acknowledge and label the feelings children have in common. Without being judgmental, help children learn that others share their feelings, and acknowledge their capacity for empathy. For example, instead of stating critically, "How would you feel if you had to wait?" a teacher might say, "You know how waiting feels when you really want to do something."

Create opportunities for children to act with empathy. Encourage children to help one another. Convey that everyone, regardless of age or ability, needs and can provide help. Caring for plants and animals also promotes empathy at home and in the classroom.

Practice perspective-taking in non-social situations. Since perspective-taking is both a cognitive and social accomplishment, encourage it in a variety of situations. *Marcus talks with his teacher, Rachel, about the class trip to the apple orchard. He says some children can ride in his father's big blue car. Others can go with Rachel or in the van. Rachel comments that the children can get there many ways. "But all to the same place," says Marcus.*

Promote perspective-taking in science, math, literacy, and the arts. Look at a bush from various positions. Gather data about preferences before mixing a batch of trail mix. Ask what characters in a book see, think, and feel. View sculptures from different angles. Let children give movement directions for others to follow, or consider an artist's choice of materials and the ideas conveyed.

Morality

Jean Piaget interviewed children about acts such as stealing and lying. Asked what a lie is, early preschoolers answered they were "naughty words" and said it was wrong to lie because it was a forbidden act. However, later preschoolers were able to explain, "Because lying isn't right," or, "It isn't true." That is, they cited simple moral reasons. Children in primary grades indicated intention as being relevant to the meaning and judgment of an act: "A lie is when you deceive someone else, but to make a mistake is just when you make a mistake."

What we know

Morality is an internal code for judging whether behavior is right or wrong, apart from external sanctions. In early stages of moral reasoning, children focus on outcomes rather than intentions, and obey rules and authority. As they interact with peers, they begin to consider behavior from other perspectives and apply rules based on reciprocity. Young children can also differentiate social conventions from moral principles. Conventional rules fluctuate, while moral behaviors do not. For example, 4-year-olds say it is wrong to wear pajamas to school (a social convention) and wrong to hit others (a moral principle). Asked which behaviors would be OK if the teachers allowed them, most say wearing pajamas would be fine, but hitting is still wrong.

Psychologists are also learning how moral development begins. Toddlers react emotionally to a violation of standards, such as a broken doll or dirty toy. They feel shame when their behavior falls short of expectations. Preschoolers wrestle with how to treat siblings and peers. They see how one person's actions affect the whole group: if they tear the pages from a book, no one can read it. Even if children do not see consequences on their own, they can if adults point them out.

Older preschoolers assess motivation and differentiate accidental harm from intentional harm. This ability is fragile — they still mostly focus on consequences — but grows with classification skills.

Families and communities play a significant role in moral development. Words, and especially actions, shape early ideas about right and wrong. Friends are also influential, though not

as much as parents. Children in stable homes usually choose peers who share their family's moral code. Those with negative or inconsistent parenting are more susceptible to harmful peer influences.

What we can do

To support children as they construct a moral framework, adults can employ these strategies:

Give simple reasons for moral decisions. Provide concrete explanations, not abstract statements; for example, it's not fair to take seconds before everyone gets a first serving. Help children differentiate moral rules from social conventions so they can adjust their behavior accordingly.

Acknowledge when children act morally. We think children who feel good about themselves will do the right thing, but it's the opposite: children who do the right thing feel good about themselves. Acknowledging moral behavior helps them become aware of their effect on others.

Acknowledge and support parents. Teachers can model ways for parents to guide children without using coercion. When home and school beliefs diverge, open communication helps teachers and parents clarify and resolve differences. It eases tension to remember that most differences reflect social conventions (for example, eating with fingers or utensils), while the underlying moral principle is the same (for example, grown-ups are responsible for feeding children healthy food).

Model moral behavior in instructional interactions with children. How we teach as well as what we teach affects moral development. In authoritarian teaching, students follow orders but do not engage in the higher reasoning that advances moral development. In inquiry-based learning, students express ideas and receive feedback from adults and peers. Teachers mediate but do not impose solutions. This type of learning models how to formulate and enact moral principles.

Conflict resolution

At small-group time, Amber says, "Teacher, she took my tape." When asked what she could do, Amber replies, "Say I don't like that." Then she gets the other child another roll of tape.

What we know

Conflict resolution involves using nonaggressive strategies to settle interpersonal differences. Young children get into conflicts when they are prevented from reaching a goal. They do not mean to misbehave, but have not yet learned to act appropriately. They may also be imitating behavior they see at home or in the media.

The capacity to resolve conflicts develops gradually and depends on children's abilities in other domains. Because strong emotions are often involved, they must recognize and regulate feelings. A rudimentary sense of time helps them delay gratification. Compromise involves perspective-taking, cooperation, and a sense of community. Children have to want to get along. Finally, resolving conflicts often rests on moral principles such as fairness and compassion. Thus, social problem-solving is not a separate strand of development, but requires growth in many areas.

What we can do

Adults are often uncomfortable with children's conflicts and impose solutions, rather than seeing them as learning opportunities. Yet when preschoolers solve problems on their own, challenging behaviors — crying, tattling, and physical aggression — decrease by as much as 40%. Learning to resolve conflicts take time and practice, but can be achieved with the following strategies:

Establish a safe environment with clear limits and expectations. Reassure children four things are safe: their bodies, feelings, thoughts (ideas and words), and work. Help them learn to calm themselves, for example, by holding a soft toy or handling soothing materials. Some programs create a permanent or temporary "peace place," or quiet spot, with soft furniture and lighting.

Use a multistep approach to conflict resolution. A conflict-resolution curriculum is a sequence of adult-guided steps to help children gradually learn to handle problems on their own. Typical steps include: stop hurtful behavior, accept children's feelings (if not a specific behavior), ask what happened (do not make assumptions), restate the problem so everyone understands, elicit solutions and choose one together. It may not be the adult's choice, but respect anything feasible: *Jacob and Sam argue over necklaces in the house area. When the teacher asks how to solve the problem, Jacob says, "We need more." Since that is not possible, the teacher is about to ask for another idea, when Sam says, "Yeah!" He gets leather thongs and beads from the art area. The boys spend the next hour making necklaces with hidden "spy phones" inside.*

Talk about solving conflicts apart from the actual situation. It is easier to absorb information when emotions are not running high. Revisit a conflict after a crisis has passed or before another occurs. Read and discuss books whose characters face similar issues.

Culturally Responsive Perspective

Tammy Mann[45]

Across the country, policymakers, economists, educators, and community leaders decry challenges on the horizon associated with changing demographics, the deplorable state of public education, and increased global competition. In fact, the prior publication *Children of 2010* challenged the field to carefully examine its work with children and to be diligent in its efforts to help prepare them to reach their full potential in an increasingly diverse society. While the early care and education field has certainly realized important gains in terms of increased programs for the very young (for example, Early Head Start) and increased access to state-funded preschool, some would say we have not done nearly enough to ensure that the professionals within the field are prepared to nurture and support children and families from diverse backgrounds.

The reasons for our slow progress are many, yet the longer it takes the field to identify and implement effective solutions, the more likely it is that we short-circuit our efforts to meet the development and learning needs of children in ways that can contribute to their health and well-being. As demographics continue to shift, the need for more skilled and informed professionals who are able to work effectively with children and families from diverse backgrounds will expand. This essay will offer perspective on the unique opportunities we have to focus on relationships and culture as we strive to nurture and support development and learning from birth through age 8.

New knowledge and its implications for practice

In 1998, the National Academy of Science (NAS) convened a committee charged with evaluating and integrating, across multiple disciplines, the science of early childhood development. The resulting publication, *From Neurons to Neighborhoods,*[46] highlighted 10 core concepts of development. Two of the concepts that most directly apply to this essay are:

- Human relationships, and the effects of relationships on relationships, are the building blocks of healthy development.
- Culture influences every aspect of human development and is reflected in childrearing beliefs and practices designed to promote healthy adaptation.

Both concepts are derived from an extensive review of the literature across many disciplines. In the case of the first point, the attachment literature and emerging neuroscience research both support the powerful role that relationships play in fostering healthy development. For more than 40 years, researchers have explored how attachment relationships provide a secure base from which young children gain a sense of confidence about themselves and others as they reach out to explore the world around them. While much of the attachment literature has focused on the mother-child relationship, recent research has also examined how young children form attachments with their fathers and other significant caregivers and siblings. For the infant and young child, having access to adults who are able to respond to their overtures for engagement increases their ability to associate meaning with their experiences. We know that at birth, all children are born wired to learn, yet without responsive, emotionally available adults, a child's physical, language, cognitive, and social and emotional development can be adversely impacted. One of the most critical advances in our understanding about the power of relationships and their impact on development comes from neuroscience research, which basically posits that the back-and-forth nature of interactions between children and adults plays a critical role in shaping the wiring of a child's brain. Nature provides the hardware, but experiences help shape how the hardware comes to express itself over time.

When it comes to understanding the impact of culture on development, unfortunately not nearly enough progress has been made to deepen our empirical understanding of its influence and how practitioners can take and use this knowledge to inform their work with children and families. While the NAS committee clearly identified culture as important for promoting healthy development and adaptation, it seemed less certain about how to empirically study and document its impact on development. With more than 100 years of research focused on child development, it's a tragedy that so little work has been devoted to examining one of the most important forces that shapes the manner in which parents and other adults interact with children during and beyond their formative years. In a national poll conducted by ZERO TO THREE, parents, across diverse racial/ethnic groups, reported that the two most powerful influences on their behavior as parents were their faith and the manner in which they were parented, when compared to other sources (parent educators, pediatricians, etc.).[47]

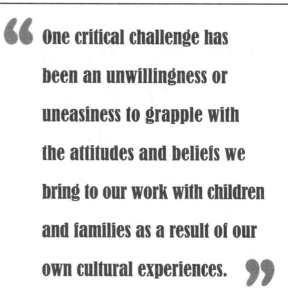

> **One critical challenge has been an unwillingness or uneasiness to grapple with the attitudes and beliefs we bring to our work with children and families as a result of our own cultural experiences.**

ZERO TO THREE has had a longstanding interest in this issue because caregiving routines such as feeding, sleeping, guidance and discipline, and toilet training during the earliest years are likely shaped by cultural values and beliefs. In 2007, ZERO TO THREE completed a literature review to understand the extent and nature of research examining the impact of culture on development for children younger than 3. The report, *The Changing Face of the United States: The Influence of Culture on Child Development*, reinforces conclusions reached by the NAS committee. In the report, culture is defined as "a shared system of meaning, which includes values, beliefs, and assumptions expressed in daily interactions of individuals within a group through a definite pattern of language, behavior, customs, attitudes and practices."[48] This definition presents important points worth expounding on:

- It stresses understanding shared meaning as a critical component of how culture is understood. All too often in our work with children and families, we have a tendency to focus more on the external ways culture is expressed (that is, customs) and miss the opportunity to explore the shared meaning associated with such practices and how they influence our interactions.

- Values, beliefs, and assumptions provide an important unspoken script to guide how we interact and behave. Many times these values and beliefs are unspoken and operate outside of conscious awareness, yet they have a powerful impact on how we interact with and relate to others daily. This element of culture demands that we focus our attention on seeking to understand these implicit values, beliefs, and assumptions as a critical element of being prepared to work effectively with all children and families, especially those coming from different cultural backgrounds. Considerable anthropological research has long documented that there are variations in how groups, depending upon their ethnic origins, value interdependence over behaviors that are more individualistically oriented. Such perspectives consequently affect how parents may approach promoting behaviors that encourage independence over those that support interdependence.

- Culture finds its expression through definite patterns of language, behavior, customs, attitudes, and practices. This point further amplifies the fact that culture finds its expression through the ways we interact with others. If we focus on how culture is expressed without seeking to understand the meaning behind behavior and practices, we run the risk of operating based on assumptions rather than verified understanding about meaning.

Relationships are the vehicles through which culture is transmitted from one generation to the next. Furthermore, core elements of this definition suggest that all individuals have a culture, and these experiences shape how we interact with others daily. It seems like yesterday's news to state that the awareness of one's own culture is the first step along the path to working with children and families from a culturally informed point of view, because this has been stated on numerous occasions by many leaders in the field. Yet the reality is that not enough attention has been paid to developing and implementing transformative professional-development experiences that equip early care and education professionals to practice from this perspective. In the sections that follow I turn my attention to why I believe our progress has been slow on this front and the opportunities before us to accelerate our progress.

Challenges associated with integrating cultural knowledge into our work

One critical challenge has been an unwillingness or uneasiness to grapple with the attitudes and beliefs we bring to our work with children and families as a result of our own cultural experiences. Since many equate culture with race, an immediate discomfort surfaces when one has to think and work from a perspective that serves as a reminder of our painful history regarding race relations in this country. Consequently, we have not developed the communication skills needed to openly discuss these tensions in ways that are constructive and offer opportunities for learning. For example, within education, some continue to rely on superficial strategies where we "recognize" the important contributions of various cultural groups on special holidays. We hang pictures and implement "special lessons" tied to these special days. Some educators have become disillusioned about the value and merit of incorporating a multicultural perspective into teacher-education programs. In *Becoming Culturally Responsive Educators*, Cathy Kea, Gloria D. Campbell-Whatley, and Heraldo V. Richards write:[49]

> *"Some schools of education have acknowledged the urgency for developing culturally competent teachers, while others grapple with ways to fit appropriate programs into their curriculum. Unconvinced of the academic merits of culturally responsive programming but not wanting to appear 'anti-diversity,'*

some will grudgingly add a diversity course to their curriculum. Overcoming this resistance is crucial to developing effective [teacher-education programs] that will provide pre-service teachers with the knowledge, skills, and dispositions needed to educate diverse learners."

Breaking through resistance and creating strategies that better equip teachers, home visitors, and other human-service professionals to commit to work from a culturally informed perspective is difficult because it requires adults to challenge their own values and beliefs. Yet there is an urgent need for progress when considering the shifting demographics of our country. Unspoken beliefs that undermine or disrespect the cultural values and beliefs that children and families bring into our programs can impact parental engagement and a child's developing self-concept because adults tend to act on what they believe.

For example, teachers who believe that all children must learn English, even at the expense of losing their home language, may be less likely to truly embrace and value implementing practices that involve utilizing home-language expressions as a part of interacting regularly with children and their parents. Some go so far as to reject bilingualism for nonnative English-speaking children even as they seek bilingual learning experiences for their own children. Countless other examples can be substituted for language in which decisions are made every day about what to value and what to disregard when it comes to addressing the learning needs of diverse groups of children. It's time that we create opportunities to openly discuss these tensions and jointly work with parents to chart a course for children that honors their culture while also preparing them to successfully participate in mainstream culture.

Opportunities to accelerate our progress

There are at least three strategies worth carefully considering that are ripe for research and evaluation to determine their impact on how early care and education professionals can develop greater capacity to work from a culturally responsive perspective:

- Increase the use of culturally relevant knowledge and content as educators support development and learning.
- Create more transformative professional-development experiences.
- Create opportunities for reflective supervision.

Increase the use of culturally relevant knowledge and content

Educating young children is as much a social process as it is about pedagogy and instructional methodology. When early childhood educators can extract knowledge from children and their families about their culture and how they approach learning, these educators are better positioned to use that information to create relevant learning experiences. To make progress educators must increase their knowledge about each child and his or her family, and the hopes and dreams these families have for their children.

That means we must examine the messages we convey to families at the very onset of their entrusting us with their children's care and education. Do we welcome them in a way that communicates that we are partners, and that our ability to individualize what we offer their children requires the parents' active input and engagement? Does our enrollment material provide an opportunity for parents to begin to share their desires for their child's identity development and what they hope their child will learn during their time in our care? How often do teachers revisit this information and seek new information to enhance their understanding of how to best support the child's development? Many other strategies can be used to actively incorporate more culturally relevant content and knowledge into our work with young children, but first, early childhood educators must value working from this perspective.

Create more transformative professional-development experiences

In 2006, the Frank Porter Graham Child Development Institute issued a report[50] evaluating the state of early childhood teacher-preparation programs in the United States. The report suggests that most programs are not focusing nearly enough time or attention on how to help teachers understand the values and beliefs they bring into their work with children and families, or on how to develop the necessary communication skills to work with parents who may come from cultural backgrounds different from than their own. Findings also revealed that less than half of all teacher-preparation programs at the associate's, bachelor's, and master's levels included an entire course that prepared educators to work with diverse children and families. More effort needs to be devoted to carefully examining preservice training programs to increase the number of educators leaving postsecondary education with the skills and experiences required to effectively engage and work with families from culturally diverse backgrounds.

In addition, because many adults who work with children and families in early care and education may have limited formal education, greater attention needs to be given to state-based professional-development programs. With access to increased federal resources, many states are working to devise a systemic approach to professional development that considers state-based standards necessary to render high-quality early care and education services. Inservice training programs that include a special focus on working effectively with diverse families need to be incorporated into these state-based professional-development systems. Furthermore, more aggressive outreach is needed to engage family child care providers in these professional-development opportunities. Because infants and toddlers are by and large served in family child care (including family, friend, and neighbor care), we need to reach out and provide opportunities to engage these providers as we seek to enhance quality. Although many such providers are not interested in becoming "professionals," a handful of reports have surfaced that suggest they value the opportunity to develop relationships with others caring for young children to reduce feelings of isolation.

Create opportunities for reflective supervision

Finally, the field needs to examine which forms of supervision and mentoring are effective

in supporting teachers. As a mental-health professional, I became acutely aware of the difference between how early care and education (along with many nonmental-health disciplines) approached supervision and how supervision is viewed when working from a mental-health perspective. In the latter instance, because mental-health professionals are working with individuals and families, supervision generally provides an opportunity for the practitioner to gain perspective from a more seasoned professional about impressions, approaches, and ways of intervening because the relationship serves as the primary vehicle through which the intervention is delivered. It's important, therefore, that practitioners have a chance to reflect on how much of their interpretations about challenges, progress, or difficulties may be tied to their own biases versus what really seems to be happening for the individual or family seeking help.

Am I suggesting here that early childhood educators need to experience a similar form or type of supervision to be effective with children and parents? No. However, I do believe that reflection and learning how to be reflective is at the core of this form of supervision, and that this skill is essential for early care and education professionals to work from a culturally responsive perspective. ZERO TO THREE has written extensively about reflective supervision and its importance within the multidisciplinary infant-family field. I believe early care and education can get closer to creating transformative professional-development experiences if it decides to devote more attention to understanding how to support staff to work from a reflective perspective.

For example, a teacher who is comfortable reflecting may be more likely to consider multiple determinants of a child's behavior rather than boiling everything down to a child's difficult temperament. Reflection requires that practitioners stop, reflect, and consider multiple factors when trying to understand the meaning of a child's behavior. Since reflection requires being comfortable with raising questions about interactions and experiences, and cultural differences are bound to surface in our work with children and families, I would argue that reflective supervision helps to support staff to work from a culturally responsive perspective.

Conclusion

A great many resources are available to support early care and education practitioners as we strive to meet the development and learning needs of all children. As the field looks ahead to 2020 and beyond, it is certain that our country's cultural and ethnic makeup will be more diversified than ever before in our history. What an awesome opportunity we have before us to ensure that our children are prepared to embrace this new reality with a sense of positive regard for how much richer our world can be because we are able to celebrate and respect different perspectives and ways of approaching learning and life rather than looking upon it with fear. May our journey to become more open, reflective, and responsive continue. ▶

About the Author

Tammy L. Mann, PhD, *Executive Director, Frederick Patterson Research Institute*
tammy.mann@uncf.org

Professional focus

Mann focuses on how experiences from birth through adolescence contribute to positive outcomes across all domains of development, especially for low-income children and families.

Hope for the children of 2020:

To ensure that children of 2020 have a future that includes access to quality education, health care, safe communities, and a stable home environment. I hope we have the courage to choose wisely — their future depends on it.

Racial Identity

10

Carol Brunson Day

African Americans are oppressed not because of anything about our African ancestry—we are oppressed because blackness is responded to negatively. For children of color these harmful responses are at the heart of their failure to thrive. Today nearly 41% of the entire child population in the United States is of Latino, Asian, Native American, and African American/ African descent. By 2020, that figure is projected to grow to 47%.[51]

It might be argued that technically these numbers do not refer specifically to the racial makeup of the population, the concept that this chapter concerns itself with, but instead to families' geographically based ethnicity or their socialization-based cultural origins. While this may be true, it seems to matter little when it comes to discussing children's racial identities in early education. For in large part, the profile data that are collected about the children with whom we work tend to use race and culture interchangeably. Furthermore, despite the fact that hard science would argue that "race" doesn't exist as a physiological phenomenon, racial designations as they are used in the United States today are real and in general closely parallel broad ethnic and cultural origins.

Therefore, for ease of discussion in the space of these few pages, we acknowledge but will put aside the real and important intricacies that distinguish them. We will use the terms "race" and "culture" interchangeably where they share traits when it comes to children's identities and responses to them. For the learning and devel-opment issues that arise for young children are quite similar, as is the good advice about how to handle them.

Whence we have come

Scholars and educators have been interested in children's racial identities for decades. In the research community, for example, Kenneth and Mamie Clark's doll studies in the 1940s were designed to examine the psychological effects of segregation on black children. Further, most notably in the early childhood education community, the work of the Council on Interracial Books for Children beginning in the mid-1960s was geared to change the way racial groups were portrayed in children's literature because of its effect on children's self-images. Widespread interest in the field, however, can be traced to the multicultural education movement in the 1970s, when conversations and articles began to appear in great number, and classroom materials reflecting diverse racial and cultural images became prolific. A touch point in that era was the 1989 NAEYC publication by Louise Derman-Sparks and the ABC Task Force *Anti-bias Curriculum: Tools for Empowering Young Children*.[52] Because of its widespread distribution, this book played a seminal role in bringing the field face to face with the idea that as children learn to make racial/ethnic/cultural distinctions, they also are learning about the values attached to each. And at ages as young as 2, they are also learning, without any explicit instruction, which characteristics are desirable and which aren't, reflecting both identity issues as well as attitudes toward others.

By this time, demographic changes due to immigration and differential birth rates were becoming widespread across the United States, and the number of racially and culturally diverse children was increasing everywhere. At the same time, more and more families with bicultural children were claiming a "new" biracial identity, and in response, the federal 2000 Census established a new classification, allowing respondents for the first time to identify themselves as more than one race.[53]

Contributing to increased visibility of these issues and their impact on young children, groups like the National Head Start Association, the Southern Association for Children Under Six, and the Association for Early Childhood Education International issued position statements and ramped up production of journal articles and materials designed to increase competence of their constituents in fostering positive responses to culture and race. One notable example during the 1990s was the Anti-Defamation League's major national initiative in cooperation with *Sesame Street* (which had been an early media pioneer in bringing multiracial characters to the screen) to deliver positive messages about racial identity and attitudes in young children.

We also experienced a shift in how we conceptualized the role of culture in the development of young children. From a theoretical vantage point, we have known for a long time — because of developmental theorists like Erik Erikson, Jean Piaget, and Zev Vygotsky — that every child is a cultural being. But with the 1997 revision of NAEYC's developmentally appropriate practice framework, the cultural child was lifted to a new position of prominence. Whereas previously that framework directed us to think about two dimensions of children's development — their universal similarities and their individual differences — we now were urged to also consider children's cultural group membership as we plan effective practice. Since

this directs us to see all children as "cultural," the voices of many researchers and writers such as Janet Gonzales-Mena, Rebecca New, Linda Espinosa, and Patricia Ramsey have been elevated in prominence as their work has contributed much to increasing our understanding about planning appropriate programs to build positive cultural identities.

This shift in conceptualization of the cultural child has also helped to bring into sharper contrast the issue of cultural bias as an obstacle to development (and by extension the issue of race bias). As a result the field has embraced goals for the cultural and racial child that include addressing bias, as evidenced by those established in the 2009 revision of NAEYC's Antibias Curriculum:[54]

- To affirm and foster children's knowledge and pride in their cultural identity.

- To foster children's curiosity, enjoyment, and empathetic awareness of cultural differences and similarities.

- To teach children to overcome any inappropriate responses triggered by cultural differences.

- To ensure that children will have accurate information about and feel comfortable with their physical characteristics linked to racial identity.

- Children will feel positive, but not superior, about their racial identity.

- Children will demonstrate appropriate skills for identifying and criticizing misinformation and stereotypical ideas about "race."

- Children will develop nonbiased responses to racial differences and beginning skills for interrupting biased behaviors and for creating fair classroom environments.

We have come a long way since Mamie and Kenneth Clark demonstrated that black children's racial identities were being harmed by segregation. But much work is still needed if we are going to thoroughly understand how children develop racial and cultural identity, and how to support positive identity development as they grow up.

Where we are today

From 1970 to 2010, early childhood education worked diligently and consistently to create educational curricula and approaches that address children's development and learning needs related to culture and race. These efforts have been multifaceted and disparate, but all contribute to where we are today as we attempt to create settings to respond to the way children see themselves in relation to their individual experiences and how they are seen by society's prevailing views of the racial and/or cultural group to which they belong. When examined through the lens of multicultural education, this journey demonstrates similar themes echoing through various approaches visible both across time and today. Most of the work observed today falls under one or more of four themes.

One consistent theme is helping children learn to appreciate others — the cultural/racial appreciation approach. This is designed to teach people about other people (presumably so that people will like each other better). The activities generally have an international flavor and are arbitrary in terms of which groups are chosen for study: it may be the teacher's favorite, or the group with the most exciting and colorful culture. The approach is a tourist one, focusing on the exotic elements of the group — the things most unlike the ways of the cultural mainstream of America.

A second theme is helping children learn to like themselves — the cultural/racial self-enrichment approach. Here activities are designed to teach children about themselves as opposed to others (ostensibly in order to change their self-image from negative to positive). The activities focus on the group of children for whom they are designed. For example, Navajo culture/language is taught to Navajo children,

usually focusing on taking pride in the historical achievements of the group and contemporary heroes, as well as learning about and honoring holiday celebrations and food practices.

A third theme, cultural/racial empowerment, teaches children in culturally consistent contexts (unlike appreciation and enrichment, where culture is taught to children). In empowerment strategies, teachers learn how to recognize and use culture to make classrooms more like the homes where children have learned to be powerful. They use the language of the child's family rather than English, and help children become proficient in their home culture and in the skills that are powerful in mainstream culture. Further, they struggle along with parents to decide how best to educate their children in a society that devalues them by demanding that they give up their culture in order to achieve.

A fourth theme, closely aligned with the third, is the antibias model, an approach that structures experiences to help children understand fairness and learn ways to take action to make change when things seem to them to be unfair. Activism and change are key to these approaches, and projects and activities often take on real-life situations and contemporary events that children and/or parents encounter as a basis to stimulate problem-solving.

Predictions for 2020

As we think about and work toward 2020, when there will be more racially and culturally diverse children, and when more biracial and multiracial children will attend early education programs, we ask what will be needed and how can we ensure that the field will be able to provide it?

One prediction is that there will be more pressure to meet the education challenges of this diverse society by closing the achievement gap and guaranteeing every child a successful start in school. We will want teachers with whom children and their families can identify. This will mean recruiting and retaining staff

whose racial and cultural heritages reflect those of their students. These adults will be important for the appropriate development of these children, serving as racial and cultural models, and facilitating language development and effective communication with families. Although I expect that by then we will have more studies and better research findings about these issues, we already know in general that the lack of racial and cultural diversity among teachers is hurting the chances of success for racially and culturally diverse students. Research reports have shown that emergent majority students tend to do better in class and face higher expectations when taught by teachers from their racial or ethnic group. Those reports have concluded that teachers of color serve as role models and cultural brokers who help students connect to school through shared identities.

While securing a culturally diverse teaching workforce is an important strategy, we also already know that cultural/racial matching of teachers and students alone is not a panacea for education. More fundamental is the issue of having teachers who understand their students' cultures and incorporate them into their interactions in class. Preparing teachers who are good

cultural matches for children is really the goal, and this cannot be assured just because a teacher is from the same cultural group as the children.

Giving definition to and creating strategies for postsecondary teacher preparation will be areas in which we will make a good deal of progress by 2020. This is what I expect to be achieved:

We will "rethink culture."[55] As we teach theory and principles of child development, we will be able to help teachers enter practice with a deep understanding of culture and how it influences development and learning. We will need to approach this from an anthropological perspective, not just an educational one, and engage students in a process that helps them think more about culture's influence on behavior and less about the artifacts that it has produced, that is, deep structural elements rather than surface ones. Certain principles are critical and will come to dominate that teaching:

- Culture is embodied in the rules that shape behavior. Cultural rules do not cause behavior; they influence people to behave similarly, in ways that help them understand each other.

- Culture is learned. What we learn depends upon the cultural rules of the people who raise us. Further, it can be well-learned by some people in the group and less well-learned by others.

- Individual members of a culture are embedded to different degrees within their cultural group. Usually members of a cultural group learn the core rules of their culture, but some families are more tradition-oriented, others less. (And of course, even though families and individuals learn the cultural rules, they may not always behave according to what they have learned.)

- Culture is dynamic. Every cultural group changes over time, and that change occurs because of individuals. So while culture influences individual behavior, individuals also influence cultural patterns. Group changes occur for a variety of specific reasons, including contact with the ideas and behaviors of outsiders, and thus some groups change more rapidly than others. Yet this dynamic element coexists with another element, that of cultural stability, which overall is more predominant at any one point in time. So while it is useful to know that culture is dynamic, it is perhaps more practical to think about culture as the group characteristics that are passed from one generation to another, although it is individual behavior within a generation that also contributes to the changes that cultural groups inevitably undergo. Neither process negates the other; they are simultaneous and interdependent.

Discussions about culture will be in-depth and long term and will build on using examples that come from the lives of the adult students, remembering that one must understand how culture influences one's own life in order to understand how culture influences others.

We will help teachers enter practice with an understanding of how racial and cultural bias contributes to children's underdevelopment and how they affect policies and practices in schools. Lisa Delpit's book *Other People's Children: Cultural Conflict in the Classroom*[56] presents this challenge through a provocative discussion related to the dynamics of inequality as they play out in cultural mismatches in the classroom. Her advice to teachers is that they understand and address the intersection of race, culture, and bias, an understanding that can be achieved through direct study.

Louise Derman-Sparks and I have made a similar case[57] that teachers should explore racism in depth and learn to use the same tools for exploring other forms of bias (ethnic, class, etc.). It is what we call antibias education, and it is based on the assumption that most educators have been taught to understand racism and other forms of bias at a very superficial level and tend to think of its manifestations in the bigoted and prejudiced behavior of individuals (for example, telling ethnic jokes and name calling).

But in order to help teachers develop a disposition to continually work on maintaining an understanding of their personal role as a participant in institutional oppression (racial and cultural), they must understand the institutional forms of bias, that is, how racism affects the mission, policies, structure, and methods of education and human-service programs. For instance, the institutional forms of bias that are manifest in monocultural, monoracial assumptions and representations in books and materials, and in testing and tracking, cause repeated and cumulative harm to children's growth and development.

We will give teachers tools and the confidence to constantly seek out authentic sources of information about various racial and cultural groups. This means finding resources that come from deep within cultural communities (in their own voice), and learning how to determine the validity of information for use with specific children and families. Teachers need skills to know how to enter and interact with ethnic and cultural communities, and how to create a climate for discussing topics that they may find difficult for fear of making mistakes or sounding racist. They must also know how to make the difficult but important distinction between stereotypes and genuine cultural characteristics of groups, and know how to weigh and use information appropriately. They must learn to make tentative hypotheses about people and not overgeneralize. Finally, they must know who they are culturally and have a healthy sense of what they do not know about others who are culturally different from them.

We will create an activist mentality and help teachers understand the importance of working for change. They must understand how to act to foster racial equity and examine how to use whatever power they have as individuals to change the oppressiveness of the larger society. For instance, we must help teachers embrace the value of having a racially and culturally diverse workforce, both for children and families and for the profession, and help them become advocates to achieve this goal. Having culturally diverse staff helps build and maintain cultural competence because diverse staffs have more opportunities to discuss culture in the workplace. They bring diverse perspectives to problem-solving and strengthen programs' capacities to use diverse ways of being in the world to promote growth and benefit to all.

Helping teachers in training understand the benefits to children's school success will help teachers to not be threatened by representative staffing. Such fears often make teachers minimize the importance of culture in development and learning, and increase the potential that culturally diverse groups of children's need will go unmet.

Conclusion

If we do these things by 2020, how differently will children and families fare when it comes to their racial and cultural identities, development, and early learning? I think there's reason to hope things will be much better. For I believe we see the signs today that people working in education and human services in general want to have a better appreciation for diverse populations and want to explore deeply to get things right. I also believe there are signs today that people are less satisfied to stay on the surface of these issues, and that as time goes on they will be more willing to push themselves past their points of comfort to find solutions. And I deeply believe there are signs of a sense of hope filling the air that this society will change its attitudes about race.

Who's to say that by 2020, our society won't have changed so much that general racism will have diminished, if not disappeared, and that by then its impact on young children will be negligible? Well, should that be the case, and I hope that it is, we shall consider our job well done and will have nothing to be concerned about. ▶

Hope for the children of 2020:

That throughout their life experiences, they will encounter institutions and individuals fully committed and prepared to contribute to the development of their full potential.

About the Author

Carol Brunson Day, *CEO, National Black Child Development Institute* cday58@comcast.net

Professional focus

Day's focus is the role of culture on the development of children and developing cultural competence in teacher education.

Language and Literacy for Bilingual and Monolingual Children

Linda M. Espinosa

One thing has become crystal clear in the last two decades: *all* young children need to learn to read and write in order to have a chance in school and later in life. We have also learned that teachers play a major role in leading children down the path to literacy in both universal and particular ways. Universally, all children need warm, responsive, and accepting relationships to benefit from the particular teaching and learning strategies best suited to a child's individual strengths and needs. There are also certain skills that underlie the ability to read. All children can learn to read if they have the opportunity to learn fundamental language skills within the context of safe and supportive personal relationships. These first and most endearing relationships are formed in the home setting and are based on specific cultural norms and values.

Very young children learn and use language to communicate for a variety of purposes: to request, control, comment, reject, express emotion, gain attention, and acquire information, among others. During the preschool years, oral language development plays a central role in early literacy development. Promoting oral language development is a major goal for virtually all early childhood classrooms and is prominent in all state early learning standards. Oral language skills include the abilities to:

- Listen to and comprehend spoken language.

- Use language to communicate with others.

- Use age-appropriate vocabulary and grammar.

- Hear and distinguish the sounds of language (any language).

Since the 1990s, all publicly funded early education programs have increased their emphasis on directly teaching early reading abilities that have been shown to predict later reading achievement. Emergent literacy skills, while including oral language abilities, also encompass these specific preschool literacy skills:

- Alphabet knowledge: knowing the names and/or sounds of printed letters.

- Phonological awareness: the ability to detect, manipulate, or analyze component sounds in spoken language, independent of meaning, such as the ability to match similar sounds (for example, find words that all begin with "m") and the ability to orally put together two syllables to form a compound word (for example, "What word do you get when you put sun and shine together?").

- Rapid automatized naming of letters/digits: the ability to rapidly name a sequence of repeating random letters, digits, or both.

- Rapid automatized naming of objects/colors: the ability to rapidly name a sequence of repeating random pictures of familiar objects or colors.

- Writing/writing name: the ability to write single letters on request or to write one's own name.

- Phonological memory: the ability to remember spoken information for a short time.[58]

It is not clear whether some of these skills should be taught during the preschool years, or whether they are part of general cognitive development and do not need to be targeted for instruction (for example, rapid naming tasks and phonological memory).

Nevertheless, preschool children need to learn when and how to communicate effectively, to speak so others can understand them, to use an increasingly expanded vocabulary and grammatical structures that accurately convey their meanings, as well as letters of the alphabet, the purposes of print, how to manipulate sounds of words, and to begin to write letters and words legibly. It is no longer a question of *whether* preschool programs should directly teach the alphabet and other literacy skills but of *how* they should teach them.

Early childhood programs can and should intentionally teach oral language skills, alphabetic knowledge, and phonological awareness skills to all children. No single skill should be taught in isolation, but multiple literacy goals should be integrated into engaging and age-appropriate approaches. Instruction that is based on warm, respectful, responsive relationships and is appropriate to the developmental, linguistic, and cultural capacities of each child is needed. In general, effective early language and literacy instruction includes these elements:[59]

- Frequent opportunities for extended conversation between adults and children. We know that preschoolers need to engage in interesting conversations with more-proficient language users, learn how to take turns, participate in multiple back-and-forth interactions, and practice new vocabulary words. This type of extended discourse promotes advanced oral language abilities that underlie reading comprehension during the upper elementary years.

- Dialogic reading with individual or small groups of children. When using this strategy, teachers actively engage children in the process of reading books by asking questions about the objects and pictures in picture books; using "what" and open-ended questions to encourage children to elaborate on their answers; and expanding on the child's response as a way to teach vocabulary and provide more background information. Dialogic reading activities need to occur at least three times per week and include small groups of children to be effective.

- Phonological awareness activities that actively engage children in analysis of words at the syllable or individual sound level with frequent feedback on the child's performance. Young children will benefit from learning that when you delete, add, or substitute sounds to words, a new word is formed, and from frequently playing with the sounds of words. These skills can be taught through a variety of language games that keep the learning process playful and not overly drill-like. It is possible to effectively teach phonemic awareness by using listening, clapping syllables, sound-word, and rhyming games. Teachers can promote these skills by learning nursery rhymes and making up their own silly, nonsense rhymes with children, and by singing songs with small groups of children every day (songs naturally break words into syllables and are a fun way to learn about word sounds). The important points are to conduct these literacy activities frequently and to keep them playful.

- Deliberately and systematically incorporating opportunities for children to learn about the alphabet. Teachers can take dictation, emphasize letters throughout the day, have children create their own books, use letters and letter sounds in transition activities, and help children learn to write their own names. All of these activities will help preschoolers attend to the shape, sound, and names of letters, and capitalize on their intrinsic motivation to communicate through print.

- Shared book reading with a focus on the print in the book can help preschoolers learn about print knowledge, concepts about print, and early decoding skills. Teachers can use books of high interest that are culturally appropriate to engage children and demonstrate the salient features of print (for example, where a word stops and starts, ordering of print from left to right and top to bottom, connecting words to pictures).

We now know that it is critically important that all children learn these early language and literacy skills, and that high-quality instruction incorporates specific practices. However, as we progress toward a greater scientific understanding of the developmental path of literacy, we need to be careful that we don't throw the baby out with the bathwater. Much of what we have known for decades and promoted as developmentally appropriate practice is still quite relevant: teachers need to be knowledgeable about child development and early learning; teachers need to actively learn about the strengths, interests, personalities,

and prior experiences of each of their students; and teachers need to understand the particular social, linguistic, and cultural contexts in which children are growing up.

Increasingly, children in our communities and our early childhood programs are learning these basic literacy skills in English while simultaneously mastering the elements of a home language that is not English. What do we know about how these children develop early language and literacy skills, and what can teachers do to promote skilled, motivated, and successful dual-language learners?

Language and literacy for young dual-language learners[60]

Across the country, early childhood programs and demographers are documenting the rapid rise of families and children who speak a language other than English in the home and whose childrearing practices reflect a wide variety of cultural backgrounds. In California, approximately 39% of the children 3 to 5 years old are identified as English language learners (also known as dual-language learners, or DLL). The federal Head Start program has documented more than 140 languages represented in its programs. Most Head Start grantees (85%) serve DLL children, and a significant number of states (36) provide services to more than eight language groups.

As with all children, dual-language learners are motivated to learn their home language within a particular cultural and highly social context. The language they are first learning provides a symbol system that allows them to understand and communicate meaning. Their first language gives them the tools to connect with important people in their environment, to share their life experiences, and ultimately to develop their personal identities and participate in the wider world.

Whether children are growing up with one language or two, there are predictable stages they progress through, and critical types of learning opportunities they need. During the preschool years, all children are extremely capable language learners (some have even called preschoolers linguistic geniuses): they learn the particular sounds of their home language and how the sounds are pronounced (phonology), how words are combined in order to express thoughts (syntax), the meanings of words (semantics), and when and how language should be used in different social settings (pragmatics). These are complex tasks that form the building blocks of listening and speaking, which are fundamental to literacy abilities. Learning these features of language usage will occur in the child's first or home language and is essential to eventually mastering these skills in English. Once young children have learned that language has specific sounds and rules, and how to use language effectively in their first language, it will be easier for them to learn these same skills in English. In fact much of what DLL children know in their home language transfers to their learning in a second language and enhances their overall linguistic development.

How do young children learn through two languages?

Most language researchers make a distinction between children who learn a second language simultaneously and those who learn sequentially.

When children learn two languages simultaneously before age 3, their language progression is similar to children who are learning only one language. They speak their first words, learn grammatical rules, and meet language benchmarks at roughly the same age as children who are monolingual.

The language development of children who learn a second language after their first language is established (usually after 2 to 3 years of age), or sequentially, follows a different progression and is highly sensitive to characteristics of the child as well as the amount and type of language exposure the child experiences. Just as virtually all children can master the features of their home language with time and opportunities, preschoolers are also capable of learning more than one language with enough support for both languages. In fact, children can thrive in both languages and experience cognitive and linguistic advantages when they have the opportunity to learn two languages during the preschool years.

When learning a second language sequentially, the basics of the children's first language have been learned. They know the features of their first language, but now must learn the specific phonology, grammar, vocabulary, and pragmatics of a new language. According to Tabors and Snow, sequential second language acquisition follows four developmental stages:

1. **Home language use.** When a child has become competent in one language and is introduced into a setting where everyone is speaking a different language (for example, a DLL child who enters an English-dominant preschool classroom), the child will frequently continue to speak his home language even when others do not understand. This period can be short (a few days), or in some cases the child will persist in using his home language even when others are unable to understand him.

2. **Nonverbal/observational period.** After young children realize that speaking their home language will not work, they typically enter a period where they speak infrequently, observe other children intently, and mainly use nonverbal means to communicate. This is a period of active language learning for the child; he is busy leaning the rules, sounds, and words of the new language (receptive language) but is not yet verbally using the new language to communicate.

Korean Counting

1 일 (Il)
2 이 (I)
3 삼 (Sam)
4 사 (Sa)
5 오 (O)
6 육 (Yuck)
7 칠 (Chil)
8 팔 (Pal)
9 구 (Goo)
10 십 (Sib)
11 십일 (Sib Il)
12 십이 (Sib I)
13 십삼 (Sib Sam)
14 십사 (Sib Sa)

This is an extremely important stage of second language learning that may also last a long time or be brief. Any language assessments conducted during this stage of development may result in misleading information that underestimates the child's true language capacity. At this point in sequential language development, children may appear to be delayed in both their home language and English, but this is usually a temporary by-product of adjusting to the demands of a second language.

3. **Telegraphic and formulaic speech.** The child is now ready to start using the new language and does so through telegraphic speech that involves the use of formulas. This is similar to a monolingual child who is learning simple words or phrases (content words) to express whole thoughts. For instance, a child might say, "Me down," indicating he wants to go downstairs. Formulaic speech refers to unanalyzed chunks of words or sometimes even syllables strung together that are repetitions of what the child

has heard. For example, Tabors reports that DLLs in the preschool she studied frequently used the phrase "Lookit" to engage others in their play. These are phrases the children had heard from others that helped to achieve their social goals, even though the children probably did not know the exact meaning of the two words (or string of sounds). During this stage of second language learning, it is easy to overestimate a child's language proficiency in the new language. DLL children can often express simple thoughts or desires — enough to engage in social interactions with others—but have limited comprehension of complex vocabulary or sentence structure.

4. **Productive language.** Now the child is starting to go beyond telegraphic or formulaic utterances to express original thoughts in unique ways. Initially the child may use very simple grammatical patterns such as, "I wanna play," but over time he will gain control over the structure and vocabulary of the new language. Grammatical errors in language usage are common during this period, as children are experimenting with their new language and learning its rules and structure.[61]

It is important to remember that there is great diversity within our DLL population. Young dual-language learners vary greatly both in their personal characteristics and their cultural, social, and language-learning environments. The rates at which they learn English, as well as their eventual bilingual proficiency, depend to a great extent on interactions between their cognitive abilities, cultural background, personality, motivation, age, and the amount and quality of exposure to English. Some young DLL children have had little or no exposure to English prior to their entry into an early education classroom and may also have had limited extended language interactions in their home language. Others may have had systematic and extensive opportunities to learn both languages from their earliest years. Some are growing up in well-resourced households with highly educated bilingual parents, while many live in homes where no one speaks English and it is a daily struggle to meet basic needs.

These economic, linguistic, and cultural differences are significant and should not be overlooked. DLL children and families should not all be lumped together and treated as though they share the same strengths and needs. It is important for early childhood educators to know about each DLL child's specific language background, what languages have been spoken in the home, by whom, for what amounts of time, and for what purposes. It is also important to find out about the parents' attitudes toward maintaining the home language and acquiring English. Finally, early childhood teachers should carefully observe DLL children to determine their proficiency in English and their home language.

Loss of home language

Research in the last two decades has also deepened our understanding of the consequences of losing one's home language while mastering a second language. We have ample evidence that as soon as a DLL preschooler enters an English-dominant classroom, he starts to prefer to speak English and loses interest in continuing to use his first language:

> "It is true that children in the preschool years can learn a language quickly and with little apparent effort. These are the years of rapid language development and children can acquire a language in a year or two simply by being in a setting where the language is in daily use. However, it is equally true that languages can be lost with equal ease during this period, especially when the language they are learn-
> ing is more highly valued than the language they already speak. Over the years, I have tracked many young children who, as soon as they learn a little English in the school, put aside the language they already know and speak, and choose to communicate exclusively in English, even at home with family members who do not speak or understand much English."[62]

This early shift to English dominance often occurs at the expense of the home language. When children lose the ability to speak their first language, the language of their home, they are at risk for multiple negative outcomes: poorer academic achievement in English, loss of cultural and personal identity, decreased ability to communicate with and learn from important family members, and the loss of their potential bilingualism. The language they have learned to interpret and understand the world, to build enduring relationships with immediate family members, and to process information is no longer relevant — at the same time they are still struggling to master the basics of English.

Recent research has also demonstrated the multiple advantages of becoming bilingual. Infants growing up in bilingual settings (which is typical in many parts of the world) have displayed the innate capacity to acquire two languages without significant cost to the development of either language. Simultaneous dual-language children generally experience the same milestones at approximately the same age as monolingual children. In addition to the capacity to acquire more than one language, there are special cognitive, linguistic, and social advantages of bilingualism. Children who are systematically exposed to two languages during the preschool years demonstrate age-appropriate development in both languages as well as specific cognitive benefits associated with bilingualism.

> **The increasing proportion of young children who are dual-language learners has major implications for the composition and preparation of the early childhood workforce.**

We now have evidence that the development of two languages benefits the brain; greater brain tissue density in areas related to language, memory, and attention is found in bilingual children. Young children learning two languages also have more neural activity in the parts of the brain associated with language processing. This increased brain activity and neural density may have long-term positive effects on specific types of cognitive abilities, such as those that require focusing on the details of a task, and knowing how language is structured and used, or metalinguistic abilities. These are important underlying linguistic competencies that promote high levels of literacy in the long-term.

These studies have also demonstrated that knowing more than one language does not delay the acquisition of English or impede academic achievement in English when both languages are supported. Research on children who learn English sequentially, after their home language has been established, has also shown that most young children are capable of adding a second language during the early childhood years with long-term benefits.

Best practice for dual-language learners

In general, high-quality literacy instruction for monolingual children is also good for dual-language learners — but it is not enough! Dual-language learners require classroom and instructional enhancements in order to thrive

and achieve at high levels. In addition to warm and responsive relationships, DLL children learn best when:

- There are daily opportunities for small-group and individualized interactions with adults in both the home language and English.

- The learning environment (for example, print, books, media, pictures, and stories that reflect the languages and cultures of the children) incorporates the cultures and languages of the children enrolled.

- Teachers are knowledgeable about second language development and instructional practices that promote both maintenance of home language and English acquisition.

- There is direct teaching of English (for example, targeted vocabulary instruction, storybook reading, use of cues, props, gestures, and scaffolding of existing knowledge for dual-language learners).

- Teachers know how to adapt their instruction and expectations based on knowledge of the child's stage of English acquisition.

- They are encouraged and supported to continue the use of their home language.

- Teachers have knowledge of each child's early language learning background (for example, first language spoken to child, by whom, extent of English exposure and usage).

- Outreach to DLL families is linguistically and culturally appropriate.[63]

Summary

All young children in the United States deserve quality instruction that provides them with the background knowledge, language abilities, and specific early literacy skills that are critical to proficient reading in English. It is necessary to know how to read and write in this culture in order to have access to a decent standard of living and participate in civic society. In the last two decades, we have learned a great deal about what young children need to know and how to teach it.

Young children who have regular and rich exposure to two languages can successfully become bilingual. Most research concludes that there may even be some general advantages of bilingualism in many areas of development. We also are identifying the features of learning environments that promote long-term growth and school achievement.

Early childhood educators need to create safe and accepting environments with positive relationships for all children; early literacy instruction can be both targeted toward specific skills and developmentally appropriate; program approaches must provide some level of support for the home language of DLLs; young DLL children can successfully learn English during the preschool years, but it must be an additive approach in which English is added to the home language, and not a subtractive approach in which English is learned at the expense of the child's home language; and specific instructional approaches must be adapted to the unique needs of children who are not fully proficient in English.

The increasing proportion of young children who are dual-language learners has major implications for the composition and preparation of the early childhood workforce. All staff, teach-

ers, support staff, and administrators will need to understand the developmental characteristics of dual-language learners, effective instructional and assessment practices, and most critically, the role of first and second language proficiency in long-term academic success. Ideally, the workforce will include professionals who are proficient in English as well as the children's home language, and are well-trained in early childhood pedagogy. In order to realize the potential of early bilingualism, we will need highly skilled teachers who have achieved proficiency in bilingualism, multicultural perspectives, and effective teaching strategies. ▶

Hope for the children of 2020

That by 2020, all children will be loved unconditionally, educated brilliantly, and hear multiple languages daily!

About the Author

Linda Espinosa, PhD, *Professor of Early Childhood Education (retired)*

Professional focus

Espinosa works passionately to improve early educational opportunities for young children who are born into poverty and/or who speak a language other than English at home.

The Mathematical Lives of Young Children

Julie Sarama and Douglas H. Clements

Three pictures hang in front of a 4-month-old girl. The first shows two circles, the others one circle and three circles. The infant hears two sounds. Her eyes move to the picture with two circles.

At some intuitive level, this infant has recognized number and has translated number from one sensory input, sound, to another, sight. There is no age too young for mathematical thought. Children often know, or can learn, far more than most curriculum developers or teachers have believed. Babies are sensitive to number and shape. Most 2-year-olds can name the number of objects in small collections (one to three) and many can count them. Three-year-olds can do simple addition in playful contexts with objects. Preschoolers know a surprising amount about shapes and the geometry of navigation — getting around in the world. Most entering kindergartners can count, recognize some shapes, make patterns, and use nonstandard units of measurement.

The early years are a critical period for learning math. Children's knowledge of math in these years predicts their mathematics achievement for years later, even into high school, just as their early literacy predicts their later achievement in reading. That makes sense, but it is interesting that early literacy predicts later achievement in reading only. Children's early knowledge of math predicts not only later math achievement, but also later reading achievement. Thus, it appears that math is a core component of cognition. Math is knowledge of quantity, number, and space, of course, but it is also a basic way of thinking.

Therefore, learning math early is important for all children. Especially important is math for children from low-resource communities, who often have not had high-quality learning opportunities.

What can we do to change the future of young children's mathematics in positive ways? First, we could recognize that too many curricula and programs teach too much of what children already know. Many programs teach the names of basic shapes, presented only in typical ways. But many children already know these shapes. Programs seldom build upon this knowledge. When they attempt to add knowledge, it is often mathematically incorrect, such as "every time you cut a square, it makes two triangles."

Instead, programs can build on the creativity and mathematics capacities of young children. After using the Building Blocks[64] preschool curriculum, one group of 4-year-olds was trying to fill a long rectangular puzzle with triangles (Figure 1a). Cory found an elegant strategy. He put four triangles together to make squares and repeated the arrangement to fill the rectangle.

Although using a pattern to solve the problem isn't highly unusual, he understood the four triangles to be a new mathematical unit created

Fig. 1b

out of smaller units (Figure 1b). Another boy saw the square structure and tried to use the idea, but he built the wrong square, using only two triangles (see the two yellow triangles the boy in the lower right is holding in Figure 1a). It is commendable that he noticed Cory's structure, and more so that, when his square didn't fit, he looked again and used four triangles.

When the boys finished, they showed their teacher (Figure 1c), who asked, "How many triangles did you use?"

Cory counted them by ones: "24"

Teacher: "24 what?"

Cory: "Triangles."

Teacher: "How many squares do you have?"

One of his friends put up four fingers on the four triangles in each new unit and counted them: "6!"

The teacher provided good materials and followed up with a short but rich discussion. Unfortunately, such good instruction is limited. Preschoolers often see little or no math. Kindergartners and primary grade students engage in math far less than they do in literacy. We can and must do better. Especially for children from low-resource communities, high-quality education results in learning benefits into elementary school.

The importance of learning trajectories

Research has provided a powerful tool that educators can use to improve the learning and teaching of math: learning trajectories. Children generally follow natural developmental paths in learning mathematics. When teachers understand these paths, and sequences activities based on them, powerful mathematics learning environments can be built.

Learning trajectories have three parts: a mathematical goal, a developmental path along which children develop to reach that goal, and a set of instructional activities, or tasks, linked to each of the levels of thinking in that path that help children develop higher levels of thinking.

Goals: big ideas of math. The first part of a learning trajectory is a goal. Goals should include the big ideas of mathematics — clusters of concepts and skills that are central and coherent, consistent with children's thinking, and generative of future learning. These big ideas have been described in the National Council of Teachers of Mathematics' *Curriculum Focal Points*[65] and the National Research Council's *Mathematics Learning in Early Childhood: Paths*

Toward Excellence and Equity.[66] For example, one goal is to be able to count objects and solve problems using counting.

Development progressions: paths of learning. Developmental progressions consist of levels of thinking that lead to the mathematical goal. The developmental progression is a typical path children follow in achieving the goal. For example, we know that young children first learn the verbal number sequence, then how to keep one-to-one correspondence between counting words and objects, and then to understand the cardinality principle — that the last number word tells "how many."

Instructional tasks: paths of teaching. The third and last part of a learning trajectory is a set of instructional tasks, linked to each of the levels of thinking in the developmental progression. These tasks are designed to help children learn the ideas and skills needed to achieve that level of thinking. That is, educators can use these tasks to promote children's growth from one level to the next. For example, simple counting finger plays and songs — if children string the number words together without interruption — can help children to develop verbal counting. But more attention must be given to developing children's skills with one-to-one correspondence, such as the activity count and move, in which children count from 1 to 10 or an appropriate number, making motions with each count. For example, say "one" (touch head), "two" (touch shoulders), "three" (touch head), and so forth.

Teachers also need to carefully monitor individual children's counting, perhaps in small group lessons, making sure they adapt activities as they develop. Teachers need to check for different stages of development by altering the size of the sets being counted and emphasizing cardinality. Computers can also help (Figure 2). Activities and games can be chosen for individual students to best meet their goals. Games are important here because the goal, and how counting achieves the goal, can be clear and important to children (Figure 3).

Learning trajectories can help educators forge paths to future success in early mathematics

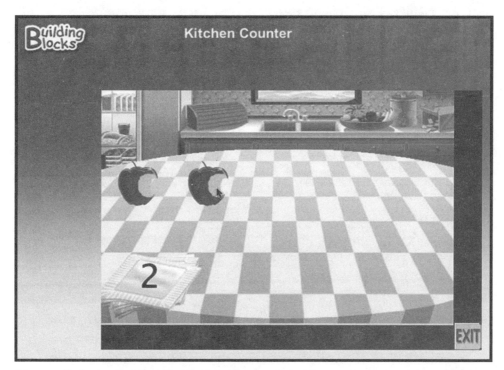

Figure 2. In the Building Blocks computer activity Kitchen Counter, children click on objects one at a time while the numbers from 1 to 10 are counted aloud. For example, they click on pieces of food, and a bite is taken out of each as it is counted.

Figure 3. Children play the Building Blocks activity Pizza Game 1 in pairs. Player one rolls a number cube and puts that many toppings (counters) on his/her plate. Player one asks player two, "Am I right?" Player two must agree that player one is correct. At that point, player one moves the counters to the circular spaces for toppings on his/her pizza. Players take turns until all the spaces on their pizzas have toppings.

education. Several randomized field trial studies have shown that curricula and professional development based on the Building Blocks learning trajectories increased children's achievement more than those that do not.

More importantly, children were able to demonstrate higher levels of mathematical reasoning in the context of developmentally appropriate activities. For example, two children were playing Pizza Game 1, with a number cube that has only 1s, 2s, and 3s on the faces. Carmen had almost filled her pretend pizzas with toppings. As she got ready to roll the number cube, she said, "I'm going to get a high number and win!" "You can't," replied her friend. "You have 4 spaces and the number cube only has 1s, 2s, and 3s on it."

Quite young children can reason logically, and mathematics is a superb context for such thinking. This is one reason why math is a core component of learning and thinking.[67] ▶

Hope for the children of 2020

That the children of 2020 are provided the chance to have rich, engaging, opportunities to learn how to make sense of their world by seeing it through mathematical lenses.

About the Authors

Julie Sarama, *Associate Professor, University at Buffalo, State University of New York*
Jsarama@buffalo.edu

Douglas H. Clements, *SUNY Distinguished Professor, University at Buffalo, State University of New York*
clements@buffalo.edu

Professional focus

Sarama and Clements conduct research on the early development of mathematical ideas and the scaling up of effective interventions.

Play

David Elkind

Over the past decade, the importance of play for human development has become a heated issue both at school and in the home. The focus upon accountability and test scores had led, in all too many elementary schools, to the elimination of recess and encouraged the transformation of the kindergarten into a one size smaller first grade. In the home childhood has moved indoors as television watching, computer game playing and internet activities have increasingly replaced active outdoor play such as bike riding and hide and seek.

The need for play is well documented

Many recent books have articulated the importance of children's self initiated play for their healthy physical, emotional, social and intellectual development. For example, Edward Zigler and his colleagues[68] analyze national policy decisions as these pertain to the importance of play for young children. Vivian Gussin Paley[69] speaks out strongly against the disappearance of time for creative play and makes the case for the critical role of fantasy play in the psychological, intellectual, and social development of young children. My book, *The Power of Play,*[70] considers the work of theorists such as Piaget[71] and Freud, noting that taken together, play, love and work are the three necessary ingredients of a full, happy and productive life. Psychiatrist Stuart Brown[72] reviewed more than 6000 case histories to explore a person's play experiences over his or her life. Among his findings was that homicidal males were severely play deprived as

children; in contrast, highly creative and successful people had a rich play life.

As individual authors highlight the importance of play, so have the works of many national organizations. The support of play has been urged in works by the Association for Childhood Education International (ACEI)[73] and the American Academy of Pediatrics. The consistent themes of these reports are illustrated in the Alliance for Childhood's booklet entitled "Crisis in the Kindergarten: Why Children Need to Play in School."[74] Here Edward Miller and Joan Almon cite European research which clearly demonstrates that when academics are substituted for play in kindergarten, the long term results on literacy and math are significantly worse not better.

While many European countries have returned to play based kindergartens, the United States has not. The negative effects of silencing play are all too evident in this country: preschool expulsion rates are three times higher than the national average for children in kindergarten through twelfth grade; boys are being expelled 4-5 times more often than girls. Kindergarten retention rates are also much higher than is true for the later grades with perhaps the exception of sixth grade.

What RESEARCH tells us about play

Despite these troubling trends, the research about play clearly illustrates its beneficial effects on both social-emotional and academic growth. Research also notes important variations in play behavior related to specific situations such as peer group and gender interactions; block play; parent play; and clinical studies.

Peer Group and Gender Interactions[75]

Peer group interaction studies elaborate on many established insights about peer group play and add new ones. Studies of gender suggests that girl's spontaneous play is more closely associated with that of adults than is true for boys whose play is more stereotyped and less adult oriented. These results are even greater when children play in groups rather than in dyads. In addition to adding to our knowledge of gender differences, studies identify the effect of the number of children at play as a significant variable as to its character. A related study indicates that outdoor play is more facilitative of complex peer interactions than is indoor play. This effect is partly due to the absence of major adult presence during outdoor play.

Studies of gender differences in play involving imaginary companions suggest that girls tend to create imaginary companions that are alter egos, and that serve as confidants. Boys in contrast seem to identify with their imaginary companions and to impersonate them. I believe this analysis is a bit misleading because imaginary companions tend to be personal and both boys and girls use them as alter egos. There are many accounts of boys having imaginary companions whom they use as the culprits for their own misdeeds.

Another study found that for girls, not boys, playing with a child at a higher level advanced the play of the child at the older level. I suggest that while gender differences are important birth order needs to be taken into account as well. A first born, for example, is less likely to learn from a last born, while a last is willing to learn from a first born.

Another variable affecting the level of play performance appears to be emotional competence with peers.[76] High social competence with peers is associated with higher levels of play than is low levels of social competence.

In another study peer play at home was a good indicator of social adaptation to peers at a child care center. A related study found that high levels of peer play at the beginning of the school year predicted good emotional regulation, initiative, and self determination and vocabulary skills at the end of the school year. In contrast, low levels of peer play at the beginning of the school year predicted negative emotional and unregulated behavior at the end of the year. These studies all suggest that the level of play is a significant measure of many different facets of adaptive early childhood behavior.

Block Play[77]

Two additional studies — one research investigation and a case history — report that block play facilitates logico-mathematical and mathematical thinking. The problem with such studies is that they are short term and have no control groups. One wonders about the impact of gender on these studies: Boys tend to play more with blocks than do girls. And girls tend to do more poorly than boys on math, at least initially. An interesting study of the effects of block play would be a longitudinal one that looked at block play by gender over time and assessed children's mathematical competence.

Perhaps the most interesting, and definitive study in this group is the one in which parents were given sets of blocks to take home and were sent periodic newsletters as to how they could engage in block play with their children. It was a controlled study and took place over a long time span. The results suggested that providing parents and children with blocks and with ways in which to play with them together can have beneficial effects upon children's language development and potentially their cognitive development as well. This study makes clear that there are relatively low cost ways to involve parents and children in constructive play with many positive results not only for the child's development but also for the parent child relationships.

Parent Child Play[78]   As might be expected, parent involvement in children's play has beneficial effects. There is evidence that when parents engage in physical and pretend play with their children, there are positive benefits for children's emotional knowledge and peer social competence. In a longitudinal study that looked at the effects of father and mother semi-structured play with their children, the play was associated with positive language and cognitive outcomes. The children's results were more beneficial for those having fathers with higher education and incomes than it was for children of fathers with less education and lower incomes. The effectiveness of mother's play with the children was also related to these variables. Perhaps, when husbands are better educated and have better incomes, mothers feel more secure and this can come through in their play with the children.

A related study looked at father-child attachment and quality of play. The results showed that children who were securely attached to their fathers played with them at a higher level than did those children who were poorly attached to their fathers. Attachment had a different effect for mothers. Mothers who were securely attached to their children were more responsive, facilitative and socially interactive with their children than were mothers who were insecurely attached. Apparently secure attachment facilitates higher level of play for fathers but higher levels of social interaction and participation for mothers.

The question as how parents interact to support children's development was explored in a study of mother-child interactions with gifted, average and deaf children. This study suggests that parents intuitively know how to support the play of their children depending upon their level of mental or sensory ability. As expected the intellectual levels of the children were reflected in their play levels. The gifted engaged in the highest level of play and the deaf children the lowest. Mothers of the average children played at a bit higher level than their children. But the mothers of the gifted children played at significantly higher levels than their children. Apparently these mothers knew about how much additional input children could take to advance to the next level.

Also, the quality of mother child interaction may be determined by the gender of the child as well as by the security of attachment. In the study that looked at mother's play with infants at three age levels the differences between their interactions with their sons and daughters was striking. At all three age levels mothers interacted more, and more directly, with their daughters than with their sons. Mothers talked more with their daughters, interpreted their play and engaged in more conversations with them than they did with their sons. The authors suggest that these differential patterns of interaction can affect gender role identity. It would be interesting to see how attachment fits into this picture.

The results of this study were further amplified by another that looked at parent and adult play with boys and girls. When parents and non-parental adults played with boys, most of the time was spent playing with masculine toys. In playing with girls, however, both parents and non-parental adults showed much more flexibility and variety in the toys they chose to play with. It was also found that the way in which parent's categorized toys by gender was different than the ways that experts categorized the same toys. In general these findings reflect the cultural bias which gives girls and women more flexibility in exploring boys toys and play than is the reverse.

Clinical Studies[79]

Specific clinical studies have found, for example, that adult interventions with children who have potential language delays have a positive effect on the children's language skills.[80] Another clinical finding is that outdoor play has advantages over indoor play for most children. But when home play is compared to classroom play, home play seems to have the advantage. This is particularly true for children with intellectual disabilities who may feel more comfortable at home than in a classroom setting. So context does affect play, but the range of possible contexts has to be taken into account.

Another finding is that children who preferred solitary play were socially, emotionally and intellectually less mature than peers who engaged in social play.[81] Solitary play is thus a marker of potential social and emotional problems at a later age. This finding corroborates many of the studies on peer interaction, where the quality of social interaction is always related to other facets of adaptation. It appears that social competence may well mediate many other achievements in young children.

New insights into the different types of play

All of the books, position papers and research on the play of young children emphasize its importance for healthy intellectual, social and emotional development. However, there are some important fresh insights into young children's play that may be noted, specifically the relationship between play and work; kinship play; and harmful play.

Play and Work

As in all of her books, Vivian Gussin Paley,[82] wonderfully illustrates how young children go about constructing their own play, resolving their own conflicts, and using play as a therapeutic vehicle for handling their emotional distress. I do have one reservation about her last book and that lies in its title, *A Child's Work*. It was Maria Montessori[83] who introduced the phrase, "Play is the Child's Work." In so doing Montessori did not mean to identify work and play, because she often contrasted the two. Unfortunately this phrase has often been taken to mean that children should be working not playing.

Paley does not make this mistake in her actual writing but by using this phrase, particularly in the title, she contributes to this misunderstanding. Jean Piaget, who himself attended a Montessori school as a child, and whose Lab School was run along Montessori lines, was nonetheless quite clear on the separation of work and play.

Piaget argued that play was pure assimilation, the transformation of reality in the service of the self. Work, in contrast, was accommodation, the transformation of the self to meet the demands of reality. When children engage in dramatic play, they transform reality by making believe they are teachers, or doctors, or super heroes. On the other hand when young children learn to eat with a knife and fork, to put on and take off their clothes, this is a form of work. Clearly work and play can be combined, and that is what Montessori had in mind. What she might well have said, is that "Play is the motivation for children's work." I try to make this point in my own book.

Kinship Play

I also introduced a different typology of play. I suggest that children's play could be described as including mastery, innovation, kinship and therapeutic activities.[84]

The novel inclusion was kinship play. By kinship play I had in mind the fact that children spontaneously play with other children of about the same size even when they are strangers. It is a little like being in a foreign country and meeting other tourists from home. Kinship is a basic way in which young children learn to deal with social relationships and skills.

Harmful Play On the other hand, one thing that I failed to deal with in my book is the fact that some play can be negative and hurtful. Put differently play has the power to do good, but also has the power to do evil. When children tease, bully or harass other children in the name of play, this is evil use of imaginative abilities. I think that I am not alone in this emphasis on the positive role of play. In the other books, certainly in Stuart Brown's book[85], and in the position papers as well, the possible negative uses of play are downplayed. Given the negative connotation of play in contemporary parlance, this emphasis on the positive is entirely understandable. But we have to acknowledge that imagination and creativity are often used for evil purposes including torture and innovative weaponry.

Conclusion

The last decade (2000 to 2010) had been witness to a great deal of attention to the play of young children. Books, and position papers have not only detailed the importance of young children's play to healthy development, they have also described the many ways in which play has been being limited, over-programmed and overscheduled. Research studies reinforce the importance of self-initiated play for social, emotional and intellectual development. Block play seemed to receive particular attention in this regard. The studies also documented the importance of parents playing with their children and many benefits that accrue from such play. Clinical studies both reinforced and qualified the normative research.

The last decade has once again provided abundant evidence for the importance of self initiated play. But the real task is to make parents, educators and legislators realize and support the importance of play for young children. The commercialization of childhood has pitted what is in the best interests of children against what is in the best interest of economic gain. It is a battle we may not be able to win, but it is one we cannot afford to lose. ▶

Hope for the children of 2020:

That we as a society will come to our senses and stop the damage being done to children and youth by our schools, the media and unscrupulous advertisers and merchandisers to the young.

About the Author

David Elkind, *Professor Emeritus of Child Development, Tufts University*

Professional focus:

Combating the unhealthy pressures on families, children and youth, by the larger society

Learning and Life Skills

14

Ellen Galinsky

For as long as I can remember, I have been interested in learning. Perhaps it was because my mother, with a few other parents, cared so much about learning that they got together and hired a tutor as a first step to creating their own school. That school, focused on dynamic, meaningful, and experiential learning, provided me with a model of the difference good schools can make. My college major in the new field of child study introduced me to the world of research. Later, I spent more than two decades at Bank Street College of Education, teaching in its Children's School, working in its research department, and eventually becoming one of the founders of the academic field of work and family life, before cofounding the Families and Work Institute two decades ago. Thus, I have spent my life learning about learning and trying to use that knowledge to fuel change.

Nevertheless, when I review my lifetime of effort and the work of so many incredible people in the decades leading to 2010, I come to a simple conclusion: much more is needed. There are at least three reasons for this conclusion:

- Our failure rate is too high. Karen Pittman, executive director of the Forum for Youth Investment[86], asks us to imagine a typical high school graduation, but her hypothetical graduation class represents our country as a whole:

  "A third of high school seniors standing at a graduation are ready to go onto the next thing — whether that's college or work. They are fully prepared.

  "A third of them has plans to go on to college or work but is not ready. They are going to get to college and find that they have significant challenges — we have about 40% of young people who go to college actually taking remedial courses.

  "And another third of those young people are not ready — they may be absent, they may not be graduating at all."

- This failure rate starts far earlier than high school — 1.2 million students drop out of school each year, and only two-thirds of students graduate on time.[87] U.S. Secretary of Education Arne Duncan explained some of his views on the dropout rate to me when he was CEO of the Chicago Public Schools:[88]

  "The [drop-outs] do not see any relevance to what they're supposed to be learning — to what they're being taught in school — to their daily lives."

- As we know, the failure rate starts well before the first years of school.[89] John DeStefano, mayor of New Haven, Connecticut, confronts this issue regularly in his efforts to revitalize his community:

"The promise of America is that everybody can be President — that everyone can be anything — but the fact is that's a lie for a lot of these kids because they start out behind, they never catch up. They never even had a chance. They lost the race — before the race even began."[90]

The first step in my journey

Despite what we have been learning from neuroscientists and child development researchers about how children learn best, the past decade had an increasing focus on school accountability that led to a pressure-cooker atmosphere and to a test-crazy nation. In response to my deep concern about what was happening to learning, I set out on an intellectual odyssey in 2001 to see what I could do to make a difference, and the result has become our mission, *Mind in the Making*.[91]

I had been conducting a series of Ask the Children studies, so I planned my next one to focus on youth and learning. As background for this study, I began by listening to the voices of children from the 6th through the 12th grades from communities all over the country. Although the children were very diverse geographically, economically, ethnically, and culturally, they told me very similar stories. They described learning as "learning stuff"—as the acquisition of facts, figures, and concepts. The learning experiences they described were primarily imposed, and their motivation was primarily extrinsic rather than intrinsic.

I asked the children to finish this sentence, "It is important to learn so I can . . . " The children I interviewed all over the country said:

"Get good grades."

"Go to good schools."

"Get a good job."

"Support myself — have a good house — have a nice car."

Their reasons echo those of 81,499 students in the High School Survey of Youth Engagement at the Indiana University.[92] When asked why they go to school, 73% said because they want to get a degree and go to college, 69% said because of their friends, and 58% said because it's the law. Only 39% said they go to school to learn.

It was not only the words of the children I interviewed that expressed how turned off to learning they were — so did their faces. Their expressions tended to be flat; their eyes were dull as they talked to me.

So I pushed. I asked children to finish the sentence, "When I am learning, I feel . . ." Those children who had experienced a broader connection to learning said things like:

"Excited. You feel like the world is moving again."

Learning draws them in, makes them want more. One boy describes this experience: "It's like going to an education buffet — you just want to keep going back for more and more."

"Proud, because I feel I've improved."

"Like I have a future."

At this point in my journey I had two starkly different images in my mind. One was of these older children who seem mostly turned off to learning, and it took my pushing to bring back any sparkle. The other image was of young children who are unstoppable learners. The fire in their eyes burns brightly.

To see how we can prevent the fire in children's eyes from dimming, I decided to delve deeply into the science of early learning to pursue the questions:

1. How do children learn best?

2. What makes them stay motivated and engaged in learning, to see themselves and to be ongoing, life-long learners?

3. What can be done to rekindle that motivation if it has been dulled?

Amazing babies

To find out, I and my colleagues from New Screen Concepts, a film production company, spent eight years filming over 70 researchers in action as they conducted their studies. One thing that became clear early on is that children's brains appear to be wired to help them understand and know about the world, and that this learning starts happening long before babies can be taught this knowledge.

For example, 9-month-old babies have what I call a language sense. Their brains operate almost like a statistical program, detecting which sounds go together in their native language (or languages). This helps them make sense of the "sea of sounds" that surrounds them, as the studies of Jenny Saffran[93] of the University of Wisconsin show. For example, when the babies were presented with a made-up language or a language they didn't know, they became bored and stopped listening. They showed renewed interest when they were presented with new combinations of sounds.

Similar studies have shown that infants 6 months old and even younger have a number sense: they can detect the difference between large and small numbers of things — such as the difference between 16 dots and 8 dots, or the difference between a large or small number of times that a puppet jumps or a car honks its horn, as seen in the studies of Elizabeth Spelke of Harvard University.[94]

And they have what I call a people sense, whereby they focus on people's intentions versus seeing what people do as random movements in space, as revealed by the studies of Amanda Woodward of the University of Maryland.[95]

Another interrelated problem — and an "aha" inspiration

So it is clear that children are born engaged in learning, and we have learned that children's brains appear to be wired to grasp onto different kinds of knowledge. At first, I saw the studies I

was filming in traditional categories — studies about social development, studies about literacy or numeracy. But then I had an "aha" moment: we have focused on the content that young children need to learn, but we have paid much less attention to their learning the life skills they need for now and for the future.

The issue of skills has been a special interest of mine for decades. It doesn't take long for employers to tell you — and tell you vehemently — that new entrants to the workforce are not well-prepared. That may sound like an old story, but these employers have been telling a slightly different story—that new employees don't have the life skills they need to succeed in the 21st century. I have explored this topic in a number of studies of employers and employees conducted by the Families and Work Institute.

All of this information eventually led to my "aha" moment:

- I could see that the life skills I have come to consider most essential for the workforce emerge in young children.

- I could see that if I focused on skills, I would be drawing on studies that cross academic boundaries, from developmental studies to neuroscience.

- They are always driven by goals.[96]

- They involve using our working memories to keep a number of different things in our minds at the same time while paying attention, thinking flexibly, and inhibiting our tendency to go on automatic pilot.[97]

- They pull together our feelings and thinking so that we can reflect, analyze, plan, and evaluate.[98]

Stanislas Dehaene[99] of the Collège de France in Paris calls the prefrontal cortex and its functions a "neuronal workspace" whose main purpose is to "assemble, confront, recombine, and synthesize knowledge," allowing "our behavior to be guided by any combination of information from past or present experience." Adele Diamond[100] of the University of British Columbia believes that executive functions predict children's achievements as well as IQ tests do or even better, because they go beyond what we know — they tap our abilities to use what we know.

- I could also see that these same skills not only will help children in the future (2020), but they help children in the present. Moreover, these skills often make a critical difference in which children come to school ready to learn and which children are behind before they even enter kindergarten or first grade. They also make a critical difference in which children remain engaged learners in school and which children don't.

- Finally, I could see that any child can learn these skills, and any adult can teach them. It is never too late.

Executive functions of the brain

Given this "aha" moment, I came to another significant conclusion: that the skills I see as essential are based, in one way or another, in the prefrontal cortex of the brain and involve what child development researchers call executive functions of the brain. Executive brain functions manage our attention, our emotions, and our behavior in order to reach our goals. They involve weaving together our social, emotional, and intellectual capacities. Here are some key aspects of executive functions:

Seven essential learning and life skills

Given this information, I offer seven essential life skills for the children of 2020:

1. **Focus and self-control.** We live in a 24/7 world where we are flooded with information, tempted by multiple distractions, and where we need to multitask more than many of us would like. In many workforce studies I've conducted, it has become clear how important focus is to work — and to life success.

   Focus and self-control involve many executive functions of the brain, such as paying attention, remembering the rules, and inhibiting one's initial response to achieve a larger goal. And focus and self-control can be taught, as shown by the studies of Michael Posner[101] and his colleagues at the University of Oregon.

2. **Perspective-taking.** The late Peter Drucker, known as the father of modern management, said that "an outside-in perspective" — seeing things as a customer would see them — is responsible for launching the most successful new businesses.[102] I call this perspective-taking.

Perspective-taking calls on many of the executive functions of the brain. It requires inhibitory control to inhibit our own thoughts and feelings to consider the perspectives of others; cognitive flexibility to see a situation in different ways; and reflection — the ability to consider someone else's thinking alongside our own.

According to Ross Thompson[103] of the University of California at Davis, this skill helps children by making the social world they live in more predictable and memorable. And Alison Gopnik[104] of the University of California at Berkeley reports that children who can understand others' perspectives do better in kinder-garten because they're better able to understand what their teachers want and expect.

Perspective-taking also affects how we deal with conflict, because children who can understand the motives of others are less likely to jump to conclusions about the behavior of others. As a result, they get into fewer conflicts.[105]

3. **Communicating.** Communicating well involves executive functions of the brain; for example, reflecting upon the goal of what we want to communicate and inhibiting our point of view so that we can understand the viewpoints of others. These are not simple tasks, as my workplace research reveals. When I asked a nationally representative group of employers in one of the Families and Work Institute's studies to name the gaps in skills they found among new entrants to the workforce, by far the largest proportions cited spoken communication skills and written communication skills.[106]

4. **Making connections.** I have described my "aha" moment, but think about your most recent one — when you suddenly understood something you didn't understand before. Chances are this "aha" moment involved seeing a new connection.

Making connections begins with sorting and categorizing — for example, young children can see that spoons and forks go together because both are used to eat. It also begins with an understanding that one thing can stand for or represent another — that a photograph of the family dog represents the real dog. This skill underlies an understanding of all the subjects we study in school, including math.

Making multiple connections is a skill that becomes possible during the later preschool/early school-age years and beyond, as the prefrontal cortex of children's brains matures. It calls on

> **One of the joys of conducting this intellectual odyssey is that I am closer to knowing how to keep the fire in children's eyes burning brightly, not only when they are young but as they move into elementary school and beyond.**

executive functions of the brain, including working memory, inhibitory control, and cognitive flexibility. Making unusual connections is the basis of creativity. Adele Diamond[107] says, "The essence of creativity is to be able to disassemble and recombine elements in new ways."

In the information-overloaded world of today and tomorrow, creative thinkers have an edge, as Kathy Hirsh-Pasek[108] of Temple University points out: "In a Google generation, where there are facts at your fingertips, the person who will later be called boss will be the person who can put those facts together in new and innovative and creative ways!"

5. **Critical thinking.** At its core, critical thinking is the ongoing search for valid and reliable knowledge to guide beliefs, decisions, and actions. Like the other essential skills, critical thinking develops on a set course throughout childhood and into adulthood, but its use must be promoted. And like the other skills, critical thinking draws on executive functions of the brain.

6. **Taking on challenges.** As we know far too well, life is filled with challenges. And challenges, even positive ones, can be stressful. The National Scientific Council on the Developing Child, directed by Jack P. Shonkoff of Harvard University, has reviewed the research on children and stress and has concluded that while there are different types of stress, the key factors in whether these experiences ultimately have a positive, or tolerable, or toxic impact on children's development are how long the stress lasts and whether children have safe and dependable relationships with people to whom they can turn for support.[109]

We tend to focus on helping children cope with or become resilient when confronted with stress, but I think it is important to move beyond respond-

ing positively to stress — to help them actively take on challenges as well. Carol Dweck[110] of Stanford University has found that children who avoid challenges have a "fixed mindset": they see their intelligence as a fixed trait and therefore are reluctant to undertake challenges that "stretch" them. Children who are willing to take on challenges have a "growth mindset," seeing their abilities as something they can develop.

7. **Self-directed engaged learning**. I began this quest to reconcile two contrasting images — one of young children who are unstoppable learners and the other of children in the 6th through 12th grades whom I interviewed about learning and in whose eyes I saw little, if any, fire.

During this journey into much of the classic and cutting-edge research on children's development and learning, I have identified seven principles that encourage self-directed, engaged learning. In brief, these are establishing a trustworthy relationship with children; helping children set and work toward their own goals; involving children socially, emotionally, and intellectually; elaborating and extending children's learning; helping children practice, synthesize, and generalize; helping children become increasingly accountable; and creating a community of learners. One of the joys of conducting this intellectual odyssey is that I am closer to knowing how to keep the fire in children's eyes burning brightly, not only when they are young but as they move into elementary school and beyond.[111]

You might ask, "Why focus on skills? Don't children have enough to do in mastering content? For that matter, don't teachers and parents already have too much on their plates?"

This is an age-old debate: content versus skill. But I think it is the wrong debate. Of course children need to learn content, but I also think they need these life skills so they can use the content they learn.

That's my wish for the children of 2020 — that they have parents and teachers who not only help them learn content but also promote these life skills. The good news is that it is never too late, and that these skills don't call for fancy equipment or new programs. They call for doing what we already do, but in different ways. There are hundreds of easy ways to promote these skills. If we fail at this juncture, we risk failing to keep the fire in children's eyes burning and to give them the life skills they need now and in the future. ▶

Hope for the children of 2020

My wish is that, in addition to content, children master life skills that will help them be all they can be.

About the Author

Ellen Galinsky, *President, Families and Work Institute*
egalinsky@familiesandwork.org

Professional focus

Galinsky's focus is conducting research that identifies what it takes for all of us — children and adults — to thrive at work, at home, in school, and in our communities, and then to use that knowledge to inspire and effect change.

Improv Workshop

Translating Ideas into Intelligent Action

Workshop Agenda
- Reflections on the knowledge articles
- Examining knowledge and values
- Developing your smart improv

Reflections on the knowledge articles

Our improv workshop for Act II asks you, as smart improvisers, to rehearse your long-term commitment to translate knowledge into intelligent action. As we read the eight knowledge syntheses, we recognize that these authors are role models demonstrating how to be explorers, profession-builders, and public intellectuals or activists.

These eight authors maintain a habit of inquiry that enables them to be career-long explorers of new information. Over time their ideas have grown and evolved. (Google their names to compare their writings ten years ago to today). Evolution in their thinking and writing can be tracked over many years because they continue to question and experiment as they seek improved results for children. They are active observers of unresolved challenges in the field who probe for more knowledge to guide practices. Their minds remain open and curious as they eagerly engage in debate and collaboration that may either challenge or validate their own assumptions.

Given their habit of inquiry, the knowledge they generate builds and strengthens the early care and education field. These authors are profession-builders who both *confirm* the historical continuity of the wisdom that guides our field and *challenge* ideas that have lost relevance or power. Profession-builders are not afraid to move into new territory, to re-examine cherished ideals, or to create alternative standards, assessments, professional preparation, policy, and public education initiatives.

A third characteristic of these authors is their willingness to be public intellectuals or activists who communicate with the public as well as with the early care and education field. The authors are willing to take action that moves us all beyond traditional thinking and practices when the evidence shows that the status quo is not benefiting — or may be harming — children. They understand that smart improv and ethical practice may require them to speak out in favor of tested wisdom as well as for inspired new ideas.

Any of us should be willing and able to play similar roles in our own communities — to be explorers, profession-builders, and public intellectuals or activists. The importance of "being willing" is underlined by six realities that confront the early care and education field:

- Our work is subject to public scrutiny, and public opinion may or may not be consistent with the research. Consider the example of play and dual-language learning.

- Smart improvisation is required. Applying knowledge to practice with children and families requires a great deal of wit, skill, information, and talent. Debate about the minimum qualifications for the early care and education workforce is one of the most strident in our profession.

- The ongoing challenge of poor compensation in the field of early care and education is even more difficult to accept given the skills and knowledge required for good practice.

- Having the "big picture" of the field in mind is important. Access to information in multiple topic areas is essential to effective, holistic practice.

- We know more than we do! There is an expanding gap between knowledge about young learners and actual practice or policy.

- The challenge of leveraging diversity must permeate all of our efforts toward intelligent action. In *Children of 2010*, we anticipated a diversity that is now a reality that we must leverage, use, adapt to, and incorporate in professional practice. Moving beyond tolerance and respect for diversity, we must deepen our sensitivity to the ways race and culture impact each of us as individuals, as well as the children and families we serve.

You, the reader, may have discovered additional themes and contrasts while reviewing the knowledge articles in Act II.

> *A teacher's purpose is not to create students in his own image, but to develop students who can create their own image.*
>
> —Author Unknown
>
> Source: www.quotegarden.com/teachers.html

I'm ready to learn from the inside out!

a) Take time to identify your own thoughts about the articles.

b) How are these articles on discrete topics interrelated?

c) Ask: Which of these ideas are directly related to my work? How can I learn more about this?

d) Think: What can I *do* with this information?

There is much new knowledge, and there are many opportunities, for improving outcomes for children. We encourage you with your colleagues to examine the field's knowledge base in view of your values. Create your own smart improv! Preparing your improv for Act II is challenging, and we have two practical suggestions to help:

- Recognize breakthroughs. Some of the information in the articles may have been "aha" moments promising exciting breakthroughs for your work. This information is a good place to conceive of smart improv, either individually or in collaboration with your colleagues.

- Recognize differences. You will find hot topics in some of the articles — information that is stimulating controversy — and some articles may be puzzling, or contrast sharply with your own experience. Follow up on these articles! You can do further reading, consult with others, or take a class.

Examining knowledge and values

Our personal beliefs and values function as filters through which we process new ideas and apply knowledge in our everyday professional lives. Each of us as readers, asked to recall key concepts from one of these knowledge articles, will most likely create very different lists. We most easily assimilate ideas that are compatible with strongly held personal beliefs and values. How might your smart improv be blinded or enhanced by your preexisting values and beliefs? We suggest that you make three lists to explore how your vision, personal beliefs, and values interact with the information in these chapters.

List 1: Explore new information.

Make a list of ideas from the knowledge chapters that hold potential for improving your ability to meet the needs of the children or colleagues with whom you work, or are likely to work in the future. How do these ideas mesh with your personal values embedded in the vision that you prepared in Act I? How do these ideas interact with issues or concerns for children with disabilities and other special needs?

List 2: Build your profession and the field's knowledge base.

Identify ideas in the articles that made you uncomfortable, or with which you strongly disagreed. It's OK to disagree, as disagreement can be the first step to help you clarify, strengthen, or change your perspectives. For example, do you have expectations for children's behavior and performance that are in conflict with perspectives presented by some of the authors? Reexamine the basis for the author's statements and contemplate if you might be hanging onto any outdated traditions or ideas that need to be reconsidered. Or, explore whether there is evidence to support your current position. Like all explorers, press for proof and greater understanding.

List 3: Share ideas publicly.

Use the articles to identify ideas that parents of the children with whom you work would not understand or endorse. What action can you take to support parent learning?

Hi, teacher!
Keep learning and
improvising, 'cause
I'm on my way!

Developing your smart improv

Your three lists can provide the script for your smart improv:

- **Your smart improv requires you to take action.** You can organize your smart improv into at least three categories — actions that:

    1. Entail revising or refining your current practices.

    2. Require you to translate totally new ideas into practices.

    3. Involve translating knowledge to public audiences such as parents and policy-makers.

    To begin implementation, prioritize your action list. You may be surprised by how much you can accomplish.

- **Form or join a learning team.** To leverage your efforts, gain access to the insights of peers, and encourage each other to keep moving toward positive changes.

Learning Teams

Learning teams provide an exciting way to explore emerging knowledge and engage in innovation that will strengthen the quality of early care and development. Teams are a powerful means of engaging teachers, administrators, professors, and other caregivers in devising detailed improvements in outcomes based on validated information. They also provide a constructive environment for questioning our own assumptions and traditions.

Keep in mind that not all of your smart improvisations will be successful, or successful right away. It is important that you identify desired outcomes when you plan the improv so you can measure or verify its effects. It may take a number of attempts before you know for sure whether the improv intervention is having the desired results. Whether it is successful or not, share your findings with others — because your well-disciplined efforts add to the profession-building that enhances the field of early care and education.

Congratulations on preparing for this act! Remember that exploring and applying knowledge is a career-long activity, and each situation may present new challenges. Continue your efforts by monitoring research, educational assessments, program evaluations, and emerging issues about children and families in your own community. ▶

Did you know I'm a genius when it comes to learning?

Act III: Strategies

Facilitating Outcomes for the Children of 2020

Commentary

Rooted in a clear vision and a sound knowledge base, the strategies we use to facilitate outcomes for children are the art of professional practice. Smart improv is the essence of being a gifted educator, both individually and as a member of a high-performing team. Successful strategies applied to intelligent improvisation are driven by context, collaboration and community.

Context. The degree to which knowledge is put to effective use is heavily influenced by such contextual factors as the settings where children interact with adults, tools that support or hamper programs, and policies that govern and fund services.

Smart improv requires us, on an ongoing basis that starts *now*, to exercise judgment based on current realities and context. Facilitating

better outcomes for the children of 2020 is very much dependent on what we do *today*. We cannot wait until the next decade to begin to create results we want to have achieved by then.

Collaboration and strategic alignment. Millions of children and families will benefit from strategic improvements in our field, yet the challenges are sometimes daunting. To achieve better outcomes for all children, there must be a comprehensive strategy for providing services, ensuring quality, connecting resources, and making the system as efficient as possible. Implementing an overarching strategy means we all need to get into the act and work together, moving beyond our historic tendency to operate each program as a separate island. Our strategies must be aligned in ways that are transparent, that transcend individual program loyalties, and that address well-defined, common goals.

Examples of Context

<u>Settings</u> where adults interact with children, whether in nurturing or debilitating ways: e.g., the family, schools and centers, informal child care, and the community.

<u>Tools</u> that support or hamper children's learning and adult's effectiveness: e.g., assessment, technology for use by children, and online learning communities for adults.

<u>Policies and systems</u> that influence the availability and quality of early care and education opportunities: e.g., federal and state-funded programs and regulations, public opinion, and public and private investments.

Our field wide strategies can occur at many levels: coteaching a class of children; communicating around children's daily or periodic transitions from program to program and grade to grade; or creating systems that ensure that children receive comprehensive services. Any of these levels of effort may be complex; the more people, programs, and services involved, the more difficult it is to achieve collaboration to the benefit of children. Such complexity intensifies the need for smart improvisation. That's why in *Children of 2020*, we emphasize the importance and potential effectiveness of adult learning communities in addressing these challenges. Fortunately, technology is now making collaboration more accessible, efficient, and powerful!

Community-wide nurturing of children.
The important work of the early care and education field is only one part of the broader spectrum of strategic efforts needed to facilitate better outcomes for children of 2020. We are only one piece of the puzzle needed for children to achieve the American Dream. Smart improvisation means that we must be more intentional about creating or advocating for community-wide networks of health and social services, and other resources. These networks, together, can effectively influence critical dimensions of strategy, including policy, regulation, and funding matters, especially when communities face competition for finite resources.

> *"Life is like a play. It is not the length but the excellence of the acting that matters."*
>
> —*Seneca*

One approach to promoting community-wide connectedness is the Pathways project, founded by Lisbeth B. Schorr, senior fellow at the Center for the Study of Social Policy (Table 1). *Pathway to Children Ready for School and Succeeding at Third Grade*[112] assembles a wealth of findings from research, practice, theory, and policy about what it takes to improve the lives of children and families, particularly those living in tough neighborhoods.

The Pathways framework does not promote a single formula or program. Rather, its emphasis is on acting across disciplines, systems, and jurisdictions to increase the number of children who are ready for school and succeeding at third grade. Pathways provides a starting point to guide choices made by community coalitions, services providers, researchers, funders, and policymakers to achieve desired outcomes for children and their families. By illustrating a comprehensive, coherent array of actions, Pathways provides an example that may be useful as your community develops its own smart improv.

 Early care and education are an important part of the overall strategy, but we are not the entire picture! Children come to ECE from someplace, and they go on to other learning environments. Along the way, their other needs must also be addressed. Strategy must encompass the whole child.

Table 1: The Pathways project, founded by Lisbeth B. Schorr

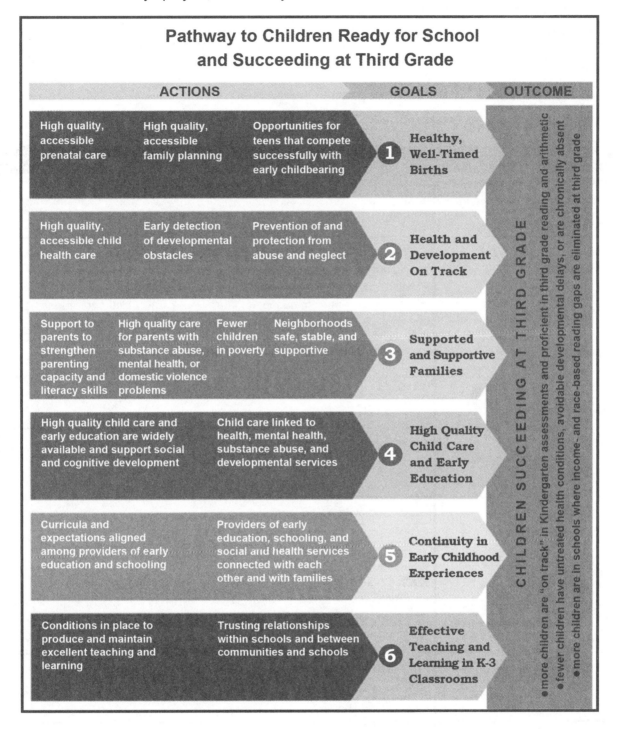

We have invited articles that provide in-depth approaches for developing smarter strategies, policies, and systems. Read each article and ask yourself:

- What results do I hold myself or my program accountable to achieve?
- How would the strategies recommended in this article impact me, my team, or my community?

The following thoughts provide a flavor of what is to come from our six commentaries, but read each strategy statement carefully and make notes for creating your own strategies.

PREVIEW OF STRATEGIES — Thoughts from Act III	
State-Funded Preschools *Barbara Bowman*	Whether children receive their preschool education in Head Start, a child care center, or a public school, the goal is that all children have the same opportunity to prepare for school.
Assessment for Teaching and Learning *Jacqueline Jones*	Can the community of early childhood professionals move beyond a reactionary stance based on the assessment-related mistakes of the past, or will it move forward into a proactive mode that tackles the big issues in the design and implementation of appropriate early childhood assessment systems?
Family Engagement *Bernice Weissbourd, Richard Weissbourd, and Kelley O'Carroll*	It is the exceptional program or school that engages families in deep, sustained ways that affect important childhood outcomes. Few programs or schools partner with a diverse range of families effectively.
Technology *Douglas H. Clements and Julie Sarama*	Promising practices encourage children to spend the time building physical, mental, and social skills with and without electronic technology.
The Role of States *Harriet A. Egertson*	Systems growth, QRIS, professional development, assessment, and data systems — all are key to seeing improvements in what children experience every day in early childhood settings.
Linking Economic Research to Public Investment *W. Steven Barnett*	Rather than viewing early care and education expenditures solely as a cost, economists see them as investments — investment opportunities with potentially large returns. The challenge is to convey this to the public and policymakers
The Learning Communities of 2020 *Pascal Kaplan*	The success of virtual learning communities depends more on the personal qualities, intentions, and goals of those who engage in them than on any particular technology.
(Excerpt) **Aliens in the Education Matrix: Recovering Freedom** *Asa G. Hilliard III-Baffour Amankwatia II*	It matters greatly how teachers think about who they are, who children are, and why they are here.

After reading the full articles about strategy to help guide future action to improve the well-being of children, continue with the Act III improv workshop. ▶

State-Funded Preschools

Barbara Bowman

As requirements for academic achievement have risen, preschool education has expanded. Two streams of research provide evidence for this connection. One group of studies has pointed out the relationship of early cognitive and social stimulation to subsequent development. This research has demonstrated that instead of the capacity for learning being fixed at birth, the brain actually changes in response to experience, helping prepare children — or not — for future challenges.[113] A second group of studies has demonstrated social and academic benefits from preschool attendance. The early gap in scholastic achievement between children from low-income families and others places them at increasing risk of school failure, failure from which many never recover. Follow-up studies of adults who were enrolled in model preschool as children show that it was instrumental in changing their social and educational trajectories as much as 40 years later.[114] Children from model programs were more successful in K–12, and their later prosocial achievements and work records were superior to their matched controls.[115] Both lines of research highlight early learning as a critical base for the development of later cognitive and social skills and knowledge. Early learning benefits both the individuals and society.

Much of the support for state-funded preschool programs has been fueled by the failure of other efforts at school reform. Over the past 50 years, the poorer academic performance of American children compared to other industrialized nations has been a concern of business

leaders, politicians, and families. A number of initiatives have been tried, but both the national No Child Left Behind and National Assessment of Educational Progress data show American children lagging. Forty years of money and effort have failed to substantially diminish the achievement gap or raise the achievement of American students when compared with those from some other countries.

Economic analysis of the research on early intervention for at-risk children (low income, special needs, and English language learners) indicates that a better educational investment is in preschool education. This research shows that while early education is not a vaccination against later academic difficulty, it is more effective than later interventions and less costly.[116] The evidence is persuasive: money spent on model preschool programs pays both educational and social dividends.

While the model programs that produced long-term results were in many ways quite different from one another, what distinguished them from other early childhood programs were their distinctly educational curricula. The programs stressed the cognitive skills that underlie school achievement, particularly language and literacy, as well as the more traditional social skills and family support. Taught by well-educated and well-trained staffs, the model programs included teacher-directed learning and presented a coherent approach to curriculum content most middle-class children learn informally at home.

It is not surprising, then, that as schools struggle to close the achievement gaps and prepare a competitive workforce, preschool is getting more attention. Over the last few years, funding for early childhood education has risen sharply, with approximately 1.2 million children in 38 states now attending state-funded programs. Despite the recession and the dire fiscal status in many states, enrollment in state-funded prekindergarten continues to rise, as does the spending per child and the total state allocation for early childhood programs.[117]

State-funded preschool is not a single model

Aside from the stress on education, state-funded early childhood programs vary across the states in populations served, auspice, curricula, length of day, teacher training, and parent involvement. Today, approximately 1.3 million children are enrolled in public schools, with 250,000 of them receiving special-education services and 200,000 receiving health, nutrition, and social services through Head Start. In addition to funding preschool programs in public schools, many states also fund programs in community agencies with grants to Head Start, child care, and other public and private early childhood programs.[118]

Age of enrollment differs among the states. Some have universal coverage and enroll as many as 90% of 4-year-olds in half-day programs, and others have as few as 10% of their preschoolers in state-funded classrooms.[119] Some states serve 3- and 4-year-old children; others enroll only 4-year-olds. Some states mix their funds with those from other sources — Head Start, the Child Care Block grant, federal ESEA Title 1 — as well as from parent tuition and private donations. State-funded programs also vary in length of day, although those located in public schools are usually one-half day or a school day, as opposed to the full work day. Curricula and activities also differ, with some programs following published curricula and others relying on teachers to make lesson

plans. Teacher education and training is equally diverse. In some states teachers have the same credentials as public school teachers; in other states they have lower levels of education and training than kindergarten teachers. Also, expectations for parent involvement vary from attending teacher conferences to volunteering in classrooms, and setting policy.

Quality is also uneven across the states. Few have invested in programs that duplicate the models that proved so successful. For example, the National Institute for Early Education Research compiled 10 standards that reflect the qualities found in model programs. Of the 38 states that fund preschool programs, only two scored a 10 on the benchmarks, indicating that few have created a high-quality early childhood system.[120]

Issues and problems

Although state-funded preschool may be on the threshold of further growth, it is not without its issues and problems. These include:

A single system or not. To meet the needs of children and families, a variety of early childhood delivery systems have evolved to provide services. Children needing 6 to 12 hours of care attend child care (centers or home-based); low-income children attend Head Start, with its stress on health and social services; children with disabilities receive specific therapies in special education; and children who speak a language other than English enroll in bilingual education. Without question, the service silos serve legitimate needs of children and families, but they also isolate children from their peers in other systems. As important, the mission and traditions of services may preclude, or make it difficult to promote, high-quality education. For example, staffs in some systems, such as Head Start, have much less education and training than seems necessary for children's academic achievement, and the cost of highly educated teachers may be prohibitive in child care.

Would it be better to deliver early education in a single system with as few restrictions as possible (as in public schools), or should we try to insert education into the different services in which children are enrolled? Each has advantages and disadvantages.

Targeted or not. Another question is whether the public should be responsible for the cost of preschool if the child is not at risk. As family income rises, the benefits of preschool intervention for individual children are smaller, and families are better able to bear the cost. On the other hand, advocates for universal preschool point out that when the middle class has a vested interest in a program, its funding becomes more stable. Some states are focusing solely on students at-risk, and others are moving aggressively toward universal coverage. Which makes the most sense?

Cost. There are long-term and short-term cost deterrents to allocating resources for prekindergarten. First, all prekindergarten expenditures are loaded on the front end of the school continuum, but educational benefits are delayed up to 12 years and societal benefits even longer. Those wishing to get results quickly have focused on the later grades: high school and middle school reform. Even primary-grade literacy has had attention, leaving preschoolers unserved or badly served.

Another cost problem is that in order to increase funding for preschool, most states need to reduce spending for K–12, pitting early childhood programs against K–12 ones. However, without the firm foundation of a well-supported first five years, later schooling costs more, and the reform effort will be less successful.

Ideology and curricula. The early learning emphasis of state-funded prekindergartens often conflicts with two popular points of view in the field. One position contends that early childhood is the time to play and that young children cannot learn formal content, and if they could, they shouldn't. The other view is that children at-risk cannot be expected to learn school-related skills and knowledge because their social environment has compromised their development; therefore, health and social services are more important than curricula for them.

Despite recent voices from Head Start and the National Association for the Education of Young Children[121] advocating a stronger educational commitment, these two viewpoints still frame the thinking of many teacher college faculty and teachers. Both of these perspectives have made establishing a coherent and powerful early learning initiative difficult. While evidence from the model programs and international studies show there is considerable flexibility in when and how children master formal learning, the failure to agree across programs and states means some children start school at a disadvantage that is difficult to make up.

Bringing young children into the K–12 domain is a new venture for the public schools and is not without risk. Traditionally, even kindergarten children have often not been viewed as serious learners. Providing principals and school administrators with information on child development, particularly the relevance of birth-through-3 programs, is essential if they are to align early childhood programs. There is an equal need for better teacher preparation and professional development.

> **If the promise of early childhood education is to be realized, states will have to be involved; parents and the federal government cannot meet the needs alone.**

Assessment. Increasing numbers of states are requiring children to undergo readiness assessments for kindergarten and are asking for evidence that the prekindergartens are increasing the number of children who are "ready." Because most states are funding preschool on the premise that more children will be ready for kindergarten, their concern with assessment is understandable. However, many in the early childhood community question

whether the goal of preschool is school readiness. Some advocates believe that public education has failed other students and, therefore, preschools should not prepare children for a broken system. Others in the early childhood community are concerned that the assessment instruments being proposed are too narrow to be useful in assessing the total readiness of children for kindergarten. And still others believe is unfair to hold preschools and teachers accountable for educational outcomes when children and their families live in such risky environments. The expectation that states will continue to increase funding for preschool without evidence of effectiveness is undoubtedly misplaced, which means the early childhood community will need to be more than naysayers in the assessment discussion.

What must we do? Should we assess kindergarten readiness? How? Should we hold teachers accountable for children's learning?

Integrate new knowledge. Despite widespread dissemination of the research on the importance of early learning, the general public is having trouble integrating this new knowledge in its thinking. Many adults, drawing on their own experience, are often not aware that education for the 21st century is different from what we needed in the 20th century. School attendance, which gained in importance throughout the 20th century, is now mandatory. Not only is more education needed

(beginning at birth), but the content has also changed, with science and technology playing an ever-more-important role.

Much of this information has not penetrated early childhood teacher education institutions, where normative child development is still the primary content. Pedagogy receives scant attention, and practice models either promote a "push down" of kindergarten curricula or free-play discovery. This means that many young teachers in public schools and community agencies have little understanding or skill in teaching the diversity of students they find in their classrooms. Revision of preservice requirements for teachers and more-robust professional development in schools and centers are essential if children are to have the opportunities to learn that are necessary for school success.

Some parents understand and are taking charge of their children's education, charting their children's way to the best schools and programs. Other parents, particularly poor and minority ones, are unaware of the kind of support necessary to advance their children's education. Educating those families about the new demands for schooling and their role as their child's ombudsman is a task for the entire community, not just parents and schools.

Provide adequate funding. Politicians must recognize that while the research says we can change outcomes for children with early childhood programs, the programs children attend must have the necessary quality to do so. Unfortunately, in most states, K–12 is not adequately funded. While we may not know all the answers to effective education for all children, we do know some of them — up-to-date teacher education, well-researched curricula, well-paid and supported staff — and they all cost money. This means that state education systems that are currently underfunded, particularly for low-income children, must increase resources and address equable funding for school districts with the poorest children. The evidence for the importance of preschool programs is overwhelming, but only if the quality matches the needs of the children involved.

Collaborate. Preschool programs must collaborate with one another if children are to be well-served. Whether children receive their preschool education in Head Start, or a child care center, or a public school, the goal is that all children have the same opportunity to prepare for school. It may, however, be impractical to arrange for high-quality learning in all settings, for instance in homes and home-based child care. In this case, state-funded preschools may be an essential link in the early childhood system.

Collaboration is also essential between educational and care systems and the social-service and health systems. Stressed children make poor learners. Professionals and data systems that communicate can make the difference between eager learners and children struggling to cope with overwhelming programs.

There are probably a number of different strategies that will permit states to tailor their programs to their unique needs. However, there are a few steps all states can take that will move their early education systems forward:

- Make a commitment to early education and a delivery system for all children.

- Develop learning standards for birth through age 8.

- Align curricula content from prekindergarten through third grade.

- Disseminate kindergarten learning expectations.

- Create an early childhood data system, aligned with public schools, and with health and social services.

If the promise of early childhood education is to be realized, states will have to be involved; parents and the federal government cannot meet the needs alone. ▶

Hope for the children of 2020:

That all children have the opportunities and supports needed to succeed in life from wherever they start.

About the Author

Barbara Bowman, *Irving B. Harris Professor of Child Development, Erikson Institute*

bbowman@erikson.edu

Professional focus

Bowman is an advocate for improved and expanded training for educators, and educational equity for minority children.

Assessment for Teaching and Learning

Jacqueline Jones

As I reflect on the past 10 years in early childhood assessment,[122] the opening lines of Charles Dickens's *A Tale of Two Cities* come to mind:

> *"It was the best of times, it was the worst of times; it was the age of wisdom, it was the age of foolishness; it was the epoch of belief, it was the epoch of incredulity; it was the season of Light, it was the season of Darkness; it was the spring of hope, it was the winter of despair; we had everything before us, we had nothing before us."*[123]

From 2000 through 2009, the early childhood community witnessed a new focus on formative assessments; the development of new observational rating systems; a stunningly contentious battle over an attempt by the Administration for Children and Families of the U.S. Department of Health and Human Services to develop and implement a standardized test, the National Reporting System, for Head Start programs; a revised position statement on curriculum, assessment, and program evaluation from the National Association for the Education of Young Children (NAEYC) in 2004; a Pew Accountability Task Force report on early childhood program accountability (2007); and a National Research Council report on early childhood assessment.

Children's learning

Over the past 10 years, the work of Paul Black and Dylan Wiliam[124] supported a strong movement that embraced formative assessments across the preschool–12th grade continuum. Teachers learned how to engage in ongoing classroom-based assessment of children's learning. They were assessing what had actually been taught and, most importantly, were using the information to guide and modify their instruction. The everyday life of the classroom provided the context for this type of assessment, and transcripts of children's conversations, samples of their drawings and representations, teachers' anecdotal notes, as well as more traditional instruments became the assessment data. Although a good deal of teacher professional development was required, formative assessments helped teachers keep track of what children were learning and how they were learning.

Classroom environments

In addition, interesting new observational tools were developed over the last 10 years. The Early Language and Literacy Classroom Observation Tool (ELLCO) evaluated the degree to which the classroom environment was supporting young children's language and literacy development. The Classroom Assessment Scoring System (CLASS) moved beyond observation of the physical environment and focused attention on those teacher-child interactions that provide emotional support and promote cognitive development. The underlying research on CLASS warned that these interactions, or the lack thereof, can go unnoticed without intentional and systematic observation. These tools provide new ways of looking at the classroom environment and a window into teaching and learning.

Early childhood programs

As these new tools were being developed, the increasing financial investment in early childhood programs was leading to a call for greater accountability. Although administration of the National Reporting System to all 4-year-olds in Head Start programs was suspended, the wounds have not yet healed from the public battle. A significant sector of the early childhood community challenged and defeated the agency responsible for funding and monitoring the nation's federally funded preschool program, Head Start. Many in the field of early childhood education have been left with a deep distrust of assessment, particularly for accountability purposes, and a lingering suspicion that the sole purpose of evaluating program effectiveness is to close programs.

There are strong feelings regarding the role of child assessments when evaluating the effectiveness of early childhood programs, and methodological questions still remain. At what point in a program's implementation should child assessments be administered? What weights should be given to child assessments in the context of the overall program evaluation? Within the early childhood community, a lively debate continues around these issues. The challenge at hand is to move beyond the mistakes of the past into a proactive stance that defines appropriate assessment procedures.

Policy

In the midst of this debate, NAEYC revised its position statement on curriculum, assessment, and program evaluation. Acknowledging the absence of a coordinated system of early care and education from birth through age 8, the statement cautioned against a rush to accountability before adequate program supports were in place; called for technically sound instruments; and proposed the use of sampling procedures to lessen the testing burden.

In addition, the Pew National Early Childhood Accountability Task Force and the National Research Council's Committee on Developmental Outcomes and Assessments for Young Children took on the accountability issues with recommendations to the field. Rather than focusing on scores from a single test, the National Research Council suggested thinking in terms of assessment systems in which the intent is that:

- Assessments are seen as a part or subpart of a larger system of early childhood care and education that addresses the multiple aspects of child development and influence.

- Selection of assessments is intimately linked to goals defined by the larger system.

- Procedures for sharing information about and using information from assessments are considered as part of the process of selecting and administering assessments.

- Different parts of the assessment system itself (standards, constructs, measures, indicators) work together."[125]

In an extraordinary turn of political events, the 2008 presidential election campaign brought early childhood education into the national discourse. Throughout the campaign, candidate Barack Obama stressed the importance of early learning. President Obama has charged Kathleen Sebelius, secretary of health and human services, and Arne Duncan, secretary of education, with implementing the ambitious goals of raising the quality of existing early learning programs and increasing access to high-quality programs, especially for disadvantaged young children. With unprecedented federal funds being targeted to early learning programs in a time of economic downturn, calls for accountability will be inevitable. What new early learning programs will be implemented? What metrics will determine if the health, social, emotional, and cognitive outcomes for young children have increased as a result of these programs?

Significant challenges to strong assessment systems remain. Instrumentation to appropriately assess social/emotional development is still wanting, and a significant amount of work is needed to develop sound policies and practices to assess the progress of language development in children who are dual-language learners. Yet, the time has never been better to pursue the development of new instruments that can highlight the talents of all young children. The field of early childhood education is at an assessment crossroads. Can the community of early childhood professionals move beyond a reactionary stance based on the assessment-related mistakes of the past, or will it move forward into a proactive mode that tackles the big issues in the design and implementation of appropriate early childhood assessment systems?

Assessment approaches that benefit young children

The important role of teachers and administrators in collecting and interpreting assessment data cannot be underestimated. Rick Stiggins'[126] call for "assessment literacy" for teachers and administers has significance for early childhood professionals. A variety of assessment-related training materials became available as data-driven decision-making became more popular. While these materials provided new ways of thinking about assessment, the field still needs to view Stiggins's assessment literacy as a critical teacher/administrator competency — one that should be a part of every teacher-preparation program.

A state strategy

As the investment in state-funded preschool has increased, several state systems have been designed to support classroom instruction.

For example, New Jersey's Abbott preschool program was grounded in the notion of supporting teachers by using classroom quality measures and classroom-based assessments in order to target professional development and to measure program improvement. An ECERS-R was administered in each classroom by a master teacher, who served as a mentor/coach to the classroom teacher. The assessment results were used to customize a professional-development program that emphasized improving classroom quality.

In addition, state funds supported the training of teachers to implement formative assessment systems such as the Child Observation Record, the Creative Curriculum Continuum, and the Work Sampling System. These assessments allowed teachers to understand each child's progress across a broad range of domains. There was a clear understanding among state administrators that ongoing professional development was the key to getting accurate and reliable information from these instruments. Once teachers were engaged in this type of formative, curriculum-linked assessment and were using the assessment data to inform their instructional practice, the state could begin to select a sample of children to participate in longitudinal studies of cohorts of children going through the preschool system and beyond. Helping classroom teachers to enhance their skills in observation, documentation, and effective interactions with young children was crucial to achieving a high-quality program that produced strong outcomes for children. Assessment for accountability consisted of a variety of approaches: samples of ECERS-R scores from the districts; traditional norm-referenced standardized measures; use of regression discontinuity methodology to compare children who participated in preschool programs with age-similar children who did not; longitudinal tracking of the progress of cohorts of children through preschool and beyond.

While by no means perfect, the New Jersey preschool model emphasized the importance of a systems approach to assessment and the use of assessment results for ongoing program improvement.

Aspirations

Currently, there is no coordinated system of early care and education from birth through third grade. If will be very difficult to think in terms of assessment systems unless a coordinated service delivery system begins to emerge that includes developmentally appropriate early learning standards, assessments that reflect the content and developmental nature of those standards, and effective and well-trained teachers.

This is an extraordinary moment in which early childhood education has a place at the federal level and in which there is the possibility of making real progress in coordinating services, providing much-needed resources, and finally coming to grips with notions of assessment, accountability, and understanding children's learning. However, it is a moment that could be lost if the field does not rise to the occasion and do the hard work that real change requires. It is a time to think broadly, to let go of the fears, and put the interest of children and families in the forefront. The basic principles of sound assessment must hold true in early childhood, and the field must reach out to other disciplines such as educational research, psychometrics, and linguistics to address the complexities of understanding and nurturing young children's learning and monitoring the effectiveness of early learning programs. ▶

About the Author

Jacqueline Jones, PhD, *Former Assistant Commissioner, Division of Early Childhood Education, New Jersey State Department of Education, and former Senior Research Scientist, Educational Testing Service, Princeton, NJ*

Professional focus

Jones's focus is the role of assessment in program improvement and in the professional development of early childhood teachers and administrators

Hope for the children of 2020

An early learning experience in which early childhood professionals and families together work to ensure that young children have everything they need to be healthy, well-adjusted, curious, and filled with wonder and endless possibilities. An experience that, as Asa Hilliard challenged the field, would nurture the genius in every child and in every teacher.

Family Engagement

Bernice Weissbourd, Richard Weissbourd, and Kelley O'Carroll

Over the last 25 years, early childhood programs, preschools, and schools have dramatically changed their approach to parents. Thirty years ago it was the uncommon program or school that sought to ally with parents in children's education and development. Sometimes parents were, in fact, considered obstacles to children's education and were intentionally kept at arm's length.

Walk into almost any early childhood program or elementary school today, and one is likely to hear quite different rhetoric about parents. Parents are now commonly viewed as children's "first teachers" and as "partners." A far wider array of programs is dedicated solely to strengthening and enhancing parents' capacity to promote their children's cognitive, social, and emotional development. In the last 30 years, a new generation of programs has emerged: family-support programs, which are explicitly designed to strengthen parents of young children and to connect these parents to each other.

Yet important as this change in stance and rhetoric is, far too often the rhetoric does not match the reality. It remains the exceptional program or school that engages families in deep, sustained ways that actually affect important childhood outcomes. Few programs or schools partner with a diverse range of families effectively. And while many programs or schools are effective in engaging parents who are functioning well, programs and schools are far less effective in engaging parents who are stressed and struggling, even though it is often the children of these parents who are also struggling the most.

The challenge, then, is both to understand the ingredients of programs and schools that are effective in engaging families and to find ways to replicate these ingredients far more widely. What practices and conditions are most effective in creating strong, sustained relationships with parents? What kinds of partnerships with parents are likely to impact critical childhood outcomes? What kinds of conditions and practices work to engage a diverse range of families and those families who are struggling the most? How can these conditions and practices be brought to scale?

The answers to these questions are, of course, complex. But at the heart of the matter is making family engagement a primary criterion rather than an afterthought, for improving early childhood programs, child care, preschools, and elementary schools. Our task is to foster an environment in which families are part of the consciousness of those responsible for children's education, so that planning, programming, and governing issues—and accountability systems—consistently include the role of families.

What the research says

Decades of research suggest that parents have a powerful influence on young children's learning and development, and a variety of programs are successfully engaging families to promote positive outcomes for young children. Their results assure us that family involvement can be done well in a host of ways and provide us with examples of effective practice.

Early Head Start, the Strengthening Families Program, First 5 California and AVANCE — programs that differ widely in their goals and scale — have been shown to bolster the home environment and parenting behavior as well as key child cognitive, language, and social-emotional outcomes.[127] Home-visiting programs, inherently designed to engage families, have been associated with improved parenting and improved child-cognitive, social, and emotional outcomes.[128] Rigorous evaluation of the well-known Nurse-Family Partnerships has shown lasting positive impacts on parenting among teenage mothers.[129] The Parent Teacher Home Visit Project[130] focuses on creating purposeful partnerships between parents and teachers from kindergarten through secondary school. Its participants have demonstrated increased parental involvement, while students have shown improved academic and social success. Taken together, these studies powerfully underscore the importance of engaging parents as real partners in achieving educational goals, especially in the first decade of life.

These high-quality programs tend to share certain characteristics. They often go beyond the mere rhetoric that a parent is a child's first teacher and develop a cogent theory of change: a set of specific strategies and activities, based on careful thought and the best evidence, designed to change a key childhood outcome. Far too many programs believe that parent involvement per se affects childhood outcomes. But outcomes typically don't change unless programs are highly intentional and laserlike in their focus, closely linking strategies and activities to outcomes. Involving parents on governance committees or as class volunteers, for instance, can be an entry into more-focused engagement but in themselves do not lead to

> **To give children a healthy start, early childhood educators should consider themselves working for the healthy development of two generations, children and their parents or caregivers.**

greater reading proficiency. These programs also tend to "correctly estimate the dose": they accurately assess the depth, intensity, and duration of interventions necessary to engage parents and support their capacities, and to improve childhood outcomes. Programs for children commonly underestimate, sometimes wildly, what it actually takes to affect parents' behavior or capacity to support learning at home.

While keeping an eye on child outcomes, effective programs ground their activities in family and community context. They sometimes collaborate with community agencies in reaching and engaging families. Effective programs promote social connections within a family's community and affirm a family's cultural identity while enhancing its abilities to function in a multicultural society.

Trusting relationships among parents and staff members define strong programs. Effective programs recognize that meaningful relationships may not happen spontaneously or easily, and staff members take ownership for reaching out to parents. Rather than just unloading information on parents, staff find significant points of entry into parents' lives, they work to understand the stresses and challenges that parents struggle with, they connect with families around families' strengths, and they remain present with families through the critical period of parenting in early childhood.

Staff members have knowledge of cultural traditions that may inhibit a parent's involvement and realize that parents' negative past experiences with institutions leave some wary of becoming involved. Staff members are flexible, creative, and persistent in helping families overcome these and other barriers to their involvement.

Staff members are also self-reflective, acknowledge dearly held beliefs as well as biases, and examine their beliefs and biases in the context of the goal of partnering with parents. In the best programs, staff members have opportunities to reflect about their biases and challenges with each other. In doing so, they begin the process of acceptance and of change, both in themselves and in the parents with whom they are involved. They are thus more able to take parents' perspectives without judging them, to coordinate their own perspectives and those of parents, and to adopt a third-person perspective, taking a more objective, "helicopter view" when things get stuck or when problems arise.

Most importantly, effective programs and schools make family engagement a priority, not an add-on but an essential. These programs and schools do not, for example, just contact parents of children presenting problems but instead give attention to all parents on a regular basis and are aware of the state of the community in which families live. Efforts to engage families are as automatic as providing good curricula or adequate facilities.

Getting to scale

Making family engagement a priority for a far wider range of providers and teachers will require placing it at the center of teachers' and providers' consciousness. Program accountability, new forms of professional development, and support for teachers and providers are keys to this challenging task.

Perhaps most important, programs that are serious about engaging families will hold themselves accountable, and those in governance and supervisory positions — whether school superintendents, regional Head Start directors, or heads of early childhood agencies — will hold schools or programs accountable for meaningfully engaging a wide range of families in ways that promote learning. Currently, it's the rare school or program that makes itself accountable for real and serious family engagement, whether

the goal of family engagement is improved parent-teacher communication, increasing parents' advocacy skills, or improving home-literacy practices. Yet program directors, teachers, and child care providers are unlikely to consistently pursue these critical forms of family engagement unless it is part of their job description and unless they are held accountable.

That means, for one thing, that schools and other programs will have to find ways to measure whether they are meeting their family-engagement goals. While assessments and measurements are topics of huge controversy in education, there is no way to assure program quality and accountability without measurement. If we are serious about engaging families, then we need to make measuring family engagement as important as measuring children's achievement gains.

For example, the Three-to-Third initiative in Boston,[131] in collaboration with ReadBoston, supports several schools in a variety of family-engagement activities, including weekly reading logs that require families to read to their children four times a week, teacher home visits twice a year, and family-literacy events. Participation in these activities is regularly measured. Schools record how many families complete their weekly reading, receive home visits, and attend family-literacy events. School principals use this data to hold themselves and teachers accountable, and our hope is that district supervisors will use it to hold principals accountable. Further, this ongoing collection of data enables schools to track their challenges and progress, and to improve their efforts. This year, for example, teachers will make follow-up, supportive, problem-solving phone calls to parents who are having difficulty completing weekly reading.

Strengthening family engagement will not be easy for teachers and providers who are often already stretched thin. What's more, teachers and providers will need support and meaningful forms of professional development to do this work effectively. Strong evidence indicates

that many important practices cannot simply be transported from high-quality programs to lower-quality programs or taught through periodic workshops. The strength of programs is deeply rooted in the innate capacities of staff and in the willingness of staff to engage in deep, continuous, hands-on professional development. That means that programs need to move away from one-shot workshops and toward creating professional cultures that are ongoing learning environments for staff. Staff and providers need, for one, periodic opportunities to discuss barriers that arise in their work with parents — whether it's parents who don't return phone calls or parents who disrespect them — and to brainstorm with each other about overcoming these barriers.

In addition to in-service professional development, preservice early childhood education and elementary school training programs should give greater emphasis to families. Many practitioners express their discomfort in working with families, a feeling often based on lack of knowledge. The desire of staff to work with families must be buttressed with education on family systems and family development, on childrearing expectations in culturally diverse families, on ways to work with families that go beyond helping to empower. Preservice education for

early childhood programs should include not only classroom information but in-depth experience in working with families. To give children a healthy start, early childhood educators should consider themselves working for the healthy development of two generations, children and their parents or caregivers.

Finally, the fact that children who live in disadvantaged communities and are most at-risk for academic failure are not attending early childhood programs, even when they are free, alerts us to the urgent need for basic outreach to families to simply let them know about the availability of programs. Families under stress and living in poor conditions are unlikely — and should not be expected — to respond to flyers inviting them to a meeting, or to an announcement of a preschool registration date. A survey in Englewood, a distressed community in Chicago, revealed that parents thought their children were not ready for school and did not need early childhood education. Thirteen percent cited the cost of preschool, clearly unaware that there is no cost for the state preschool program.[132] Because lack of awareness of the value and availability of preschool education is a barrier to enrollment, the State of Illinois has promoted home-visiting programs starting at infancy.

These changes will not transpire quickly or easily, and some changes will clearly be expensive. Most obviously, a vital aspect of recruiting and retaining high-quality child care and preschool providers is taking on the huge challenge of greatly increasing compensation for providers. It's also critical that family-engagement efforts don't dilute the vital work of improving instruction and provider-child and teacher-child relationships in early childhood settings. We need to maintain a pointed focus on improvements in these crucial areas. Yet powerful instruction and powerful family engagement can be woven together.

Just as public will was created to support early childhood programs and legislation, so our task now is to promote public understanding that high-quality programs that take seriously the work of engaging families are far more likely to produce positive and lasting results for children, and such programs require funding for professional development, adequate compensation, and serious, carefully crafted accountability systems. The good news is that, unlike the rhetoric, these changes stand a real chance of strengthening families and improving the arc of young children's lives.[133] ▶

Hope for the children of 2020:

That we create the public will to fulfill a moral imperative to close the growing gap in opportunities between affluent and poor children, attacking the problem on multiple levels: economic, educational, social, and health. —B. Weissbourd

That we dramatically improve the prospects of children facing poverty and other disadvantages, and that we raise children who are capable, productive, humane, and energized to improve the world. —R. Weissbourd

That all children and their families have unqualified access to excellent education and that we guide children to become confident and engaged in their world. —O'Carroll

About the Authors

Bernice Weissbourd, *President, Family Focus*
Weiss2737@aol.com

Richard Weissbourd, *Lecturer in Education, Graduate School of Education, Kennedy School of Government, Harvard University*
Weissbri@gse.harvard.edu

Kelley O'Carroll, *Doctoral student, Harvard University Graduate School of Education*
Kelley_ocarroll@mail.harvard.edu

Professional focus

Bernice Weissbourd's focus is promoting public awareness and policies that assure family-support resources are as integral to every community as are libraries.

Richard Weissbourd's interests are risk and resilience in childhood, moral development, effective schools and preschools for children.

Kelley O'Carroll's interests are family-school relationships in early childhood and elementary school, family support, and immigration.

Technology

Douglas H. Clements and Julie Sarama

In the Reggio Emelia class, children were working together to represent the idea of "city." They arranged recycled and new materials on a scanner, covered the arrangement with a large piece of white paper, closed the lid, and scanned the image. They evaluated the image on the computer screen collaboratively, returned to the scanner to revise their construction, and rescanned and reevaluated until they were satisfied. Then they printed their representation.

Episodes such as this have convinced many teachers that technology can play a significant, positive role in the lives of young children. Others believe that technology has overwhelmed a more "natural" childhood. We begin this article by addressing three questions.[134]

- How important is technology to young children — and how important should it be?

- What are constructive uses of educational technology?

- What are promising professional-development initiatives?

We conclude this article with visions of the future.

Importance of technology to young children

Technology will become increasingly important to young children, but not in the way many people think. Some believe that young children must be trained on computers to get high-paying jobs of the future. This is not a good reason to use technology with young children. Technology will change considerably by 2020, and even more by the time today's youngest children join the workforce. More importantly, early education should not be limited to job training! Use of computers should focus on realizing their potential across the many critical areas of development, including the cognitive and social-emotional domains. When technology contributes to this development, it should be used. When it does not, it should not be used. The following sections discuss how to use technology to positively contribute to children's development.

Social-emotional development.

Used wisely, computer technology actually promotes positive social interaction. In one example, children at a computer spent nine times as much time talking to their friends while on the computer than while doing puzzles. Children display positive emotions when using computers and show more positive affect and interest when they use computers together. Further, working on computers can promote new instances and forms of collaborative work, such as helping or instructing, and discussing and building upon each other's ideas. With the right software, they play cooperatively at the computer as much as in the block center. Indeed, the computer play can spill over into new, friendly, sustained interaction in other classroom centers, especially between boys and between children with disabilities and their normally developing peers.

Of course, these benefits depend on high-quality technology environments. For example, open-ended educational programs and those designed for cooperative work or play are particularly useful in supporting collaboration. Unsurprisingly, violent video games can increase aggression and should be avoided.

Computers can also stimulate learning. Computers environments can, more so than other learning centers such as art or block centers, increase cognitive and social interactions, each to the benefit of the other. Using the right technology can increase creativity and learning in several content areas.

Creativity. Perhaps the most surprising positive effect of computers on young children is enhanced creativity. For example, using Logo to draw on the screen has been shown to increase children's creativity. Logo is a simple computer programming language in which children can command a pictured "turtle" to draw lines. In one study, preschoolers used simple key presses (pressing "f"' to make the turtle go "forward" and "r" to make it turn to the right) to make the turtle draw. These children learned to create more-elaborate pictures and later transferred these new ideas to artwork on paper. In a series of studies of our own, primary-grade children show increases on tests of creative thinking after working for a semester with Logo. We wondered, was it just that creating figures by directing the Logo turtle (forward 100, right 90, forward 50 right 90 . . .) enhanced the children's visual vocabulary? Further research of ours and that of others has shown that Logo experiences also *increase* verbal creativity. Originality has been consistently and positively affected in a string of Logo studies. Other studies have shown that using computers to read or write, or to acquire knowledge and insight into science, math, and other areas through design, can support the expression and development of creativity. High-quality computer experience enhances higher-order creative processes.

Language and literacy. Children use more language when social interaction increases due to using computers. Preschoolers' language activity is twice as high at the computer as at any of the other activities, including play dough, blocks, art, or games. Computers also help special populations.

Computer-assisted instruction drills and tutorials are not designed to increase creativity and conversations, but they help students develop prereading and reading skills. The computer's

visual displays, animated graphics, and speech, feedback, record-keeping, and individualization can make a unique contribution, from 4-year-olds through children in the primary grades. Computer-assisted instruction drills and tutorials can help children develop a wide variety of skills, including phonological awareness, letter and word recognition, listening, and abilities to predict, sequence, and make judgments.

Creativity and conversations in print can be facilitated with computers, especially using word processing or other applications to support "authentic" writing. For example, children plan, write, discuss, and revise. Even young children use more-descriptive phrases and create better plots with climaxes and character descriptions.

Math and reasoning. As with literacy skills, computer-assisted instruction drills and tutorials can help children practice math skills and foster deeper conceptual thinking. High-quality software can even promote valuable cognitive play. For example, children can break apart and put together shapes and sets in ways difficult or impossible to do with physical manipulatives. As another example, children doing Logo move their bodies and then command the Logo turtle to move in similar ways to create geometry paths, shapes, and complex, often surprising, designs. In this way, Logo encourages children to play and explore in a mathematical environment. It also develops children's explicit awareness of geometric motions, properties of shapes, and the meaning of measurements.

Conclusions

To the long lists of reported positive effects of computer use with children on literacy and math, one can add:

- Problem-solving skills.
- Decision-making ability.
- Understanding of cause and effect.
- Self-regulation and longer attention spans.
- For children with special needs,

gains in the areas of social-emotional development, sharing, taking turns, focusing, and self-help skills; fine-motor and gross-motor abilities; and communication and cognition.

Promising professional practices

Used well, technology can make substantial contributions to early childhood educational settings. Too often, however, technology is not used well. Several recent initiatives help teachers use effective strategies that make all the difference.

Most teachers underuse technology for vague "enrichment" or "rewards." It is often a free-choice learning center without much guidance, which can become dominated by a small number of children, often boys.

In contrast, successful teachers integrate technology in their existing programs. Conceptual learning tools and games, integrated into the curriculum and mediated by teachers aware of their goals, will show the largest performance and achievement results.

Successful teachers also influence families. Parents overestimate the extent to which their children use the Internet for educational purposes and underestimate the extent to which they use it for entertainment. Educators need to find new ways to work with parents to change this pattern.

Successful use takes time. Some researchers estimate that it takes teachers three to six years to fully integrate information technologies into their teaching activities. (Start now: by 2020, you'll be guiding others!)

What professional-development initiatives have been promising? Research indicates that:

- Teachers need regular access to computers and professional development over years to experience significant changes in their instruction. Sometimes they need to confront deeply held beliefs about learning and teaching — for example, finding that children can construct significant

- knowledge when guided to working in open-ended computer environments.

- Teachers need ongoing support regarding teaching and technology.

- Student teachers need supervising teachers who use technology well.

- Teachers of young children need concrete suggestions regarding how to put computers to work in classrooms and how to integrate them into other types of classroom activities.

- Professional-development staff should examine successful models for taking professional development and effective use of technology to large-scale use, such as the TICKIT, TRIAD, and ECCTS programs.

The future

Futurist and writer Arthur C. Clarke said, "Any sufficiently advanced technology is indistinguishable from magic."[135] We are certain to see amazing technology tools in the next 10 years. However, the future of high technology defies simple prognostication. These tools may include extensions of present-day software. In math and reading, for example, we will see better tools for understanding children's thinking and learning, and for using formative assessment in our teaching easily and effectively. Technological devices will become ever-more helpful teachers' assistants. Ever-more effective computer manipulatives and activities may invite children to explore these and other subjects, such as the scientific and social worlds. Electronic books will invite new ways of interacting that "grow" with children. The way children and adults interact with technology may be more natural and ubiquitous.

The futures of educational technology and of children can and should be designed and guided by those who care about children.

> " **Technological toys should invite, not suppress, creativity, exploration, and doing the work of good play.** "

What future might we strive to create?

Equity. The digital divide separating children from high- and lower-resource communities has been called mammoth. We need to work together to build a future that will provide all children fair access to all types of educational resources — especially community-based or school educational resources. Technology is a small but significant component of educational resources.

In another vein, technology offers critical benefits for children with certain disabilities. We expect the future to bring even greater benefits to children with a wider range of physical disabilities. Technology miracles are possible — if we demand them.

The positive path. Limit the total time children spend in front of screens. Commercial TV and inappropriate video games are the largest contributors to such time, with children ages 2 to 7 spending from two to three hours per day in front of a screen. We must work with families to decrease this time. Instead, positive uses such as those discussed and new ones to be created should be promoted. These, too, should be limited to no more than one to two hours a day, so children experience a wide range of learning situations. However, strict time limits in an early childhood classroom (for example, 5 or 10 minutes per child) are not wise. Such strict rules generate hostility and isolation instead of the usual positive effects of computers on social communication. The strict limits keep children from communicating and sharing. Child-centered control was again the more positive path.

The future will bring technological toys that will interact with children without screens, and these may be useful. But they should not replace play with basic toys, from clay to wood to interactions with the nature world. And technological toys should invite, not suppress, creativity, exploration, and doing the work of good play. In summary, promising practices include discouraging children's use of mind-numbing technologies, including junk TV, narcissistic ("Look at me") Web sites, technological toys that discourage creativity, and violent or non-educational video games. Also, promising practices encourage children to spend the time saved from not playing those noneducational games in building physical, mental, and social skills with and without electronic technology.

Invest wisely. When high-priority goals can be achieved well with specific computer applications, then detailed planning should precede any purchase. Determination of the type of technology-enhanced educational activity desired should precede any purchase of hardware. Further, extensive, high-quality professional development should be considered a necessary expense. Policymakers should realize that market forces alone will not provide high-quality content; funding for research and development is needed to fill noncommercial content and the needs of all members of our society.

Collaborate in conducting studies in teams of university-based researchers and teachers. We end with a prediction born in optimism: renewed emphasis on truly research-based education will help and encourage teachers to reject inappropriate and ineffective applications of technology and adopt, adapt, and help create those that benefit children. Some of these uses will support existing practices, but a small number for most teachers, and a large number for some teachers, will lead to innovative approaches not possible without the new technology. Children, teachers, and researchers all learn by designing educational strategies, computers programs, and other curricular tools. We need linked development and research to enable the vision, invention, and implementation of effective and appropriate educational technology.

To maximize the potential, and minimize misapplications, educators from the federal and state levels to the classroom level need to collaborate to use (and help produce) research guidelines as they design, test, and incorporate technology-enriched environments.

An observation attributed to many futurists is that people tend to overestimate the short-term effects of a new technology and underestimate its longer-term effects. Let's work together to create the best educational environments we can for young children, considering the profound transformations in technologies we shall see. ▶

Hope for the children of 2020

That the children of 2020 are provided the opportunities to engage with the natural world, as well as a range of technologies, to learn about their world, and to create new worlds for the future.

About the Authors

Douglas H. Clements, *SUNY Distinguished Professor, University at Buffalo, State University of New York*
clements@buffalo.edu

Julie Sarama, *Associate Professor, University at Buffalo, State University of New York*
Jsarama@buffalo.edu

Professional focus

Sarama and Clements conduct research in computer applications, the early development of mathematical ideas, and the effects of social interactions.

The Role of States

Harriet A. Egertson

The amount spent on state-supported early childhood programs has doubled every decade since 1990. Because of this, more than one million children (not including the nearly one million participating in federally funded Head Start) can participate in some form of early learning program in all but nine states. State funding of prekindergarten programs grew from under $1 billion in 1990, to nearly $2 billion in 2000, and to more than $4 billion in the first decade of the new century. The pace at which state investments in early childhood programs rose in the first decade of this century is a tribute to many years of hard work by state-based and national advocates of all kinds. Nonetheless, access to a high-quality early learning program continues to elude too many low- and lower-middle-income families with prekindergarten-age children.

However, as the first decade of the 21st century comes to an end, the nation is just waking up from a deep and lengthy recession that will continue to have particularly serious consequences for state government budgets well into the next decade. Legislatures in several states with large early childhood initiatives have yet to enact a budget for the coming year, and other states have either kept funding flat or already enacted cuts to early childhood programs of all kinds. The glass that is only half full to begin with is already threatened with becoming emptier in a growing number of states previously known for expanding early childhood programming. The most optimistic view in 2010 is that the present will represent the low point, and by 2020 the concerns expressed here will appear quaint.

The nature of the early learning opportunities developing in the states is diverse, complex, and still evolving. The most common form of state-supported programming is an early learning program for 4-year-olds just prior to kindergarten entrance. This is what is typically understood as state preK. In a few states, the programs extend to six hours or more, but most are much shorter. The majority of state preK programs are operated through public schools, but most states encourage locating programs in existing community-based programs, including Head Start. In those cases there is a far greater likelihood that children can stay in one setting for their parents' full working day. A few states supplement Head Start directly with state dollars. A growing number permit serving both 3- and 4-year–olds, and a very few states are notable for their commitment to serve all 3- and 4-year-olds. Rarely are state preK funds used for programming for infants and toddlers. These estimates do not include the programming that all states provide for young children with disabilities, since most of those services are supported with federal funds, but increasingly, children with disabilities are served in inclusive settings.

The number of states combining an early learning initiative for 4-year-olds with a broader distribution of funds through counties or multi-county regions (similar to the North Carolina Smart Start model) is increasing. In these instances, states allow funds to support an array of services, including child care quality support activities, local early literacy programs in libraries and other community agencies, preventive health services, and professional development for early care and education staff. These initiatives are primarily designed to improve the quality of child care programs and working conditions for caregivers/teachers. Such efforts are critical because upwards of 75% of American children younger than school age are in some form of out-of-home program that enables their families to participate in schooling or work. Overall, U.S. child care has been demonstrated to be of such low quality and so woefully underresourced that three-quarters of children who participate are unlikely to be enrolled in a program that benefits them. The wages of many early childhood staff who work in private sector child care meet poverty guidelines.

Some states are building an early learning system intended to serve all of the state's 4-year-olds regardless of family income or other risk factors, but the majority of states target their early learning programs to children whose life circumstances put their school success at the greatest risk. How states define this risk varies widely, but family income typically plays some role. These examples of the nature of state prekindergarten early learning efforts further illustrate their diversity and the gaps in their reach. Differing perspectives on which populations should be served are also reflected across the advocacy community. The early childhood field has a long history of dichotomous perspectives (for example, child care or preschool; part-day or full-day kindergarten; bachelor degrees, associate degrees, or Child Development Associate credentials; public or private sponsorship), and the tension between those advocating for universal preschool versus programs targeted toward vulnerable children risks further fragmenting the historically fragmented advocacy community.

The National Institute for Early Education Research[136] annually surveyed the states during much of the last decade to document the growth of state preK activity. It frames state preK programs as those "funded and administered by the state with a primary goal of educating 4-year-olds who are typically developing and who are in classrooms at least 2 days per week," and has identified 10 indicators it believes are characteristic of programs equipped to offer children a quality early learning experience. The results of the annual surveys document wide variance across the 10 indicators across state initiatives. The variance is so marked as to defy brief description. That state efforts vary widely is not by itself a problem except as it makes it difficult for policymakers to agree on what program-quality characteristics should be supported with public resources. The situation is a gift for researchers; there is no shortage of questions to be answered. The positive news is that the number of quality indicators being met by the states is rising.

The amount of money available to support the participation of children in early learning programs also varies widely across the states, ranging from nearly $11,000 per child to less than $2,000 per child in 2008. The optimum amount needed to assure an effective program is open to debate, but most of the states spend on average far less per child on early learning programs than the federal government spends for Head Start or states spend for K–12. Of particular concern is the persistent disparity in salaries for teachers in state preK programs. Often such teachers earn considerably less than their similarly educated and credentialed colleagues in a district's elementary and secondary classrooms, and they may not have access to full benefit packages.

Longstanding parsimony with public resources contributes to continuous tension about the best ways to increase and improve early care and learning opportunities for young children. In their interaction with policymakers, advocates find themselves continuously dancing between working to increase participation and/or ensuring effectiveness. Policymakers want both, but often fund neither. Over the most recent

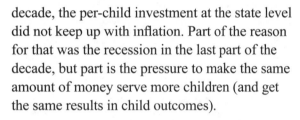

decade, the per-child investment at the state level did not keep up with inflation. Part of the reason for that was the recession in the last part of the decade, but part is the pressure to make the same amount of money serve more children (and get the same results in child outcomes).

How state early childhood funding is distributed and combined with other funding streams is another example of variability that at once enriches and plagues the field. The growth of state preK enables schools to place children with disabilities in more inclusive settings. When Head Start programs are augmented with state funds, the comprehensive services of Head Start can be extended to a greater number of low-income children. Some states make it possible for child care funds to be incorporated into local preK budgets so the day can be extended to help families with child care needs. Combined funding is both a boon and a bane for program administrators at the state and local levels. The multiple funding streams combine the funds and the administrative requirements of each of the sources, creating significant challenges for local administrators, often a sort of regulatory fatigue.

Promising approaches and practices

This brief description of current state early childhood efforts obscures their richness but highlights the constant in describing their nature: they are so diverse that making generalized statements about the nature of state efforts

is difficult and probably risks misrepresentation. Noting this diversity is not a suggestion that greater uniformity would be desirable. In fact, the varying ways states have chosen to solve problems related to disparate funding, sponsorship, and administration creates a vibrant laboratory for learning among them. Unfortunately, some of the most promising practices arise from one or another of the field's bifurcated perspectives. Unless the next decade leads to genuine merging of these perspectives, progress could be largely cosmetic. The decade between now and the year 2020 will see further development of more systematic approaches to state administration and program oversight, program and child assessment, more inclusive professional development, and data systems aligned and coordinated with K–12 systems.

The emergence of new forms of governance. The growth in publicly funded early learning programs has taken place in the context of an existing nonsystem of profit and nonprofit home- and center-based child care, private and public part-day preschools, federally administered Head Start, and both inclusive and segregated programs for children with disabilities. Reflecting a wide variety of sponsorship, funding, and quality, programs are located in freestanding centers, storefronts, homes, public and private schools, and faith-based facilities. The interactions among program leaders can often most charitably be described as reflecting parallel play, and the growth of state-funded preK has served to highlight the dichotomies and the inequities as public schools have assumed a greater role. In the past decade, several states have created new administrative configurations to address challenges in forming a cohesive early childhood system that, according to the National Early Childhood Accountability Task Force, should incorporate early learning program quality standards, a program-improvement system, professional development, and data management and reporting. Ironically, the nature of these new agencies or coordinating structures is as varied as the program components themselves and are so young that predicting how successful they will be in creating more effective administrative structures awaits a next decade.

Although many states had already begun their own work to bring about greater coordination with various forms of coordinating bodies, in 2008, Congress enacted legislation that calls for the formation of state early learning councils with defined responsibilities and participation across agencies. The next decade will witness the extent to which these councils will contribute to bringing diverse perspectives and purposes into more cohesive working relationships.

The widening state role in early learning efforts, the creation of new governance structures, and the prospect that universality will become even more common raises new questions about whether maintaining the federal administration of Head Start contributes to the creation of equitable, cohesive, and efficient state systems. As Head Start reaches a half century of service to low-income children and families, it is time to initiate new conversations about how the iconic program can be restructured to contribute more fully to widening opportunities for the most vulnerable children and families. Bold ideas have already emerged, such as enlarging the Early Head Start program and envisioning Head Start for 3- and 4-year-olds as wraparound health and social services, with the early learning responsibility devolving to state preK programs.

 Assuring the best opportunities for children to grow and learn requires the infrastructure to make it all work. "

More systemic professional-development efforts. The trend is for qualifications for early childhood staff to increase across the decade, influenced by higher qualifications for teachers in state preK programs and Head Start, and the effect of T.E.A.C.H.® While salaries for teachers in state preK do not always reflect parity with K–12 teachers, they are significantly better than in child care or Head Start.

Efforts are under way to help states develop more systematic approaches to preservice and in-service education of early childhood staff. NAEYC defines an integrated early childhood professional-development system as a comprehensive system of preparation and ongoing development and support for all early childhood education professionals working with and on behalf of young children. These efforts, focused primarily on those working in birth-through-5 settings, are closely tied to similar efforts to support states in the development of Quality Rating Improvement Systems. The Early Childhood Inclusion Project at the Frank Porter Graham Institute has been an important collaborator, signaling an intense effort to ensure that knowledge about how to work effectively with children with disabilities is a major emphasis of the states' professional-development systems. The effort could be strengthened by more effort to involve the states' professional-development initiatives for public school teachers, both in preK and K–3.

The growth of Quality Rating Improvement Systems (QRIS).

The field of early childhood uses the term "quality" as shorthand for program characteristics that must be represented to make sure children will benefit from participation. The past decade has seen rapid growth (now 22 states) of Quality Rating Improvement Systems intended to improve quality and compensation, and to communicate to parents and the public about the need for and nature of effective programs. Thus far the QRISs have been thought of primarily as mechanisms to improve the child care system, but they rarely incorporate state preK initiatives or a state's Head Start programs. Requiring all programs to participate would require a reconfiguration of the levels and would help promote a more cohesive early childhood care and learning system. Well-designed and implemented QRISs hold the potential to improve the effectiveness of programs, the status and remuneration of early childhood staff, the coherence of mechanisms for monitoring and the establishment of definitions of program quality that could help erase the real and perceived differences between child care and education programs.

Measured approaches to measurement.

Other chapters in this book discuss assessment in some depth. For this chapter, it is important to note that both program and child assessment have received significant attention in the states in the past decade. All of the states that offer preK programs evaluate them in some way through regular monitoring, the use of program assessment tools, and child assessment. Increasingly, policymakers are requiring child assessment to demonstrate that the public investment in state preK is effective. New federal early childhood initiatives will also play a role, with the potential for significant funds for the development of new tools. The next decade will see important work among the states to create new tools and processes to measure program effectiveness and children's status at the time of school entrance. Since significant challenges remain in the use of direct assessments of children, the challenge will be to help policymakers understand what can and cannot be learned from testing children.

Greater attention to data systems.

At this juncture, state-level data systems in early childhood education are in their infancy. That picture will change significantly in the next decade. There is already wide recognition in the K–12 community that understanding how to carry out reform at both the school and system level cannot take place in the absence of systems to collect data. That understanding is now moving toward early childhood. Data-systems designers need to come to understand both that the data needs in programs and services for young children are very different than those in the K–12 system, and that there are complexities involved in connecting them. The initial revelation will be how much more complicated the early childhood system is than K–12. The challenge will be to temper the zeal to use data to connect and align standards and assessments in ways that benefit children and their teachers.

These brief descriptions of some of the challenges and opportunities in states are intended to show that these topics are all connected: systems growth, QRIS, professional development, assessment, and data systems. All are key to seeing improvements in what children experience every day in early childhood settings of all kinds. The greatest error would be to fail to make optimum investments in the development of these systems along with making greater funding available for additional children to participate. Assuring the best opportunities for children to grow and learn requires the infrastructure to make it all work. What will early childhood education look like in another decade? Will the availability and quality of early learning programs in the states still be characterized by the phrase "vary widely"? Will families looking for early learning and care continue to see the same virtually unmanageable mélange of programs and services — whether they are blended, braided, or whatever the process — whereby too much of the energy of staff goes toward satisfying the administrative requirements and standards and assessments of multiple funding sources? Until the recession at the end of the decade of 2010, state efforts were trending toward solving some of these problems. We enter the next decade with hope buoyed by real progress in the last one.   ▶

Hope for the children of 2020

That grownups come to understand that we owe the best to all our children because they are our children, not because they are instruments for the betterment of the future economy.

About the Author

Harriet A. Egertson, PhD, *Retired State Early Childhood Specialist*
haegertson@gmail.com

Professional focus

Egertson's focus is on contributing to making the most beneficial development and learning opportunities available to the nation's children.

Linking Economic Research to Public Investment

W. Steven Barnett

The wealth of a nation is determined more by the capabilities of its people than by its financial capital and natural resources. Inadequate investments in human development are a principle cause of lost human potential and national wealth. No one has calculated a comprehensive estimate of the national cost of inadequate investments, but it is well above $100 billion, perhaps even $1 trillion, for each birth cohort in the United States. A substantial body of research now documents the damage done, the potential for public programs to produce better results, and the economic returns on these public investments. If the public is made aware of this evidence and acts upon it, the children of 2020 are much more likely to be healthy, wealthy, and wise, to use Ben Franklin's words.

The immediate consequences of inadequate investments in young children and their families are well known: high rates of infant mortality and morbidity, and developmental lags that leave far too many children already behind when they enter kindergarten. The longer-term consequences are also well known: wide gaps in school achievement between those who are best and worst prepared, and an overall performance that is mediocre by international standards; high rates of school failure, special education, and high school dropout; far too many Americans with poor physical and mental health; lagging economic productivity; and high levels of delinquency and crime.[137]

All of these human consequences of underinvestment in young children have economic dimensions. The United States spends a great deal of money on health care, from neonates to the elderly, for problems that are largely preventable by improvements in health behavior. The costs of education are driven up by remediation, grade repetition, and special education, as well as by the need to pay more to attract and retain teachers for children who are poorly prepared for school. The costs of failure continue after school; by one calculation, each high school dropout costs the nation more than $200,000.[138] According to official reports, the United States has the highest rate of incarceration in the world, and the costs of corrections are small compared to the costs of crime to victims.[139]

Economist Alfred Marshall articulated the rationale for public investment in education over a century ago in terms today's early childhood educators would appreciate:

> *"The schoolmaster must learn that his main duty is not to impart knowledge, for a few shillings will buy more printed knowledge than a man's brain can hold. It is to educate character, faculties, and activities; so that the children of even those parents who are not thoughtful themselves may have a better chance of being trained up to become thoughtful parents of the next generation. To this end public money must follow freely. And it must flow freely to provide fresh air and space for wholesome play for the children in all working class quarters."[140]*

Since Marshall wrote those words, we have accumulated a considerable body of evidence that fills in the details with estimates of the economic returns to early investments in the kind of public education that Marshall advocated.

Rather than viewing early care and education expenditures solely as a cost, economists see them as investments. Viewed in this light, public investments in preschool programs are investment opportunities with potentially large returns. The challenge is to convey this to the public and policymakers so that policies will be formulated that realize the return on investment from the near-term and long-term gains produced by high-quality early care and education programs. One of the challenges in developing such policies is that benefits may take many years to be realized, while costs are incurred immediately. The temptation then is for elected officials and other policymakers to cut costs at the expense of program quality and coverage while continuing to promise benefits that will never materialize.

The relevant economic research falls into four general categories:

- Benefit-cost analyses based on longitudinal studies of early care and education.

- Extrapolations and extensions of benefit-cost results to state and national policy.

- Benefits of child care for parents, communities, and the labor force.

- Positive macroeconomic impacts of investments in early care and education with implications for long-term economic growth.

Three major benefit-cost analyses

Rigorous cost-benefit analyses have been conducted based on three longitudinal studies of the effects of early education through adulthood. These studies are the most-often-cited research on the value of educational investments in young children. Together they constitute a kind of Rosetta stone for translating into economic terms the broader evidence from hundreds of studies of the effects of early care and education. Therefore, it is important to understand these studies. Their findings are summarized in Table 2, and they are briefly described below. All three studies were conducted in the United States to assess the effects of classroom-based education before age 5 on children from low-income families. Although each of these cost-benefit analyses is important, they are even more useful when considered together in the context of the larger research literature. Findings from these studies regarding effects on children's learning and development, school success, and later adult social and economic success have been replicated in other studies. These three studies pull all of the strings together and provide overall estimates of economic returns.

All three studies used rigorous methods to estimate the effects of high-quality programs. The High/Scope Perry Preschool program, in Ypsilanti, Michigan, was a two-and-a-half-hour-per-day education program offered to small numbers of children in the public schools during the school year for one or two years. Effects were estimated with a true randomized trial. The Abecedarian program, in Chapel Hill, North Carolina, delivered education in classrooms for up to 10 hours per day over 50 weeks and served children from younger than age 1 to age 5. With this schedule and age range, it was the only one of the three programs that met the child care needs of parents working full-time, or even long part-time hours. Again, effects were estimated using a true experimental design. The Chicago Child-Parent Centers study compared children in matched neighborhoods to estimate the effects of a part-day, public school preschool program. This study provides a "real life" test of early education on a large scale in the Chicago Public Schools, with teacher-child ratios and costs achievable by public preschool programs across the nation.

In all three studies, preschool education was found to produce gains in long-term academic achievement and educational attainment (for example, completing secondary school). And there were other indications of positive effects on school progress: all three decreased the need for special education, and two decreased grade repetition (when children fail and must repeat a grade). Only the Abecedarian program was shown to produce permanent gains in IQ, but all three interventions produced permanent increases in achievement test scores. This finding may say more about the limitations of IQ tests as measures of cognitive abilities than about the capacity of early education to produce long-term gains in children's abilities in the areas of language, literacy, math, and science. These results have been replicated by many other studies. Program effects are not always as large in other studies, but the programs studied often have been weaker and more poorly funded.

All three studies investigated effects on crime, but only two found such effects. Both half-day programs found decreases in arrests. The full-day program did not. There are at least two plausible explanations for this result. One is that some curricula have stronger effects on social and emotional development and behavior than do others. Several randomized trials have found that curricula can vary greatly in their influence on executive function, self-regulation, and social skills and behavior even if they have similar effects on achievement. The other explanation concerns differences in context. The Abecedarian study took place in a community with a much lower rate of crime than the others. In general, if there is a low rate of a problem to begin with, programs will have little impact on the problem. Remarkably, a randomized trial of enriched half-day preschool education in Mauritius replicated this finding of crime reduction in young adults.

The economic analyses in these three studies meet accepted standards for benefit-cost analysis. To make all costs and benefits comparable, adjustments are made for inflation and timing (a benefit next year is worth more than the same benefit 20 years later). Thus, the costs and benefits in Table 2 are the discounted present value of the estimated streams of costs and benefits over time (calculated using a real discount rate of 3 percent). The calculation of discounted present

value essentially takes into account that public funds could have been invested in other ways, and an annual return of 3% above inflation is factored out. All three studies found that the discounted value of benefits greatly exceeded costs. In fact, the results are robust to the use of even higher discount rates, particularly for the part-day programs. There are other ways to portray the findings, for example, in terms of an estimated annual rate of return. Double-digit rates of return have been estimated for the part-day preschool programs, which far exceed the historical averages from private-sector investments.

Although the Abecedarian program may not appear to have as strong an economic return as the two part-day programs, this interpretation should be approached with caution. On the benefit side, differences in the estimated benefits can reflect differences in local circumstances and children served rather than in the size of program impacts. However, one key difference is that the Abecedarian program is the only one of the three to provide child care that facilitated parental employment. The Abecedarian study indicates that the long-term impacts on maternal earnings can be substantial. Even though full-day, year-round programs are more expensive, they generate additional economic benefits through their effects on employment and long-term productivity. Parents who take less time out of the labor force are more productive.

These benefit-cost studies go beyond simply indicating that there is a high rate of return to investments in high-quality early care and education programs. These studies reveal that there is a need for public investments in preschool education. Why? Many of the economic benefits are what are called spillovers, benefits to others in society outside the families of the children who attend good preschool programs. These are school-cost savings, reductions in crime, and costs of the criminal-justice and welfare systems. There is no reason for parents to take such spillover benefits into account when deciding how much to spend on early care and education. It follows that parents will spend too little on high-quality preschool education even if they

Table 2. Three Benefit-Cost Analyses

	Carolina Abecedarian	*Chicago Child-Parent Centers*	*High/Scope Perry Preschool*
Year began	1972	1983	1962
Location	Chapel Hill, NC	Chicago, IL	Ypsilanti, MI
Sample size	111	1,539	123
Research design	Random assignment	Matched neighborhood	Random assignment
Ages	6 weeks to age 5	Ages 3-4	Ages 3–4
Program schedule	Full-day, year-round	Half-day, school year	Half-day, school year
FINDINGS *(% Experimental Group vs. % Control Group)*			
Increased IQ short-term	Yes	Not collected	Yes
Increased IQ long-term	Yes	Not collected	No
Increased achievement long-term	Yes	Yes	Yes
Special education	25% v. 48%	14% v. 25%	37% v. 50%
Retained in grade	31% v. 55%	23% v. 38%	35% v. 40%
High school graduation	67% v. 51%	62% v. 51%	65% v. 45%
Ever arrested as juvenile	45% v. 41%	17% v. 25%	16% v. 25%
Mean number of adult arrests	1.7 v. 1.5 (age 21)	Not yet available	2.3 v. 4.6 (age 27)
Adult smoker	39% v. 55% (age 21)	Not yet available	42% v. 55% (age 40)
COST-BENEFIT RESULTS *(2002 dollars, discounted at 3%)*			
Cost	$63,476	$7,417	$15,386
Child care	27,621	1,829	919
Maternal earnings	68,728	0	0
K–12 cost savings	8,836	5,377	8,556
Post-secondary ed. cost	- 8,128	- 615	- 1,309
Abuse and neglect cost savings	Not estimated	329	Not estimated
Crime cost savings	0	36,902	173,959
Welfare cost savings	196	Not estimated	774
Health cost savings	17,781	Not estimated	Not estimated
Earnings	37,531	30,638	65,455
Second generation earnings	5,722	Not estimated	Not estimated
Total benefits	$158,278	$74,981	$248,354
B-C ratio	2.5	10.1	16.1

can afford such programs, though those who are least able to afford expensive programs have children who would benefit most. If the government does not intervene, too few children will attend high-quality programs, and the taxpayer will lose out.

The spillover problem is not the only reason that government should become involved in funding early care and education. Even relatively high-income families face a daunting problem in identifying programs of sufficiently high quality. The nature of the service is that it is provided in the parent's absence, and young children cannot adequately report on the quality. Surveys of parents find that parental report on program quality does not correspond well with expert measurements of program quality. Studies of program quality also reveal that very few private programs are good enough to produce the kinds of effects found in these three long-term studies. Even if parents had the means and inclination to purchase intensive high-quality early care and education, they are unlikely to be able to do so on their own. Thus, there is a strong economic case that government should fund preschool education and ensure that programs are of the quality needed to produce the desired benefits.

Beyond the "big three"

In recent years, a growing number of studies have filled in more of the details of the economics of early care and education. These include studies that both elaborate on theory and the connections linking short-term and long-term outcomes. Prominent among these are publications by James Heckman, a University of Chicago Nobel laureate in economics. Other economists have estimated additional cost savings to taxpayers and other benefits from early care and education that were not included in the three benefit-cost analyses studies discussed above. Clive Belfield at Columbia University estimated a number of significant cost savings in education not previously taken into consideration. Mildred Warner at Cornell University and others have examined in much more detail

the economic impacts of child care per se on families and communities, and this work makes it clear that it is important for public-policy planning and development to consider child care and child development needs together.

Another set of publications, a number of them quite recent, build upon the three benefit-cost analyses discussed above by examining the consequences of national policies that would provide high-quality preschool programs on a large scale. These necessarily extrapolate from the results of these studies to much larger populations of children and programs. Robert Lynch at Washington College provides estimates of the costs and benefits of investing in quality preschool education for the nation as a whole and for each individual state with calculations of the numbers of years that must pass before the annual benefits exceed the annual costs. Separate calculations are provided for total benefits and for government cost-savings alone, for both targeted and universal programs. The estimates are based on the results of the Chicago Parent-Child Center program, with benefit estimates lowered for children who are not from low-income families and would already have had access to a preschool program. For the nation as a whole, annual benefits are estimated to exceed annual costs within six years for a program targeted to disadvantaged children only, and nine years for a universal program.

The notion that public funding for early care and education should be viewed as an investment in economic development has been further advanced by a number of other economists. Art Rolnick and Rob Gunewald at the Minneapolis Federal Reserve Bank emphasize that the rate of return to the Perry Preschool program is about 16% annually, while the rate of return to many public investments made to spur economic development is quite low. Tax breaks for businesses to relocate, or public subsidies to build sports stadiums, may have return rates that are close to zero. By moving these resources to investments in early care and education, the public earns a much higher rate of return. Other economists (for example, Belfield and William Dickens, Brookings Institution) have estimated the effects of investments in high-quality preschool programs on economic growth. This is useful because tax increases generally have negative effects on economic growth, and these studies point out that public funds spent on quality preschool education and parenting programs are likely to increase economic growth, resulting in higher gross domestic product in the future even if taxes must be raised to finance them.

When developing public policies for early care and education, a key question is whether the program should be available only to children in poverty (or near-poverty) or to all children. Although it is clear that the public benefits from quality preschool programs are likely to be higher for children from low-income families than for their more-advantaged peers, this doesn't mean that there is not still a good return to be earned from investing in quality programs for other children as well. This issue is addressed by Lynn Karoly and James Bigelow in a Rand Corporation report on the costs and benefits of universal preK in California, and a comparison of the returns to targeted and universal programs by Barnett. Underlying these studies is evidence that there is no clear dividing line between low and high income at which the problems addressed (for example, school failure or crime) or the gains produced (for example, improved cognitive abilities and character) disappear. Instead, there is a gradual decline as income rises. Longitudinal studies of universal preschool programs in Oklahoma and outside the United States have contributed to this understanding.

Much remains to be done to bring federal, state, and local policies for early care and education into sync with the economic evidence. Too few public programs deliver the quality and intensity of services demonstrated to produce substantial long-term impacts on child development. Public programs fail to cover many of the children already eligible for such programs. Policy and programs are still developed separately for child care and early education. There is little doubt that by bringing better information from economic studies and analysis into the policymaking process, we can develop policies that will better meet the needs of children, families, and taxpayers. Key resources to help with this are available on the Web and in print, and are listed in the endnotes to this article.[141]   ▶

Hope for the children of 2020

That the young children of 2020 have high-quality education and health care, and strong families and communities to help them grow up healthy, wealthy, and wise.

About the Author

W. Steven Barnett, *Board of Governors Professor of Education and Co-Director, National Institute for Early Education Research, Rutgers University* sbarnett@nieer.org

Professional focus

Barnett's research focuses on the economics of investments in early learning and development.

The Learning Communities of 2020

Pascal Kaplan

"The future is already here. It's just not very evenly distributed."

—William Gibson

The year 2020 is an eye blink away. Not even an eye blink: it is here today, unfolding itself minute by minute, day by day, through pockets of people who already live the reality that, spreading out slowly over time and space, will become the widely shared present of 2020. These are the natural leaders whose thoughts, actions, relationships, and consciousness breathe the fresh breezes of tomorrow. If we attune ourselves to these same currents, we can envision today how those called to serve young children a decade from now will engage professionally and personally in rich lives of service.

"Learning organizations," "communities of practice," "professional learning communities," and "appreciative organizations" are terms coined in the 1990s for a set of transformative processes that seek to engage people in continuous learning, professional improvement, innovation, and organizational change.[142] The appeal of each of these approaches is at heart a call for personal transformation, new ways of seeing, of joining with others collaboratively, setting aside older competitive, controlling, and self-centered ways of interaction for the sake of shared understanding and common action for a higher good.

With the advent of interactive Web communities, the support and engagement offered by professional learning communities has begun expanding well beyond small groups of people who work in the same physical location. The barriers to expanded communication posed by physical space and time are dissolving in virtual space. Between now and 2020, as this trend accelerates, the distinction between in-person and online professional learning communities will also dissolve, because of at least three convergent forces:

- Positive personal experiences in both localized and online learning communities will confirm the value of actively engaging in shared learning with others whose professional experiences and cultural backgrounds are different from and complementary to our own.

- The exponential rate of innovation related to how we communicate with others at a distance will make it possible to develop meaningful relationships and have increasingly rich interpersonal experiences with people we have never met physically. Being with someone "in-person" or "face-to-face" will not always mean that we are with them in the same physical space.

- The globalization of professional networks will make it increasingly impractical to depend on traditional conference settings and meetings to share insights, participate in formal and informal learning sessions, and interact socially with colleagues. Physical convention halls are too small, and the cost, time, and inconvenience associated with travel to a central location are so great that traditional conferences will increasingly be thought of as parochial gatherings. The historical role that conventions and conferences have played in introducing early childhood education and care professionals to new ideas and to new colleagues will shift to online and blended venues that will serve the same purposes, but at less cost, at greater convenience, and with more expansive opportunities for learning and networking.

Characteristics of the 2020 learning community

Ask an early childhood education and care professional in 2020 to describe his or her learning community, and you will likely hear:

It's globally accessible. Low-cost wireless Internet access is now available in most countries. Language differences are no longer a hindrance to communication, thanks to an array of instant translation technologies. This means that preschool staff and early care providers in different parts of the world can communicate with one another freely. Moreover, parents and grandparents who are non-English speakers can participate fully in classroom activities, as well as in the global learning community.

The so-called digital divides that separated the more impoverished members of society and members of the older generation from the riches of the Internet no longer exist. Digital literacy is now as pervasive as the use of the telephone was in the latter part of the 20th century.

It's nonhierarchical. The learning community has no central, controlling authority. The millions of teachers, aides, administrators, parents, grandparents, policymakers, child advocates, community leaders, and others committed to the welfare of young children who meet together online provide its life, structure, and organization. Originally launched by an alliance of forward-looking organizations and individuals, it quickly broadened into its current egalitarian form thanks to skilled facilitation and a creative and flexible design.

Leadership roles are no longer necessarily intertwined with organizations or hierarchies within organizations; instead, the learning community's leaders emerge naturally from among those who evince certain personal characteristics through their ongoing participation in the learning community:

- A gift for collaborating with others by creating safe, accepting environments where people can express their views and engage in keen discussion without personalizing outcomes or becoming defensive and ego-invested in their points of view.

- A sincere conviction that the input of every individual has value regardless of myriad differentiators—such as position, education, social or economic status, gender, and cultural heritage — that formerly disenfranchised many.

- A natural recognition that the purpose of collaboration is to develop a broad, shared understanding of core issues in a spirit of respect for divergent viewpoints.

- An abiding concern to represent and honor the interests of all stakeholders, even when they are not present "in the room."

- A wish to deepen the wisdom of the group for the sake of productive, localized action.

The learning network itself is regarded as the source of expertise and knowledge-creation in the field of early childhood education and care. Those who have mastered the field's formalized informational content continue to be respected, as do those who have demonstrated mastery of the early childhood education and care practitioner's craft. But there is universal recognition that expertise is not the sole province of these specialists, that knowledge emerges through collaborative approaches that welcome diverse stakeholders to contribute large numbers of ideas, extract meaning from those ideas, and present them as actionable insights and strategies.

It's multidimensional. The early childhood education and care learning community of 2020 is richly textured in layers of interaction, dialogue, discussion, and relationship. Colleagues connect together in their local workplaces and connect to the family members of students (whether they live nearby or at a distance), and to anyone from early childhood education and care settings or specialties anywhere in the nation and the world. Relationships developed online strengthen and enhance workplace learning communities by expanding the perspectives of colleagues with whom one works on a daily basis. Members engage in the online learning community at different levels and for various purposes:

- To obtain immediate assistance answering a factual question, identifying a learning resource, or otherwise addressing a pressing issue.
- To maintain ongoing relationships, for example with a mentor.
- To discuss a current hot topic or child-development or staffing issue.
- To attend an online course or a virtual conference.
- To work on a project geared to taking action for positive change in the profession.

Dimensions of the 2020 learning community

Our early childhood education and care practitioner of the future might report that he or she participates in an online learning community through the following range of engagement opportunities:

Clarify-All (the transactional dimension). Clarify-All is an information request-and-receive system that allows quick callouts for a specific piece of information and quick replies from others in the community. Clarify-All is transactional in the sense that this level of communication is primarily about information rather than relationship — a helpful response to a specific request. As early as the 1990s, listservs often provided this function, but in 2020, the reach and richness of the responses have been dramatically enhanced. Questions to the learning community can be spoken into Clarify-All, and responses are automatically synthesized into a weighted outline for review. The program intelligently links professionally prepared text, and audio and video resources, to the responses to enable the user to explore more deeply any of the lines of thought opened up by the responses.

Mentor-Me (the mentoring dimension). Mentor-Me is a no-cost system for early childhood education and care professionals that extends algorithms originally developed in the early 2000s for personal matchup programs (like match.com). Now in 2020, these algorithms are used to help match young early childhood education and care teachers and caregivers with mentors. Experienced teachers who are grateful for the mentoring help they received years earlier register with the service to help sustain the cycle of mentoring in the profession.

Course Central (the formal learning dimension). Course Central is a clearinghouse of site-specific, blended, and online courses available to the early childhood education and care professional. The searchable list of public and private university, association, commercial, and ad hoc course offerings includes curriculum and instructor ratings by former students, syllabi, and sample course assignments (including excerpts of readings, and audio and video clips). Prospective students identify the issues and/or skills they are most interested in studying, and Course Central provides a ranked list of learning opportunities tailored to the individual.

Spiraling Cohorts

(the informal learning dimension). In response to research that showed that only 30% of what someone needs to know for a job is learned in structured training programs and the remaining 70% is learned informally in conversation and observation,[143] Spiraling Cohorts was devised as a virtual forum to provide enhanced informal learning opportunities for early childhood education and care professionals.

It is open to all early childhood education and care stakeholders, including staff from schools, child care centers, federal and state agencies, unions, advocacy groups, professional research organizations, foundations, associations, and public corporations, as well as family members of children younger than 5. Assignment to a particular 12-member cohort is based on a questionnaire that elicits data on professional background and interests, current and previous work settings, and professional aspirations. The algorithms the system uses ensure not only members' compatibility with one another, but equally important, ensure sufficient diversity among members to introduce broad experience and divergent points of view into the cohort's explorations. Cohorts can be organized around predetermined topics, such as understanding children's learning styles, exploring approaches for participating productively in staff meetings, or ways to apply the array of new technological devices available for the classroom. Alternatively, members can opt to join an agendaless cohort where members allow their conversations and explorations to emerge organically.

Most cohorts meet virtually every two weeks for six months. At the end of the six months, the cohort dissolves, and each participant has the option of joining another cohort for another six months. This cycling characteristic, which has led to the term Spiraling Cohorts, exposes members of the learning community over time to a wide range of viewpoints about what is important for young children. The learning from cohort participation deepens appreciation for the complexity of the early childhood education and care profession. Because cohorts are multinational and multicultural, they also sensitize participants to the subtleties of preparing the next generation to live productive, authentic, and fulfilling lives in a global society.

Flourishing Connections (the social/

caring dimension). Flourishing Connections are unstructured groups that often develop informally in the learning community when members resonate and bond with colleagues at levels that transcend intellectual pursuits and practical projects or objectives. After meeting in formal courses, in Spiraling Cohorts, or on project teams, members occasionally develop special friendships and choose to remain connected through self-organizing subcommunities. Flourishing Connections clusters meet online informally according to their own rhythms; they also tend to find ways to gather together at nonvirtual conferences and conventions. Among all the groups in the learning community, these Flourishing Connections clusters are the most successful in brainstorming creative and outside-the-box solutions to seemingly contentious policy and pedagogical issues: the trust engendered within the cluster allows for a free exchange of ideas without the customary social filters and professional guardedness that tend to hinder creativity.

Collaborative Action Projects, or CAPs (the action dimension). A broad range of practical projects — data-gathering efforts, curriculum-development experiments, research studies, parent/family-involvement facilitation guides, etc. — emerges organically from discussions and interactions in the Spiraling Cohorts and Flourishing Connections groups. These are offered as options to the learning community as a whole, and, following the CAPs methodology, which is expansive and seeks wide inclusion of learning community members, CAPs often energize large numbers of people to become change agents in the early childhood education and care community.

By 2020, facilitation of these CAPs has become a new leadership art form. Rather than being structured as task forces with top-down leadership, these projects are guided by coordinating teams that see their role as conveners and guardians of a broadly shared knowledge-creation and learning-facilitation process.

Because of the broad involvement of the early childhood education and care learning community, these CAP initiatives often attract public and private funding and lead to more-effective innovations than projects spawned by individual agencies or organizations.

In Situ-Plus (the local dimension). The global early childhood education and care learning community finds its grounding and its points of greatest impact in strengthening local work settings. Each school, center, agency, association, or other stakeholder group can set up a private workspace within the overall online community environment to foster and support communication, coordination, and collaboration. The goal is to expand capacity and enhance the learning of staff, members, and local stakeholders. Integrating the global online learning community with virtual workspaces at the local level aligns the support, learning, and growth provided by a global community of profession-

als with the day-to-day experience of caring for young children.

Communication technologies in 2020

One lesson that has already been learned in 2010 is that the success of virtual learning communities depends more on the personal qualities, intentions, and goals of those who engage in them than on any particular technology. Nonetheless, it is also true that the more-accessible an online learning community becomes through advanced technologies, the higher the level of engagement is likely to be.

The landscape of the learning communities of 2020 described in this chapter assumes that certain advancements will occur in their enabling technologies. Though many may find them hard to imagine, a spate of technological breakthroughs, almost all of which are already available in nascent form in 2010, can be expected to become commercially viable and widely adopted as we approach 2020. A sampling of the new and enhanced tools and capabilities we are likely to see in one form or another in the next decade includes the following:

- Smartphones will continue to become smaller and lighter, and will likely sport foldout, paper-thin, high-definition, true-color screens. They will provide 24/7 Internet access and never need charging because their batteries will be powered by ambient light.
- Skype-like conference-calling capabilities will enable dozens of people at a time to join fully interactive videoconferences from their pocket devices.
- Speech-recognition software that in 2009 already provided 98 to 99% accuracy under optimal conditions will deliver 99+% accuracy, even for heavily accented speakers and under noisy conditions. A major turning point for learning communities will occur when speech-recognition

software integrates with translation software, enabling anyone to speak into a pocket device in his or her own language and be heard in the preferred language of the listener. Some companies today already provide translation services into more than 75 languages, and that number will continue to increase in the next decade. When voice-recognition programs are integrated with translation programs that in turn incorporate text-to-speech capabilities, it will be possible to speak in one language and have someone hear you in another. Language barriers that have long interfered with productive communication will start to dissolve. Not only will this kind of technology bridge geographical divides, but it will help monolingual, foreign-born parents or grandparents of young children participate more fully in their children's classrooms and enable teachers to work collaboratively with families who speak a language other than the one they speak themselves.

- Content-analysis software will develop that can read voice and even video content in addition to text. Using such software, high-speed computers will be able to quickly parse hundreds of thousands of posts and inputs and to synthesize and organize the results in increasingly meaningful ways. Though earlier collaborative efforts such as World Vision's 2004 "Big Ideas" change initiative[144] enabled 5,000 employees to submit electronic feedback to a planning session in Bangkok attended by 150 executives, it required a group of organizational development graduate students and consultants to spend night after night reading and summarizing their submissions for the feedback to be useful. By 2020,

content-analysis software will make massive collaborative endeavors possible by categorizing, sorting, and helping surface the meaning of feedback and other contributions that would otherwise be impossible to handle manually.

While these and related technical innovations can be expected to affect communication in dramatic ways by the year 2020, two other factors will magnify these effects further:

Usability innovations. Computers, cell phones, and other electronic devices are currently immature products. They provide innovative functionalities — which in the context of the history of mankind are momentous accomplishments, not to be demeaned — but they have not yet reached a state of performance that is elegant and transparent to those using their functionality. Like a young skier whose sole focus is getting down a slope without falling and does so without the style and grace that will only come after much practice, so do the devices and software of the first decade of the 21st century accomplish their mission, but without grace or ease of use. The result is the often-heard complaint, "I can't figure out how it works." The grand accomplishment of technological advancement in 2020 will be in the area of usability: hardware and software products will become transparent because they will have matured in their design sufficiently that they will disappear from awareness, just as the telephone as an instrument disappeared from awareness several decades ago. Once the telephone became standardized and easy to use, we did not need to think about it. Making a call, we could concentrate on the nuances of a business conversation or of a chat with a loved one. In the same way, the technologies that will underlie the learning communities of 2020 will similarly disappear from awareness, as will the resistance that many feel today to using those technologies.

Reaching critical mass. The second milestone that will be reached by 2020 is attaining critical mass of usage of the technologies underlying communication, coordination, and collaboration. When only a few people had a telephone or a television or a personal computer, those technologies had little impact. Once telephones, televisions, and personal computers became ubiquitous in the United States, their impact on social, psychological, educational, economic, political, and even religious and spiritual dimensions of life was transformative. Similarly, by 2020, the penetration of the Internet, data access via mobile devices, online real-time video streaming, and collaborative technologies will near saturation, not just in the wealthiest nations, but almost everywhere on the planet.[145] Once everyone is connected and the technology has been used sufficiently to become transparent, the barriers of location, time, and language will dissolve. At that point a new era of being present to one another will begin. There will be challenges — new forms of etiquette, privacy protection, and security safeguards will be needed — but these will get worked out as the opportunities for professional and personal growth and learning continue to inspire people to persevere in perfecting these enabling tools.

The future is already here

Novelist William Gibson's observation that, "The future is already here. It's just not very evenly distributed," is true on many levels.

Those early adopters who began using the telephone in the early 1900s were already experiencing a time decades in the future when everyone in developed countries would have at least one or more telephones.

Those who are committed today to transforming their own competitive and self-interested tendencies in order to unite with others in the service of a common higher purpose are already living in a future in which collaborative processes and collaborative learning will simply be the modus operandi of all organizations and social networks.

And the early childhood education and care professionals worldwide who today work with, care for, and develop strategies to nurture the youngest children in the human family see the face and heart of the future every day in the eyes of each child they care for. And they create the future every day in the way they respond and give of themselves to these young embodiments of our future.

The learning communities of today, the learning communities of tomorrow, and the learning communities of 2020 are designed to provide each teacher, each practitioner, each researcher, and each policymaker with opportunities to imbibe the fresh currents of the new age of collaborative living that is even now unfolding on our planet. The early childhood education professionals of 2020 will engage in these learning communities as a natural part of life; we have the privilege of enlivening that future for them today. ▶

Hope for the children of 2020

That they learn to trust and act upon their highest intuitions, those that will lead them to lives of service and kindness to all.

About the Author

Pascal Kaplan, PhD, *Chief Executive Officer and Co-Founder, iCohere, Inc.; and Adjunct Professor of Transformational Studies, John F. Kennedy University* pascal@icohere.com

Professional focus

Kaplan's focus is the personal and organizational change processes that contribute to building successful online learning communities.

(Excerpt) Aliens in the Education Matrix: Recovering Freedom*

Asa G. Hilliard III-Baffour Amankwatia II

We end Act III with excerpts from one of the last essays written by Asa G. Hilliard III (Baffour Amankwatia II) before his untimely death in 2007. Hilliard, a lifelong teacher, psychologist, and historian, prompts us to focus on the children we nurture rather than the institutions we serve. He stirs us to take responsibility for examining knowledge and improvising strategies that empower children to learn successfully. As Dr. Hilliard concludes:

> ". . . millions of our genius children, some wearing the false labels of 'retarded,' 'at-risk,' 'attention deficit disordered,' 'oppositional defiant disordered,' etc., are waiting for the next generation of teachers. I have already seen many in the next generation of teachers who are ready now for a new space, place, mission, and who will settle for nothing less."

Such a vision challenges us all to free ourselves of outdated assumptions, to join together, and improvise strategies that meet the needs of each of our wonderful children.

"I have come to a frightening conclusion. I am the decisive element in the classroom. It is my personal approach that creates the climate. It is my daily mood that makes the weather. As a teacher I possess tremendous power to make a child's life miserable or joyous. I can be a tool of torture or an instrument of inspiration. I can humiliate or humor, hurt, or heal. In all situations it is my response that decides whether a crisis will be escalated or de-escalated, and a child humanized or dehumanized."[146]

Being a teacher is simply one of the greatest things in the world! Is it a job? Is its purpose to prepare students for the world of work? Yes and yes, but those things are minimal. It matters greatly how teachers think about who they are, who children are, and why they are here. It is my fondest hope that those who intend to enter teaching will learn early about its enormous power, its awesome rewards, its value to students and their families, and its personal fulfillment for teachers.

---

*Reprint permission for these excerpts from *Aliens in the Education Matrix: Recovering Freedom,* granted by the Asa G. Hilliard family. The full essay was originally published in *The New Educator,* 2:87-102, Taylor & Francis. For information about this, and all other materials written by Asa G. Hillard, contact: N. P. Hillard-Nunn at makare@mindspring.com.

Summary biographical information about Dr. Hilliard is at http://en.wikipedia.org/wiki/Asa_Grant_Hilliard_III.

Over 30 years ago, Ginott, quoted above, was correct. His analysis is as valid today as it was then. Teachers are the decisive element in their classrooms. Failing "innovations," today called "school reforms" are ubiquitous. The negative impact of the "innovations" or "school reforms," especially on poor ethnic minority schools, has been acute. This entire approach to education suffers from invalid assumptions, theories, and analyses. Certainly, the low international ranking of achievement results of the United States among "developed nations" should give the United States, the leader in "innovations" or "school reform," great cause for pause.

The power twins, Lindsey and Ewing-Bouquett

Recently I learned about the outstanding work of two master teachers, in one of the most common locations for reporting of excellence in urban schools. No, it was not in a journal on staff development or educational research. It was in a daily newspaper, this time in the *Atlanta Journal Constitution*.

Over an eight-year period, Stephanie Lindsey and Kimberly Ewing-Bouquett, teachers at the C. W. Hill Elementary School in the Atlanta public school district, on their own initiative, collaborated to produce a powerful approach to teaching reading. They were so successful that their work was featured in a promotional videotape for the school district, "Great Expectations."

The work of Lindsey and Ewing-Bouquett grew out of their deep dissatisfaction with the all too common low achievement of the children, mostly low income African children. They reported that many teachers repeat, "Kids can't, kids can't, kids can't." And yet, in these two master teachers' opinions, the published standards for achievement were far too low for kindergartners. For example, being required to learn only "one letter a week and one color a week," or to count only from "0 to 20 initially,

and 0 to 100 later," were tasks far below children's capabilities. They noted that children in some schools were required to do projects, even though they were not able to read, and that grammar was not taught along with reading skills. Yet they knew that these things were well within reach of their students.

They said, "We require our children to write every day, and some of our children are working at the third grade level," and as a result, "Our kids actually beg us to take the tests." Remarkably, when I asked if they had been visited by teacher educators, or if they had been assigned student teachers, they said no.

Lindsey and Ewing-Bouquett also expressed a strong dislike of a widely used scripted program, Success-For-All. Instead, they produced and published their own reading instructional materials, which are being used increasingly within the school district, with interest from teachers outside the district as well. To celebrate their children's success, they approached the superintendent, Dr. Beverly Hall, who found funds to support their request to take the children on a trip to Sea World. Both the superintendent and their principal, Ms. Walters, were said to be "extremely supportive, and gave us leeway to use our own system."

Many lessons can be learned from teachers like Lindsey and Ewing-Bouquett. Unfortunately, although there are many other equally well prepared and creative teachers, they tend to exist on the margins, unknown and unused in advanced staff development or in initial teacher training. Even more exciting, Lindsey and Ewing-Bouquett work with the lowest income African students, who have succeeded marvelously in spite of the many challenges in their high-poverty neighborhoods. Yet, the successes of such teachers seldom inform the work of cognitive psychologists and psychometrics experts, who tend rather to use the student's initial IQ and low achievement scores to make false or invalid predictions about the student's "innate" capacities. Typically, policymakers accept these results.

I have observed many successful schools and teachers for several decades. These schools demonstrate repeatedly, given good teaching, virtually all students can reach the highest levels of academic achievement. Even students who are years behind their peers, can catch up and even surpass students who have a head start, in a relatively brief period of time. Yet, educational planning and practice is not often based upon these realities. I want new teachers to know what their top performing peers are doing, and that as new teachers, they too can become one of those.

The matrix

Most educators live in a "matrix," an ideological prison that determines how they work. Many educators, educational support personnel, and policy makers have long ago accepted the matrix-determined pessimistic view of teacher and school power, and an equally pessimistic view of the children's innate abilities. Unfortunately, infrastructures are in place, with inertia that is almost impossible to overcome. Worse still, the powerful and influential position of the United States is such that these toxic structures within the matrix are being sold to and copied by the world. These toxic infrastructures stand as models that throw doubt into the minds of new teachers, who can become quickly socialized into an acceptance of the toxic condition as the normal, even inevitable, state of affairs. Then, teachers often lose their own valid human instincts for nurturing learners.

It is sad to see the pontifications of professionals, who have passed all of the professional tests required inside the matrix, accumulating credentials and prestige associated with these symbols of legitimacy. Yet, most often they are unable to match the performances like those of teachers like Lindsey and Ewing-Bouquett, who simply got into the trenches and figured out how to be successful with their children. The great tragedy of the matrix is that it sucks the joy out of life, and distorts the humanity of its inhabitants, producing little success for students. Ignorant of these facts, educators and policymakers usually blame student factors for low achievement.

Excellence in teaching and learning existed long before colleges of teacher education and teaching as a profession. All over the world, many parents, family, and community members have nurtured the learning and development of their children in deep and profound ways. Universally, children have demonstrated their genius, virtually effortlessly. In fact, some anthropologists have studied the learning and development of all primates, and have seen many similarities in the ease of learning among them by their young, simply by being placed in environments where they are exposed to good models.[147] Under normal nurturing, teaching and learning are joyful experiences, contrary to the low results achieved with scripted standardized programs.

> **I dream that the new teachers will crack the walls of the matrix, to go over and beyond, around beneath, and far above those of us who are stuck in neutral and spinning our wheels in a bad place.**

The development of the professions of teaching, and of teacher education should result in much higher achievement than that produced by untrained teachers. Otherwise, there is no justification for the enormous resources that are provided for required teacher education. Teachers must be educated for high achievement, not to fit the matrix.

Now it is well known that many children's achievements are far below the idyllic picture that I have just painted. Many students never learn to read, write, quantify, or solve even the most basic traditional academic tasks, whether taught by trained or untrained teachers. Many students never complete a common school curriculum or develop habits that enhance their life's potential, grow up to be dysfunctional adults. How does that happen?

Having been a teacher for many years, with my own view of human values and human destiny, I have been concerned deeply about the evolution of common practices in schools, especially in public education that serves the masses of our children. This evolution follows from the changing aims in education that radiate from the power centers in the world, and the world/value views linked to those power centers. Eventually these changes have a profound influence on educators' beliefs, behaviors and structures globally. In one of his last speeches, Dr. Martin Luther King charged that three mega-defining values of *materialism, militarism*, and *racism* permeated United States culture, the current source of greatest power and influence in the world. To the extent that this was and remains true, everything will be affected by those values, including educational aims and teaching. So "reform of education" must start with a commitment to particular values, hopefully to democratic human values. Current popular educational reform efforts have proceeded with little attention to and examination of and the development of a consensus on world/value views. No matrix is consistent with democratic human values.

The "matrix," is an "invisible," structured, *virtual* reality that sets limits or boundaries on what we perceive as possible and desirable in everything, including teaching and learning, schooling, and socialization. It is a matrix if those who live within it have little or no awareness of life's possibilities outside of common habits and practices, which tend not to be questioned at any fundamental level. Serious attention to alternative views in a matrix is rare. Most important of all, the enormous power potential of teachers and schools is now compromised severely, because of a matrix that conveys the belief in a world of low expectations, for both students and teachers, and a false

belief in their low capabilities. In fact, often the *very systems and structures that we design for enhancement and healing in schools have come to be instruments of mass destruction, recently through mass instruction.* This condition is not natural. It does not serve human interests, nor is it inevitable.

The path to the matrix and the path for escape

Educational excellence is driven first and foremost by belief, by a combination of world/value views, and secondarily by *intent*. It is after we settle on where we stand on belief and intent that less critical matters of particular techniques, methods, organizational structures, tests and assessments, instructional materials, teacher education approaches, etc. It is a fundamental error to proceed to address any of the foregoing secondary matters, without clarity on the educators' world and value views, and their purposes and intent for students' lives and in education. New teachers in particular can make the best professional choices by gaining as much clarity as possible on their world/value-views and their intent. Then they must ally themselves and apprentice themselves with those who share their beliefs and intent. By doing so, they will enhance their chances of becoming people of power and joy.

The main part of world/value-view is *who* human beings are, and why are we here. Is human genius universal? Do students have virtually unlimited potential? Is spirit the essence of our students? Do we really find that guesses about a student's innate potential is a worthy use of professional time? Are communities vital to human societies? Are relationships central to schooling and socialization? These are not mere philosophical or theoretical matters. They are integral to a matching set of practices as well. For example, Dr. James Comer is the creator of a "school reform" approach.[148] I wrote the following recently in a draft of a review of Dr. Comer's book, *Leave No Child Behind*:

"The 'mental health' orientation in the Comer approach is apparent when Dr. Comer observes that, 'Teachers tend to practice in isolation from each other, and they need to talk with each other.' Schools structures and expectations tend not to support opportunities for this type of activity at all.

"Comer calls attention to the need for schools to respond appropriately to children's physical, cognitive, psychological, linguistic, social, and ethical needs. For this to happen, teachers must be taught how to 'read' child behavior. I believe that at least two other needs are paramount, the spiritual and cultural needs of students and teachers. Though he does not say so explicitly, I think that Dr. Comer would agree. Finally, he argues persuasively that the centrality of relationships means linking school, family, neighborhood, and heritage, in creation of the nurturing context for the school.

"Dr. Comer argues that current school reform models are flawed, actually 'creating dysfunction in schools.' Current models 'mimic business, judicial processes, and emphasize efficiency.' More explicitly 'school reform' models place great emphasis on school 'management,' punitive accountability, shaming and naming failing schools, competitive marketplace structures, alien leadership, limited focus on curriculum, scripted teaching, devaluation of development, devaluation of relationships, preoccupation with the student capacity question, retaining students who fail, and minimum competency goals, as standardized state tests reveal."

Dr. Comer's example is of immense importance, since his "reform" approach is one of the most successful, producing the highest academic achievement, although it centers on relationships, *with no standardized instructional component at all*! It is Dr. Comer's world/valueview that sets him apart, an implicit view that embodies an optimistic assessment of human potential, and recognition of the need for a social and spiritual bond of belonging and collaboration among students and teachers. World/valueviews vary considerably. Most important, they determine practice.

I hope that the madness of the matrix has run its course, and that the new teachers will not come to it seeing their task mainly as getting *credentialed*, or *qualified* simply to serve in it. Like Marylyn Cochran-Smith,[149] I am fearful of the embrace of educational "outcomes," as they are conceived in popular terms. I worry about which outcomes are enshrined, and which ones are missing. Who is asking for *character, critical consciousness, and social responsibility*? I dream that the new teachers will crack the walls of the matrix, to go over and beyond, around beneath, and far above those of us who are stuck in neutral and spinning our wheels in a bad place. Teeming millions of our genius children, some wearing the false labels of "retarded," "at-risk," "attention deficit disordered," "oppositional defiant disordered," etc., are waiting for the next generation of teachers. I have already seen many in the next generation of teachers who are ready now for a new space, place, mission, and who will settle for nothing less. They are coming to reinforce teachers like the heroic ones described above. They will be free. They will be human. They will be connected, not aliens. They will demand a place to stand. They are the ones for whom our children are waiting.

It's time for a change. Goodbye matrix. ▶.

Improv Workshop

Translating Ideas into Intelligent Action

Workshop Agenda
- Reflections on the strategy articles
- Examining the Harlem Children's Zone
- Crafting and implementing your smart improv strategies
- Applying your strategies

Reflections on the strategy articles

The articles you have just read connect the developmental needs of children with realities about the workforce, family engagement, financial resources, bureaucratic institutions, technology, and more. The authors' discussion of barriers and challenges reveals that they do not turn a blind eye to the world as it is, and the challenges you face, but they also believe that improvements can and should be made.

Smart improv will require us to commit to the long-term task of exploring, experimenting, and rehearsing how to translate promising innovations into smarter strategies, policies, and systems. As a starting point, we reflect upon the themes of accountability, a comprehensive approach to nurturing children, and cultural sensitivity and flexibility. You will want to add more key points based on your individual and collaborative review of the articles.

Accountability. The authors hold both individuals and institutions such as schools accountable for successfully supporting child development and learning. They articulate innovative strategies and examples of collaborative leadership for institutional change that are needed to provide all children with opportunities. The theme of accountability is focused on responding effectively to children's needs by introducing specific innovations and tools that we can apply in our own settings and community environments.

Comprehensive approach to nurturing children. No one person or program can respond to all the needs of each child, or to the needs of all children, nor to the entire range of birth through 8 years. Implementing a comprehensive strategy that serves all children requires a coordinated early childhood system. Smart improv in Act III requires you to work collaboratively, acting in concert with others in the early care and education field — and indeed with many others in the community who are committed to better outcomes for the children of 2020.

This is where your improv goes beyond your work as an individual actor. You will need to reach beyond your child development center, program, and agency. Since Act III calls for you to collaborate with others in your community, we suggest that you "put your heads together" and identify and learn from examples of coordinated strategies. To help you get started, we are summarizing one example here, the Harlem Children's Zone (HCZ). Like HCZ, specify the results you intend to accomplish, and in preparing your improv, you should also identify additional models for coordinated early childhood strategies. Make sure they are culturally sensitive and flexible, which is the next key point.

Cultural sensitivity and flexibility.

The articles in Act III emphasize that effective programs and services are culturally sensitive and flexible. In developing a comprehensive strategy, we must constantly hold ourselves responsible for keeping the standards and rules governing our programs adaptable, dynamic, and supportive rather than biased, obstructive, or irrelevant. This calls for us to keep our eyes on the goal: supportive environments for children's development and learning. Specific policies, strategies, and pet ideas must never obstruct our ultimate goal of healthy development for all children.

Examining the Harlem Children's Zone

The Harlem Children's Zone as an example of comprehensive strategies

The Harlem Children's Zone (HCZ), conceptualized and led by Geoffrey Canada, is an example of comprehensive collaboration that is paying off with considerable success for children and their families in New York City's Harlem neighborhood. It is a coordinated strategy for the entire community environment, beginning with healthy births, safe neighborhoods, and quality learning. HCZ emphasizes accountability for successful outcomes in the areas of health, quality child care and education, social services, supported and supportive families, and more. It links the early years to ongoing academic achievement and personal development for each child. HCZ is a comprehensive strategy, focusing on the whole child, providing continuity for services, and demanding robust evaluations to validate accountability and successful outcomes for children.[150]

HCZ demonstrates that coordinated comprehensive services can be achieved and result in astounding improvements. The two fundamental principles of the HCZ project can serve as important guidelines for work in our own communities: (1) support children in a sustained, comprehensive way, starting as early in their lives as possible, and (2) surround children with a critical mass of adults who understand what it takes to help children succeed.

Obviously, many children may not require the HCZ intense level and array of services, but it would be important for communities to have the capacity to provide an array of supportive opportunities for any children who do need them if we are to achieve both excellence and equity by 2020. Access to high-quality services is an achievable goal for all children in our American Dream.

Crafting and implementing your smart improv strategies

Each of us has a responsibility to be informed and stay current about documented evidence of strategies that improve opportunities that support children's development. Still, preserving the American Dream for all children is a task far beyond the scope of our individual capabilities, and a successful strategy calls for collaboration and knowledge sharing. What's more, we must put our shared knowledge into action — as a cooperative, community-wide cast of smart improv actors.

This means we need to do what we know and share what we know with others. As a community of public intellectuals and activists, we can start with staff and colleagues in close-to-home settings and branch out to circumstances calling for change in the broader arena.

The articles in Act III provide a wealth of information to organize into briefing/talking points and action strategies on a variety of topics. Many circumstances will call for our active involvement:

- efforts to increase constructive family engagement,
- reviews of curriculum or assessment procedures,
- appeals for increased funding,
- revisions of standards or regulations,
- input into teacher-preparation guidelines,
- testimony before school boards or legislative committees,
- initiatives to influence public opinion, and more.

Connecting the articles in Act III with an overall plan of action for your community is a major undertaking, and that is why collaboration and teamwork is required. You may find it helpful to follow the step-by-step approach outlined by the Pathways[151] initiative (Figure 4):

Acts I and II, on vision and knowledge, have helped to prepare you to "See the Big Picture." Collaboration about strategy, policy, and systems — Act III — will help your community advance through Pathways steps for the remaining three categories: "Plan and Make Choices," "Implement," and "Track Progress." Note that collaborating and building a knowledge base about your community will provide the critical input of "Local Wisdom."

Implementing the ideas for your improv will be a continuing process, and your strategy will need to be a dynamic one that is updated regularly. As you track progress, you will find ongoing improvements. You will also discover additional innovations and change issues to address in the years ahead, as we anticipate the children of 2020.

Are you getting ready for me?

Figure 4.

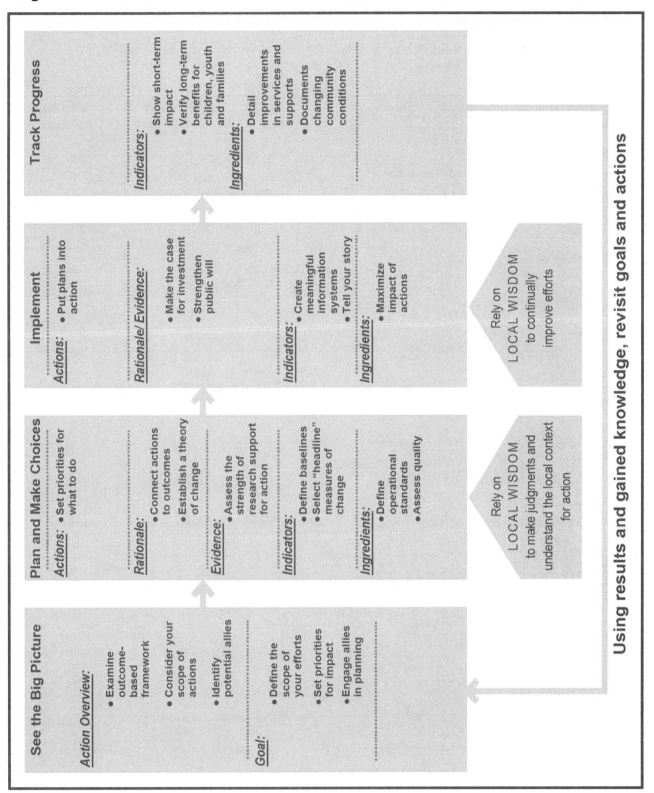

See the Big Picture

Action Overview:

- Examine outcome-based framework
- Consider your scope of actions
- Identify potential allies

Goal:

- Define the scope of your efforts
- Set priorities for impact
- Engage allies in planning

Plan and Make Choices

Actions: • Set priorities for what to do

Rationale:

- Connect actions to outcomes
- Establish a theory of change

Evidence:

- Assess the strength of research support for action

Indicators:

- Define baselines
- Select "headline" measures of change

Ingredients:

- Define operational standards
- Assess quality

Implement

Actions: • Put plans into action

Rationale/ Evidence:

- Make the case for investment
- Strengthen public will

Indicators:

- Create meaningful information systems
- Tell your story

Ingredients:

- Maximize impact of actions

Track Progress

Indicators:

- Show short-term impact
- Verify long-term benefits for children, youth and families

Ingredients:

- Detail improvements in services and supports
- Documents changing community conditions

Rely on LOCAL WISDOM to make judgments and understand the local context for action

Rely on LOCAL WISDOM to continually improve efforts

Using results and gained knowledge, revisit goals and actions

Applying your strategies

1. Using ideas from the strategy articles, what new strategies would you use to create new policies and practices in several areas? Place these new strategies in the box below:

NEW STRATEGIES I WOULD LIKE TO TRY in these areas ...	... to change policies	... to change practices	... to advance our field
a. Communication with families			
b. Assessments that help teachers plan instruction to match the needs of individual children			
c. Professional development and mentoring			
d. Cultural competence			
e. Other			
f. Other			
g. Other			

2. With your new strategies identified, can you identify and list other people and groups who need to be involved if you want to create change?

   a. _____

   b. _____

   c. _____

3. What are the next three things you can do to actually begin to implement some of these new strategies?

   a. _____

   b. _____

   c. _____

Act IV: Denouement

Taking Personal Responsibility
for the Children of 2020

de • noue • ment, *n*.[152]

1. a. The final resolution or clarification of a dramatic or narrative plot.

   b. The events following the climax of a drama or novel in which such a resolution or clarification takes place.

2. The outcome of a sequence of events; the end result

Commentary

For the children of 2020, denouement is a call to action — a dynamic process, a resolution to take responsibility for the future we create by what we do today. Our role in this act is to take responsibility, both individually and as a profession, for the denouement. Will we implement clearer vision, current knowledge, and effective strategies to continue the viability of the American Dream for the children of 2020? The denouement depends on your action, both now and in the coming years.

Many of the challenges faced by young children — and by our profession — were highlighted in the book *Children of 2010*. During the subsequent years, we have achieved great progress in advancing early care and education, and we have witnessed remarkable breakthroughs in the science of early education and brain development. In both books, we emphasize the importance of excellence and equity for all children as essential to our democ-

racy and the American Dream. On behalf of our wonderfully diverse nation, *Children of 2020* is an urgent call for a significant increase in smart, intentional action from each of us.

Some of the improvisations we need to do are not new: there is a persistent perennial call for greater family engagement and comprehensive services, for example. Other recommendations, however, represent new knowledge and approaches as described by the authors of the chapters in this book.

> ### *For Democracy's Sake, We Must Educate Well*
>
> *If we intend to have a democracy in this country, we must educate well. If we are committed to one America for all people . . . we must give every child equal access to a real education.*
>
> —Geoffrey Canada
> *Children of 2010*, page 144

But whether we move on to finally implement established knowledge, or move forward with new information, the denouement message is the same:

- Make the challenge a personal one.

- Visualize the faces of *all* children, and put your good intentions to work.

- Be willing "to embrace the distinctive values and moral obligations of the field of early childhood care and education"[153]

- Accept leadership.

- Take personal responsibility for the children of 2020.

A movement moving forward

We believe that taking responsibility will result in nothing less than a focused movement for the right of all young children to quality early care and education. While this right presents a formidable challenge, it is attainable. If the past is prologue, we quickly realize that daunting barriers to the well-being of children have been successfully challenged throughout the history of the United States. This is already a movement that evolves, is dynamic, and moves forward (see timeline below).

Timeline: *Moving Forward for Children's Rights in America*

1836 Massachusetts creates the first state child labor law, requiring that children under 15 working in factories attend school for at least three months per year.[154]

1863 First federally sponsored day nursery for mothers working in Civil War hospitals and factories opens in Philadelphia.[155]

1869 In one of the first court rulings on child abuse, the parents of Samuel Fletcher, Jr., are arrested, convicted, and fined $300, establishing recognition of children's right to be protected by law against abuse and cruelty.

1912 U.S. Children's Bureau is established, publishing seven child care-related documents from 1919 to 1944.

1929 The National Association for Nursery Education (NANE) is formally established; it is incorporated in 1931.

1938 The Fair Labor Standards Act places limits on many forms of child labor.

1942 The Lanham Act revisions allow public works money to be used for child care in war-impacted areas. All families, regardless of income level, are eligible. Child care, although federally funded, is viewed as a war need only. Federal support is gradually withdrawn after World War II ends.

1954 The U.S. Supreme Court in Brown v. Board of Education rules that "segregation of white and colored children in public schools has a detrimental effect upon the colored children,"[156] launching a long, slow struggle to remedy educational inequities.

1954 The Internal Revenue Service allows tax deductions for elected child care expenses.

1964 NANE becomes the National Association for the Education of Young Children (NAEYC).

1965 Head Start begins as a summer program in an antipoverty initiative.

1974 The Child Abuse Prevention and Treatment Act is enacted.

Child Labor

An eight-year-old newsboy in St. Louis, 1910. *Photo, U.S. Library of Congress (via Wikipedia).*

1975	Congress enacts the Education for All Handicapped Children Act.
1975	The Indian Self-Determination and Education Assistance Act curbs a practice of sending thousands of Native American children to Indian boarding schools, where they were often forbidden to speak their native languages and forced to abandon their cultural identities.[157]
1984	NAEYC publishes Accreditation Criteria and Procedures; voluntary accreditation begins in 1985.
1988	The Family Support Act of 1988 offers the first open-ended entitlement for eligible child care for parents in mandatory work and training programs, and a year of transitional child care to parents leaving welfare for the workforce.
1989	President George H. W. Bush's Education Summit, led by then Governor Bill Clinton of Arkansas, adopts six goals, the first of which is that all children will start school "ready to learn."
	The United Nations adopts the Convention on the Rights of the Child.
1990	President Bush signs into law the Child Care and Development Block Grant, the first U.S. law that specifically addresses child care funding support.
1997	An agreement based on the Flores, et al. v. Janet Reno lawsuit sets a national policy for the detention, release, and treatment of children in immigration custody based on the premise that authorities must treat children in their custody with "dignity, respect and special concern for their vulnerability as minors."[158]
2002	Pre-K Now is founded to assist national and state leaders and the public in the design and implementation of policies that support voluntary access to high-quality prekindergarten for all 3- and 4-year-olds in the United States.
	The National Institute for Early Education Research is founded to conduct and communicate research to support high-quality, effective, early childhood education for all young children.
2009	The American Recovery and Reinvestment Act (the federal stimulus package) appropriates funds for children's programs, including Head Start, Early Head Start, Child Care Development Block Grants, the Individuals with Disabilities Education Act, and others.

As we write *Children of 2020*, states across the country are experiencing dire financial situations.[159] We are encouraged, however, when we:

- Consider the timeline describing our work over many decades; we recognize that the rights of children continue to advance.

- Keep in mind that by working individually and together, we can do much to make access to quality development and education a right for all young children.

- Recognize that there are many of us in this movement, moving together over time. You are not alone.

Sometimes, it will seem like the little advances each of us makes are frustratingly small steps on a long journey. At times, it will seem like we're being asked to compromise — accepting partial solutions when we want total success. Sometimes, we may even face setbacks. However, the script — the collective results of our smart improv — has been and will continue to be powerful. Rosa Parks's famed bus ride was a courageous but small, smart improv act; yet the force of an entire movement was behind her, and she helped shatter the status quo. Working together, our small day-to-day actions — our performance — truly makes a difference. It is up to us to perform with excellence!

Performing with excellence: using vision, knowledge, and strategies to advance your work on behalf of children

By completing Acts I, II, and III, your script is complete. You have developed or refined your smart improv script comprising your vision, your knowledge base, and new strategies. So take action; don't wait for a perfect solution. Take action to eliminate gaps in children's access to a nurturing environment, quality education, health care, and community services. Who else will create and lead change for our youngest learners — and for our profession?

To *create* change we need our script — the smart improv vision, knowledge, and strategies — focused on making the American Dream accessible to all, regardless of race, class, or income. To *lead* change we must perform that script with excellence — an excellence that is visibly embedded with both culturally responsive and developmentally appropriate vision, knowledge and strategies. We hope that the following suggestions support you in the dynamic process of performing with excellence.

Imbed Culturally Responsive Vision, Knowledge, and Strategy in Everything You Do

Developing the capacity to work with children, families, and other professionals from a culturally responsive perspective is an overarching goal to be applied in all of the suggested guidelines for advancing work on behalf of children. Specific challenges include:

Approach challenges with positive expectations

- In increasingly diverse classrooms and professional circles, have confidence to continuously learn about and adapt to cultural differences.

Build your capacity and performance as an ECE professional

- Expand your knowledge about how values, beliefs, and assumptions influence every aspect of human development.

- Set goals for your work with children that honor their culture and also prepare them to participate in the mainstream culture.

- Apply developmentally appropriate practices that incorporate appreciation for the three interrelated dimensions of a child's development: universal similarities, individual differences, and cultural group membership.

- Advance strategies to achieve a culturally diverse teaching workforce and a workforce where all teachers are competent in working from a culturally responsive perspective.

Deepen your capacity to collaborate with others outside the ECE profession

- Strengthen collaborative relationships with community organizations, including cultural institutions, ethnic service organizations, and faith communities.

- Recognize broad institutional forms of bias that harm children's growth and development, and work to support constructive changes.

Reflect on and revise

- Increase your sensitivity to the cultural attitudes and beliefs that you bring to all your interactions with children and families.

Approach challenges with positive expectations

Have confidence. As early care and education professionals, we are responsible for being the architects of change for children, because by definition, their every act of developing and learning is change. We will succeed by maintaining our habit of inquiry, using wisdom in our improvisation, and applying cultural understanding in our interactions with children, coworkers, and families. Bringing about change over the long term requires persistence from day to day, from year to year. Continue to dream. Continue to act.

There will be cycles of achievements and disappointments. Recognize these cycles, rebalance, and move forward! This does not mean turning a blind eye to realities: we recognize policy and economic cycles, and we practice flexibility in focusing on what can be done now. Resist thoughts that we cannot take meaningful action because of fears about our limited financial resources, lack of consensus among ourselves, or narrow community connections. Children depend on us to keep pushing forward, and we revamp our strategies to areas where we can keep making progress.

Build your capacity and performance

Taking action also means recognizing and taking pride in the esteemed value of our field. Acknowledge that you are in a dynamic profession that produces a constant flow of new information from research studies, professional practice, community wisdom, and reactions of children and families. This flow of new information nourishes our professional roots and builds our advancing field.

Each of us connects to this flow of new information by investing in professional development for ourselves, our team, and our programs. As with any profession, a commitment to lifelong learning that builds our capacity and performance requires ongoing study, trial, feedback, change, and refinement. Smart improvisation guides you as you apply new knowledge

and promising practices in your professional setting. Many of your colleagues will pick up the contagious excitement of professional growth and the satisfaction of enhanced outcomes for children. So bring others with whom you work along on this journey — create learning teams to support this change process.

Here are specific suggestions to help you advance along your journey:

- Promote transformative professional-development experiences. The cultivation of both self-reflection and peer learning is at the heart of effective pre- and in-service educational experiences. For example, the CAYL Institute organizes intensive, confidential cohorts of professionals to learn, observe, share, assess, and practice their leadership skills.[161]

- Participate in collaborative initiatives. Identify or create endeavors in your community that focus on broad issues of policy and practice. Some examples of local and state initiatives include BUILD, Thrive in Five, and Success by Six.

- Utilize professional association resources: Our professional associations are active organizers of collaborative initiatives — be an active participant.

- Be knowledgeable about and take advantage of high-quality, vetted, professional-improvement resources and opportunities developed by professional associations in our field.

In addition to our own professional development, there is an urgent need to build bridges between the islands among us: we work in a wide variety of contexts and settings. As professionals committed to a movement — the right of all our children to high-quality early care and education — we must avoid the trap of being beholden to our specific island and feeling protective or competitive with others who work in other venues. Focus on the overarching goal we we hold in common: meeting the learning and developmental needs of children. Seek and make opportunities to share information and support common goals. Finally, acknowledge that valuable ideas and knowledge are emerging from the "other islands," and take time to listen, and to consider how your own children and families could benefit.

Finally, we can leverage collaboration and information sharing by embracing technology. A potential rich resource, technology offers a wealth of options that multiplies our capacity for communication with others: parents, team members, experts. It removes many inconveniences and costs that obstruct our access to information or opportunities for collaboration. It also challenges us to work in our learning teams to make wise judgments about the appropriate selection and use of technology with adults and with children.

Deepen your capacity to collaborate with those outside the field

Achieving our vision for the children of 2020 will require reaching beyond our own profession and taking action with others. Truly improving outcomes for children necessitates respecting, and becoming knowledgeable about, the valuable contributions of parents and professionals in related disciplines. Here are some ways to start:

Engage families. Our field is often admired for its relative strength in partnering with families compared to other education venues, but we can, and must, do better. It is imperative that we constantly recognize and respect parents as each child's primary caregiver and teacher, always honoring their role. We must make it a constant goal to engage parents as partners to the benefit of children. Lip service and good will are not enough. We must continually cultivate the vision, knowledge base, and specific skill sets to actually achieve more effective parent engagement. Beginning with the mindset that learning involves multiple constituents, we sharpen the potential for insights about and deeper relationships with each child and family.

Collaborate with professionals in related fields. Interdisciplinary collaboration is a broadly recognized goal, particularly for special-needs children and those living in low-income families. Even so, effective implementation continues to be a challenge. Additionally, as we move toward 2020, we need to broaden our focus on multidisciplinary services to include all children.

Collaborating with professionals in related disciplines helps us achieve our vision for children; our knowledge base alone won't get us there. Some of these collaborative efforts involve the direct provision of health, nutrition, and social services to children in our programs. Other initiatives focus on improvements in neighborhoods, communities, counties, and states. Closest to home, many improvements can be made by enhancing educational, social, and recreational services, and making locations more accessible to children and families. Any of these initiatives requires intentional focus on mutually established goals, as well as frequent assessments to see if you are getting the desired outcomes and determining where adjustments need to be made.

Technology for Collaboration

Many professional associations, non-profits, and universities offer online support for collaboration. Above is the main page for NAEYC's online community, www.naeyc.org/community. You can also join groups and discussions at places like Facebook and Twitter.

Influence public policy. Many policies have an immense influence on our ability to improve opportunities for children's development and learning, including:

- Standards, regulations, and funding that directly affect the operation of early care and education programs. For example, school policies have the potential to increase the continuity in education across grade levels.

- Standards, regulations, and funding that directly affect a child's nonschool environment. For example, early learning is clearly affected by substandard housing and other neighborhood issues that put children at risk. In all cases, you, using smart improvisation, can promote policy changes consistent with your vision, knowledge base, and strategic collaborations.

Expand public will. As we share our vision, knowledge, and strategic goals, we are, by definition, working to expand public will to realize the rights of all children to quality early care and education. Our resounding message is that our entire nation benefits when we invest in every child's foundational years. The investment requires many forms of support, including those that directly target families, children's programs, and the professional workforce.

Between now and 2020, we envision that financing quality early care and education arrangements will be increasingly recognized as a public, not just a parental, obligation. This involves challenging taxpayers to rebalance priorities so that we consider budgets in view of their impact on young children. It also calls for enhancing and expanding public respect for the helping professions in our communities.

Reflect on and revise

Smart, successful improvisations on behalf of children require diligent evaluation of our efforts. Not every idea will work well, and some potentially good improvisations will need substantial refinements. We have to step back and examine evidence of how well our efforts are achieving our goals. Here are important professional habits and processes for making smart improv work well:

Habit of inquiry. We need an ongoing passion and respect for questions about child development and learning strategies. We must be willing to examine objectively the basis for, and effectiveness of, our habitual and traditional practices with children and families.

Reflective practice. We must find time to examine and reconsider our work, ideally in collaboration with trusted colleagues or mentors. We welcome reflection as necessary for professional growth. We face down the fear of making mistakes, embracing the insights they provide and seeking opportunities to learn from and with others.

Ethical conduct. All professionals face multiple daily decisions that have moral and ethical implications. There could be no better document to guide your reflection and revision than the NAEYC Code of Ethical Conduct. The code presents valuable guidelines from which to make decisions that reflect your ethical responsibilities to children. The guidelines are comprehensive in nature and demand thoughtful study and frequent review to internalize them into your daily practice.

Commitment. We are asking you to make a commitment to the children of today and tomorrow. We are asking for a commitment to make drastic improvements in outcomes for children, through individual and group action. In addition, we are asking for your commitment to support closing the gap in access to quality education and the American Dream, to promote excellence and equity for all. An appropriate starting point is the NAEYC Statement of Commitment (see text box, next page). What will you do — individually and as a community — to leverage significant changes for children? What will you commit to do for children over the next ten years?

Core Values for Ethical Behavior

Standards of ethical behavior in early childhood care and education are based on commitment to the following core values that are deeply rooted in the history of the field of early childhood care and education. We have made a commitment to

- Appreciate childhood as a unique and valuable stage of the human life cycle

- Base our work on knowledge of how children develop and learn

- Appreciate and support the bond between the child and family

- Recognize that children are best understood and supported in the context of family, culture,* community, and society

- Respect the dignity, worth, and uniqueness of each individual (child, family member, and colleague)

- Respect diversity in children, families, and colleagues

- Recognize that children and adults achieve their full potential in the context of relationships that are based on trust and respect

----

*The term culture includes ethnicity, racial identity, economic level, family structure, language, and religious and political beliefs, which profoundly influence each child's developmentand relationship to the world.

Copyright © 2005 by the National Association for the Education of Young Children

Statement of Commitment

As an individual who works with young children, I commit myself to furthering the values of early childhood education as they are reflected in the ideals and principles of the NAEYC Code of Ethical Conduct. To the best of my ability I will

- Never harm children.

- Ensure that programs for young children are based on current knowledge and research of child development and early childhood education.

- Respect and support families in their task of nurturing children.

- Respect colleagues in early childhood care and education and support them in maintaining the NAEYC Code of Ethical Conduct.

- Serve as an advocate for children, their families, and their teachers in community and society.

- Stay informed of and maintain high standards of professional conduct.

- Engage in an ongoing process of self-reflection, realizing that personal characteristics, biases, and beliefs have an impact on children and families.

- Be open to new ideas and be willing to learn from the suggestions of others.

- Continue to learn, grow, and contribute as a professional.

- Honor the ideals and principles of the NAEYC Code of Ethical Conduct.

----

*This Statement of Commitment is not part of the Code but is a personal acknowledgment of the individual's willingness to embrace the distinctive values and moral obligations of the field of early childhood care and education. It is recognition of the moral obligations that lea to an individual becoming part of the profession.

Copyright © 2005 by the National Association for the Education of Young Children

Creating tomorrow by what you do today

We, early care and education professionals, are enablers of the American Dream whose contributions to the lives of young children are increasingly important to the future of democracy in the United States. Because we create tomorrow by what we do today, there can be no hesitation to take action if we are to transform the American Dream into a vibrant reality that enables democracy to flourish in a remarkably diverse nation.

For the children of 2020, early care and education must become a civil right. We sustain our belief that this dream is possible because we have a history of ongoing progress, and because millions of solutions exist. Our vision, knowledge, and strategies for working with young children and their families must be clear, purposeful, and aligned.

Let this book be a starting point for you, renewing your commitment to excellence as we act together. Working on behalf of an unknowable future, our work is an improvisation. Our work is also smart because it is rooted in a strong knowledge base. Be inspired — and inspire others. Realize, once again, that it is within our power to make a difference for young children. ▶

Perform With Excellence

- Imbed culturally responsive vision, knowledge, and strategies in everything you do.
- Approach challenges with positive expectations.
- Build your capacity and performance as an early care and education professional.
- Deepen your capacity to collaborate with others outside the early care and education field.
- Reflect on and revise your smart improv. Leadership is *dynamic*.

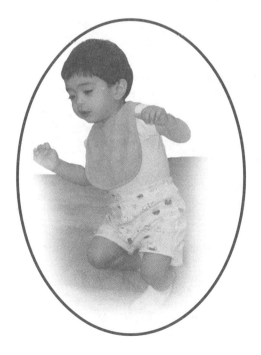

Practice Makes Perfect

Each step is going to be a challenge.
If I lose my balance and fall, I may
cry a little. But I'll stand up again
and keep trying until I get it right.
Will you do the same for me?

Notes

1. Washington, V., and J. D. Andrews, eds. 1998. *Children of 2010.* Washington, DC: National Association for the Education of Young Children, 1.

2. Goffin, S., and V. Washington. 2007. *Ready or not: Leadership choices in early care and education.* New York: Teachers College Press,

3. Ibid.

4. Each author contributed equally to the completion of this vision statement and therefore is listed alphabetically.

5. Lansford, J.E., K. Deater-Deckard, and M. Bornstein, eds. 2007. *Immigrant families in contemporary society.* New York: Guilford Press, 1–6.

6. Coleman, J.S. 1987. Families and schools. *Educational Researche*r 16 (6): 32–38.

7. As cited in Darling-Hammond, L. 2006. Securing the right to learn: Policy and practice for powerful teaching and learning. *Educational Researcher* 35 (7): 13–24.

8. Dewey, J. 1916, copyright renewed 1944. *Democracy in education.* New York: Macmillan.

9. Pianta, R.C. 2007. Early education in transition. In R.C. Pianta, M. J. Cox, and K.L. Snow, eds. 2007. *School readiness and the transition to kindergarten in the era of accountability* (pp. 3–10). Baltimore: Brookes Publishing.

10. Meisels, S. 2007. Accountability in early childhood: No easy answers. In R.C. Pianta, M.J. Cox, and K.L. Snow, eds. 2007. *School readiness and the transition to kindergarten in the era of accountability* (pp. 31–47). Baltimore: Brookes Publishing.

11. "A community school is both a place and a set of partnerships between the school and other community resources. Its integrated focus on academics, health and social services, youth and community development and community engagement leads to improved student learning, stronger families and healthier communities. Schools become centers of the community and are open to everyone — all day, every day, evenings and weekends." Coalition for Community Schools. 2009. http://www.communityschools.org/index.php?option=content&task=view&id=6&Itemid=27#WhatCS. Accessed February 16, 2010.

12. See Harlem Children's Zone at http://www.hcz.org/. Accessed February 16, 2010.

13. See Comer School Development Program at http://medicine.yale.edu/childstudy/comer/.

14. Fine, M., M.E. Torre, K. Boudin, I. Bowen, J. Clark, D. Hylton, et al. 2003. Participatory action research from within and beyond prison bars. In P.M. Camic, J.E. Rhodes, and L. Yardley, eds. 2004. *Qualitative research in psychology: Expanding perspectives in methodology and design.* Washington, DC: American Psychological Association/American Educational Research Association.

15. Henderson, A., and K. Mapp. 2002. *A new wave of evidence: The impact of school, family, and community connections on student achievement.* Austin, TX: National Center for Family and Community Connections with Schools.

16. He, W., and F. Hobbs. 1999. *The emerging minority marketplace: Minority population growth: 1995 to 2050.* Washington, DC: U.S. Department of Commerce, Minority Business

Development Agency. http://www.mbda.gov/
documents/mbdacolor.pdf. Accessed October
3, 2009.

17. Doucet, F., and J. Tudge. 2007. Co-construct-
ing the transition to school: Reframing the
novice versus expert roles of children, parents,
and teachers from a cultural perspective. In
R.C. Pianta, M.J. Cox, and K.L. Snow, eds.
2007. *School readiness and the transition to
kindergarten in the era of accountability* (pp.
307–328). Baltimore: Brookes Publishing.

Durand, T.M. 2008. Celebrating diversity in
early care and education settings: Moving
beyond the margins. *Early Child Development
and Care.* Advance online publication. doi:
10.1080/03004430802466226.

18. Ethnic minority is defined here as the com-
bined population of people who are black,
American Indian, Eskimo, Aleut, Pacific
Islander, or of Hispanic origin.

19. Rogoff, B. 2003. *The cultural nature of human
development.* New York: Oxford University
Press.

20. Doucet, F., and J. Tudge. 2007. Co-construct-
ing the transition to school: Reframing the
novice versus expert roles of children, parents,
and teachers from a cultural perspective. In
R.C. Pianta, M.J. Cox, and K.L. Snow, eds.
2007. *School readiness and the transition to
kindergarten in the era of accountability* (pp.
307–328). Baltimore: Brookes Publishing.

21. Foundation for Child Development. 2008.
America's vanishing potential: The case for
preK–3rd education. October. http://www.fcd-
us.org/resources/resources_show.htm?doc_
id=711495. Accessed February 16, 2010.

22. Chang, H.N., and Mariajose Romero. 2008.
Present, engaged, and accounted for: The
critical importance of addressing chronic
absence in the early grades. National Center
for Children in Poverty. September. http://www.
nccp.org/publications/pub_837.html. Accessed
February 16, 2010.

23. Hoover-Dempsey, K, et al. 2005. Why do parents become involved?: Research findings and
implications. *The Elementary School Journal
106*, no. 2. Chicago: University of Chicago.

24. For more information about the parent engagement toolkit developed by America's Promise
and The Annie Casey Foundation, see www.
americaspromise.org/parentengagement. Accessed February 16, 2010.

25. For more information on promoting family
economic success, see Chynoweth, J. 2007.
What works: Family strengthening and economic success. California Family Resource
Association, September. http://www.california-
familyresource.org/_pdf/CFRA_FES_BRIEF.
pdf. Accessed February 16, 2010.

26. For information about the CAYL Institute, see
www.cayl.org.

27. Collins, Jim. 2001. *Good to great.* New York:
Harper Collins.

28. General information about No Child Left
Behind can be found at http://ed.gov/nclb/over-
view/intro/4pillars.html.

29. Fielding, Lynn, Nancy Kerr, and Paul Rosier.
2007. *Annual growth, catch-up growth.* Ken-
newick, WA: page 205. New Foundation Press.

30. Collins, *Good to great,* page 119.

31. Ibid., page 186.

32. Fielding, et al., *Annual growth,* page 236.

33. Shore, Rima. 2009. The case for investing in
preK–3rd education: Challenging myths about
school reform. *Policy to Action Brief,* January.
New York: Foundation of Child Development.

34. Ibid., page 6.

35. Fielding, et al., *Annual growth,* page 203.

36. Dr. Martin Luther King, Jr. 1968. Speech
delivered at Masonic Temple, Memphis, TN,
March 18.

37. Dr. Martin Luther King, Jr. 1967. "Beyond
Viet Nam: A time to break silence." Speech
delivered at Riverside Church, New York City,
NY. April 4.

38. All data in this article are from official federal
government sources. Calculations done by the
Children's Defense Fund.

39. Much of this article is drawn from Bredekamp,
S. 2010. *Effective practices in early child-
hood education: Building a foundation.* Upper
Saddle River, NJ: Pearson.

Other sources to which the reader may refer
are: Barbarin, O.A., and B.H. Wasik, eds.
2009. *Handbook of child development and
early education: Research to practice.* Baltimore: Brookes Publishing.

Hyson, M., C. Copple, and J. Jones. 2006.
Bringing developmental theory and research
into the early childhood classroom: Thinking,
emotions, and assessment. In W. Damon and
R.M. Lerner, series eds., and K.A. Renninger

and I.E. Sigel, vol. eds. *Handbook of child psychology: Child psychology in practice*, 6th ed., vol. 4 (pp. 3–47). New York: Wiley.

40. National Research Council and Institute of Medicine. 2000. *From neurons to neighborhood: The science of early childhood development.* J.P. Shonkoff and D.A. Phillips, eds. Committee on Integrating the Science of Early Childhood Development. Board on Children, Youth and Families. Washington, DC: National Academies Press.

41. Bodrova, E., and D.J. Leong. 2007. *Tools of the mind: The Vygotskian approach to early childhood education.* New York: Merrill/Prentice Hall.

42. National Research Council. 2009. *Mathematics learning in early childhood: Paths toward excellence and equity.* Committee on Early Childhood Mathematics, C.T. Cross, T.A. Woods, and H. Schweingruber, eds., Center for Education, Division of Behavioral and Social Sciences and Education. Washington, DC: National Academies Press.

43. This article is based on a book by the author; the book covers two other areas: respect for diversity and collaborative play. See Epstein, A.S. 2009. *Me, you, us: Social-emotional learning in preschool.* Washington, DC, and Ypsilanti, MI: National Association for the Education of Young Children and HighScope Press.

44. Ibid.

    Additional references supporting the ideas in this article:

    Elias, M.J., J.E. Zins, K.S. Weissberg, M.T. Frey, N.M. Greenberg, R. Kessler, M.E. Schwab-Stone, and T.P. Shriver. 1997. *Promoting social and emotional learning: Guidelines for educators.* Alexandria, VA: Association for Supervision and Curriculum Development. Goleman, D. 1995. *Emotional intelligence.* New York: Random House.

    Goleman, D. 2006. *Social intelligence: The new science of human relationships.* New York: Random House.

    Hyson, M. 2004. *The emotional development of young children: Building an emotion-centered curriculum,* 2nd ed. Washington,

DC: National Association for the Education of Young Children.

Katz, L., and D. McClellan. 1997. *Fostering children's social competence: The teacher's role.* Washington, DC: National Association for the Education of Young Children.

Riley, D., R.R. San Juan, J. Klinkner, and A. Ramminger. 2008. *Social and emotional development: Connecting science and practice in early childhood settings.* St. Paul, MN: Redleaf Press, and Washington, DC: National Association for the Education of Young Children.

45. Disclaimer: The views and opinions reflected in this essay represent the author's perspectives and not those of the Patterson Institute at the United Negro College Fund.

46. National Research Council and Institute of Medicine. 2000. *From neurons to neighborhood: The science of early childhood development.* J.P. Shonkoff and D.A. Phillips, eds. Committee on Integrating the Science of Early Childhood Development. Board on Children, Youth and Families. Commission on Behavioral and Social Science and Education. Washington, DC: National Academies Press.

47. Maschinot, B. 2008. *The changing face of the United States: The influence of culture on child development.* Washington, DC: ZERO TO THREE.

48. Ibid. Also see Kea, C., G.D. Campbell-Whatley, and H.V. Richards. 2006. *Becoming culturally responsive educators: Rethinking teacher education pedagogy.* National Center for Culturally Responsive Educational Systems.

    Derman-Sparks, L., and J.O. Edwards. 2009. *Anti-bias education: For young children and ourselves.* Washington, DC: National Association for the Education of Young Children.

49. Kea, et al. 2006. Also see Maxwell, K.L., C.-I. Lim, and D.M. Early. 2006. *Early childhood teacher preparation programs in the United States:* National report. Chapel Hill, NC: The University of North Carolina, Frank Porter Graham Child Development Institute.

    Scott Heller, S., and L. Gilkerson, eds. 2009. *A practical guide to reflective supervision.* Washington, DC: ZERO TO THREE.

50. Maxwell, et al., *Early childhood teacher preparation.* Also see Heller, et al., *Practical guide to reflective supervision.*

51. Child Trends Data Bank. Racial and ethnic composition of the child population. http://www.childtrendsdatabank.org/?q=node/234. Accessed February 16, 2010.

52. Derman-Sparks, L., and ABC Task Force. 1989. *Anti-bias curriculum: Tools for empowering young children.* Washington, DC: National Association for the Education of Young Children.

53. Maschinot, B. 2008. *The changing face of the United States: The influence of culture on child development.* Washington, DC: ZERO TO THREE.

54. Derman-Sparks, L., and J.O. Edwards. 2009. *Anti-bias education for young children and ourselves.* Washington, DC: National Association for the Education of Young Children.

55. Maschinot, *The changing face.* 2008.

    Also see Derman-Sparks and Edwards, *Anti-bias education for young children and ourselves.* 2009.

56. Delpit, L. 1996. *Other people's children: Cultural conflict in the classroom.* New York: New Press.

    Also see Harris, Y.R., and D. Bergen. 2008. *Children and families of African origin: A guide for educators and service providers.* Olney, MD: Association for Childhood Education International.

57. Derman-Sparks, L., and C.B. Phillips. 1996. *Teaching/learning anti-bias education: A developmental approach.* New York: Teachers College Press.

58. Many of the ideas in this article are adapted from Espinosa, L. 2009. *Getting it right for young children from diverse backgrounds: Applying research to improve practice.* Upper Saddle River, NJ: Pearson. Also see National Early Literacy Panel. 2008. *Developing early literacy: Report of the National Early Literacy Panel.* Washington, DC: National Institute for Literacy.

59. Adapted from Espinosa, *Getting it right.*

60. Dual-language learners are children 3 to 6 years old who are learning a second language while still developing basic competency in their first language. These children are also referred to as English language learners or sometimes as English learners.

61. Espinosa, *Getting it right*, 62–103. Also see Tabors, P.O. 2008. *One child, two languages.* Baltimore, MD: Brookes Publishing. S.B. Neuman and D.K. Dickinson, eds. 2001. *Handbook of early literacy research.* New York: Guilford Press.

62. Fillmore, L.W. 2000 autumn. Loss of family languages: Should education be concerned? *Theory into Practice,* 203–210.

63. For a fuller description of quality practices for DLLs, see Castro, D., L. Espinosa, and M. Páez. (in press). Defining and measuring quality early childhood practices that promote dual language learners' development and learning. Chapter in forthcoming book by Brookes Publishing.

64. Clements, D.H., and J. Sarama. 2007. *Building blocks — SRA real math, grade preK.* Columbus, OH: SRA/McGraw-Hill.

65. National Council of Teachers of Mathematics. 2006. *Curriculum focal points for prekindergarten through grade 8 mathematics: A quest for coherence.* Reston, VA: National Council of Teachers of Mathematics.

66. National Research Council. 2009. *Mathematics in early childhood: Learning paths toward excellence and equity.* Washington, DC: National Academies Press.

    Also see Clements, D.H., and J. Sarama. 2008. Mathematics and technology: Supporting learning for students and teachers. In O.N. Saracho and B. Spodek, eds. *Contemporary perspectives on science and technology in early childhood education* (pp. 127–147). Charlotte, NC: Information Age Publishing.

    Clements, D.H., and J. Sarama. 2009. *Learning and teaching early math: The learning trajectories approach.* New York: Routledge.

67. The research reported here was supported in part by the Institute of Education Sciences, U.S. Department of Education, through Grant No. R305K05157 to the University at Buffalo, State University of New York, entitled "Scaling Up TRIAD: Teaching Early Mathematics for Understanding with Trajectories and

Technologies," and by the National Science Foundation under Grant No. ESI-9730804, "Building Blocks — Foundations for Mathematical Thinking, Pre-Kindergarten to Grade 2: Research-based Materials Development." The opinions expressed are those of the authors and do not represent views of the U.S. Department of Education.

68. Zigler, E.F., Dorothy G. Singer, and Sandra J. Bishop-Joseph, eds. 2004. *Children's play: The roots of reading*. Washington, DC: ZERO TO THREE.

69. Paley, V.G. 2004. *A child's work*. Chicago: University of Chicago Press.

70. Elkind, D. 2007. *The power of play*. Boston: Da Capo. This article draws heavily from this book.

71. Piaget, J. 1951. *Play, dreams and imitation in childhood*. Norton: New York.

    Piaget, J., and Alina Szeminska. 1952. *The child's conception of number*. London: Routledge and Kegan Paul.

72. Brown, S. 2009. *Play: How it shapes the brain, opens the imagination and invigorates the soul*. New York: Avery.

73. Isenberg, J.P., and N. Quisenberry. 2002 fall. Play: essential for all children. Position paper of the Association for Childhood Education International. *Childhood Education* http://www.acei.org/playpaper.htm. Accessed February 16, 2010.

74. Miller, E., and J. Almon. 2009. *Crises in the kindergarten*. College Park, MD: The Alliance for Childhood.

75. For more information about peer group and gender interaction, see Carlson, S.M., and Marjorie Taylor. 2005. Imaginary companions and impersonated characters: Sex differences in children's fantasy play. *Merrill-Palmer Quarterly* 51 (1): 93-118.

    Also see Fabes, R.A., C.L. Martin and L.D. Hanish. 2003. Young children's play qualities in same-, other-, and mixed peer groups. *Child Development* 74 (3): 921–932.

76. See Fantuzzo, J.S., Y. Sekino, and H.L. Cohen. March 2004. An examination of the contributions of interactive peer play to salient classroom competencies for urban Head Start children. *Psychology in the Schools* 41 (3): 323–336.

    Lindsey, L.W., and M.J. Colwell. 2001. Preschoolers emotional competence: links to pretend and physical play. *Child Study Journal* 33 (1): 39–52.

77. See Christakis, D.A.Z., J. Frederick, and M.M. Garrison. 2007. Effect of block play on language acquisition and attention in toddlers. *Archives of Pediatrics and Adolescent Medicine* 161 (10): 967–971.

    Also see: Cohen, L., and J. Uhry, 2007. Young children's discourse strategies during block play: A Bakhtinian approach. *Journal of Research in Childhood Education* 21.

    Park, B., L. Jeong, and B.F. Boyd. 2008 winter. Young children's block play and mathematical learning. *Journal of Research in Childhood Education,* vol. 23, 157n2.

    Miyakawa, Y., C. Kamii, and M. Nagahiro. 2005 summer. The development of logico-mathematical thinking in ages 1-3 in play with blocks and an incline. *Journal of Research in Childhood Education* 19, no. 4, 292.

78. See Lindsey, E.W. and J. Mize. 2000. Parent-child physical and pretense play: Links to children's social competence. *Merrill-Palmer Quarterly* 46 (4): 565–587.

    Ginsburg, K. 2007. The importance of play in promoting healthy child development and maintaining strong parental bonds. *American Journal of Pediatrics* 119 (1): 182–191.

    Wood, E., S. Desmarais, and S. Gugula. 2002. The impact of parenting experience on gender stereotyped toy play of children. *Sex Roles* 47 (1–2): 39–50.

    Morelock, M.J., P.M. Brown, and A.-M. Morrissey. 2003. Pretend play and maternal scaffolding: Comparisons of toddlers with advanced development, typical development and hearing impairment. *Roeper Review* 26 (1): 41–51.

    Tamis-LeMonda, C.S., J.D. Shannon, N.J. Cabrera, and M.E. Lamb. 2004. Father and mother's play with their two-year-olds: Contributions to cognitive and language development. *Child Development* 75 (6): 1806–1820.

    Kazura, K. 2000. Fathers' qualitative and quantitative involvement: An investigation of attachment, play and social interaction. *Journal of Men's Studies* 9 (1): 41–57.

Clearfield, M.W., and N.M. Nelson. 2006. Sex differences in mothers' speech and play behavior with 6-, 9- and 14-month-old infants. *Sex Roles* 54 (1-2): 127–137.

79. See Malone, M.D. 2006. Differential expression of toy play by preschoolers with and without mental retardation. *Journal of Research in Childhood Education* 21.

80. Craig-Unkefer, L. A., and A.P. Kaiser. 2002. Improving the social communication skills of at risk preschool children in a play context. *Topics in Early Childhood Special Education* 22 (1): 3–13.

81. Coplan, R.J.W., C. Wichmann. and D.G. Lagace-Sequin. 2001 spring/summer. Solitary-active play behavior: A marker variable for maladjustment in the preschool. *Journal of Research in Childhood Education* 15 (2): 164-172.

82. Paley, *A child's work*, 2004.

83. Montessori, M. 1964. *The Montessori method.* New York: Schocken.

84. Elkind, *The power of play*, 2007.

85. Brown, *Play,* 2009.

86. Karen Pittman, interview with the author, June 30, 2006.

87. *Education Week*, June 5, 2008. "Diplomas count 2008: School to college, can state P-16 councils ease the transition?" 2.

88. Arne Duncan, interview with the author, March 3, 2002.

89. West, J., K. Denton, and L. Reaney. 2001. *The Kindergarten Year.* NCES 2001–023. Washington, DC: National Center for Education Statistics.

90. John DeStefano, interview with Hank O'Karma, November 14, 2002.

91. Much of the material in this chapter is adapted from Galinsky, E. 2010. *Mind in the making: The seven essential life skills every child needs.* New York: HarperStudio.

92. Minth-Yazzie, E. 2007. *Voices of students on engagement: A report on the 2006 High School Survey of Student Engagement.* Bloomington: Indiana University.

93. Saffran, J.R. 2001. Words in a sea of sounds: The output of infant statistical learning. *Cognition* 81, no. 2: 149–169; B. Pelucchi, J.F. Hay, and J.R. Saffran. 2009. Statistical learning in a natural language by 8-month olds. *Child Development* 80, no. 3: 674–685; J.R. Saffran, R.N. Aslin, and E.L. Newport. 1996. Statistical learning by 8-month-old infants. *Science* 274, no. 5294: 1926–1928.

94. Xu F., and E.S. Spelke. 2000. Large number discrimination in 6-month-old infants, *Cognition* 74, no. 1: B1–B11.

95. Woodward, A.L. 1998. Infants selectively encode the goal object of an actor's reach, *Cognition* 69, no. 1: 1–34.

96. Philip David Zelazo, interview with the author, December 8, 2008.

97. Adele Diamond, interview with the author, October 4, 2008

98. Zelazo interview.

99. Dehaene, S. 2009. *Reading in the Brain: The science and evolution of a human invention.* New York: Penguin, 318.

100. Diamond interview.

101. Michael Posner, interview with the author, June 26, 2008; M.R. Rueda, et al. 2005. Training, maturation, and genetic influences on the development of executive attention, *Proceedings of the National Academy of Sciences* 102, no. 41: 14931–14936,

102. Edersheim, E.H. 2007. *The Definitive Drucker.* New York: McGraw-Hill, 45.

103. Ross Thompson, interview with the author, September 28, 2001.

104. Alison Gopnik, interview with the author, November 29, 2001. Capage, L., and A.C. Watson. 2001. Individual differences in theory of mind, aggressive behavior, and social skills in young children. *Early Education and Development* 12, no. 4: 613–628. Watson, A.C., et al. 1999. Social interaction skills and theory of mind in young children. *Developmental Psychology* 35, no. 2: 386–391.

Gopnik was referring to the research of Janet Wilde Astington of the University of Toronto. See, for example, Astington, J.W., and J. Pelletier. Theory of mind, language, and learning in the early years: Developmental origins of school readiness. In B.D. Homer and C.S. Tamis-LeMonda, eds. 2005. *The development of social cognition and communication* (pp. 205–230). Mahwah, NJ: Erlbaum.

105. J.L. Aber, interview with the author, August 2, 2006.

Also see Aber, J.L., et al. Resolving conflict creatively: Evaluating the developmental effects of a school-based violence prevention program in neighborhood and classroom context. *Development and Psychopathology* 10, no. 2: 187–213.

Jones, S.M., J.L. Brown, and J.L. Aber. Classroom settings as targets of intervention and research. In M. Shinn and H. Yoshikawa, eds. 2008. *Toward positive youth development: Transforming schools and community programs* (pp. 58–77). New York: Oxford University Press.

106. Families and Work Institute. 2005. *National Study of Employers* (unpublished data). New York: Families and Work Institute.

107. Adele Diamond, e-mail to the author, August 16, 2009.

108. Kathy Hirsh-Pasek, interview with Amy McCampbell, February 22, 2005. Kathy Hirsh-Pasek, e-mail to the author, August 6, 2009.

109. National Scientific Council on the Developing Child. 2005. Excessive stress disrupts the architecture of the developing brain. (working paper no. 3). Cambridge, MA: Harvard University, National Scientific Council on the Developing Child. http://www.developingchild.net/pubs/wp. html. Accessed February 16, 2010. National Research Council and Institute of Medicine. 2000. *From neurons to neighborhood: The science of early childhood development.* J.P. Shonkoff and D.A. Phillips, eds. Committee on Integrating the Science of Early Childhood Development. Board on Children, Youth and Families. Washington, DC: National Academies Press.

110. Carol Dweck, interview with the author, April 17, 2008. Dweck, C.S. 2006. *Mindset: The new psychology of success.* New York: Ballantine. Diener, C.I., and C.S. Dweck. 1978. An analysis of learned helplessness: Continuous changes in performance, strategy, and achievement cognitions following failure. *Journal of Personality and Social Psychology* 36, no. 5: 451–462.

111. Galinsky, E. 2010. *Mind in the making: the seven essential skills every child needs.* New York: HarperStudio. Galinsky, E. 2006. *The benefits of high-quality early childhood education programs: What makes the difference?* Washington, DC: Committee for Economic Development. www.ced.org.

112. From the Pathways Mapping Initiative of the Center for the Study of Social Policy. http://www.cssp.org/major_initiatives/pathways.html. Accessed February 16, 2010. The 191-page Pathway to Children Ready for School and Succeeding at Third Grade may be downloaded at http://www.cssp.org/uploadFiles/3RD GRADE PATHWAY PDF 9-07.pdf. Accessed February 16, 2010.

113. National Research Council and Institute of Medicine. 2000. *From neurons to neighborhood: The science of early childhood development.* J.P. Shonkoff and D.A. Phillips, eds. Committee on Integrating the Science of Early Childhood Development. Board on Children, Youth and Families. Washington, DC: National Academies Press.

114. Schweinhart, L.J., J. Montie, Z. Xiang, W.S. Barnett, C.R. Belfield, and M. Nores. 2005. Lifetime effects: The High/Scope Perry Preschool study through age 40. *The State Yearbook.* 2009. National Institute for Early Education Research.

115. Reynolds, A.R., J.A. Temple, D.L. Robertson, and E.A. Mann. 2001. Long-term effects of an early intervention on educational achievement and juvenile arrest: A 15-year follow-up of low-income children in public schools. *JAMA* 285 (18): 2339–2346.

Campbell, F.A., C.T. Ramey, E.P. Pungello, J. Sparling, and S. Miller-Johnson. 2002. Early childhood education: Young adult outcomes from the Abecedarian Project. *Applied Developmental Science,* 6: 42–57

116. Heckman, J.J., and F. Cunha. 2006. *Investing in our young people.* Chicago: University of Chicago Press.

117. Barnett, W.S., D.J. Epstein, A.H. Friedman, J. Stevenson Boyd, and J.T. Hustedt. 2008. The state of preschool 2008. *State Preschool Yearbook.* New Brunswick, NJ: Rutgers University, National Institute for Early Education Research.

118. Ibid.

119. Ibid.

120. Ibid.

121. Copple, B., and S. Bredekamp. 2009. *Developmentally appropriate practice in early childhood programs serving children birth through age 8.* Washington, DC: National Association for the Education of Young Children.

122. This article was written prior to the author assuming her current position with the United States Department of Education.

123. Dickens, C. 1908. *A tale of two cities.* New York: Harcourt Mifflin.

124. Black, P., and D. Wiliam. October 1998. Inside the black box: Raising standards through classroom assessment, *Phi Delta Kappan,* vol. 80, 139–44.

    Also see National Early Childhood Accountability Task Force 2007. *Taking stock: Assessing and improving early childhood learning and program quality.* Washington, DC: Author.

    National Research Council, ed. 2008. *Early childhood assessment: Why, what, and how?* Committee on Developmental Outcomes and Assessments for Young Children. Washington, DC, Board on Children, Youth, and Families, Board on Testing and Assessment, Division of Behavioral and Social Sciences and Education.

125. National Early Childhood Accountability Task Force. 2007. *Taking stock.*

126. Stiggins, R.J. 1991. Assessment literacy. *Phi Delta Kappan,* 72 (7): 534–539.

127. Administration for Children and Families. 2006. Early Head Start benefits children and families: research to practice brief, April. http://www.acf.hhs.gov/programs/opre/ehs/ehs_resrch/index.html. Accessed November 23, 2009.

    Johnson, D., and T. Walker. 1991. *Final report of an evaluation of the Avance parent education and family support program.* Report submitted to the Carnegie Corporation. San Antonio, TX: Avance. AVANCE: Unlocking America's Potential. n.d. http://www.avance.org/. Accessed February 16, 2010.

    SRI International. 2007. *Statewide evaluation of First 5 California.* Menlo Park, CA: Author. Strengthening Families Program. n.d. http://www.strengtheningfamiliesprogram.org/ publications.html. Accessed February 16, 2010.

128. Sweet, M.A., and M.I. Appelbaum. 2004. Is home visiting an effective strategy?: A meta-analytic review of home visiting programs for families with young children. *Child Development,* 75 (5): 1435–1456.

129. Olds, D. 2006. The nurse-family partnership: An evidence-based preventive intervention. *Infant Mental Health Journal* 27 (1): 5–25.

130. Rose, C. 2009. The parent teacher home visit project. *FINE Newsletter* 1 (1). Cambridge, MA: Harvard Family Research Project. http://hfrp.org/family-involvement/publications-resources/the-parent-teacher-home-visit-project. Accessed October 28, 2009.

131. This project is a partnership between the Harvard Graduate Shool of Education, the Boston public schools, and the Boston mayor's office. No published information exists about this project. Please contact author Richard Weissbourd for more information.

132. Williams, D. 2009. More than just a welcome mat. *Catalyst Chicago. Independent Reporting on Urban Schools XX* (4): 4–7. Accessed February 16, 2010 from http://www.catalyst-Chicago.org/news/index.php?item=2584&cat=23.

133. Additional material that may be useful includes Bernard, J.K., A. Winsler, C. Bleiker, J. Ginieniewicz, and A.L. Madigan. 2008. "Read my story!": Using the early authors program to promote early literacy among diverse, urban preschool children in poverty. *Journal of Education for Students Placed at Risk* 31 (1): 76–105.

    The Early Authors Program. n.d. www.ryerson.ca/~bernhard/early.html. Accessed February 16, 2010. http://www.ryerson.ca~bernhard/bilingual1.html. Accessed February 16, 2010.

    Korfmer, J., B. Green, F. Staerkel, C. Peterson, G. Cook, L. Roggman, et al. 2008. Parent involvement in early childhood home visiting. *Child Care Youth Forum* 37: 171–196.

    Lonigan, C.J., and G.J. Whitehurst. 1998. Relative efficacy of parent and teacher involvement in a shared-reading intervention for preschool children from low-income backgrounds. *Early Childhood Research Quarterly* 13 (2): 263–290.

Raising a Reader. n.d. http://www.raisinga reader.org/. Accessed February 16, 2010.

U.S. Department of Health and Human Services. *The home-based supervisor's manual for the Head Start home-based program option.* Washington, DC: Early Head Start National Resource Center @ ZERO TO THREE.

134. For further information related to the ideas in this article, please see:

Behrmann, R.E. 2000. Children and computer technology. Special issue, *The Future of Children* 10.

Clements, D.H., and J. Sarama. 2002. Teaching with computers in early childhood education: Strategies and professional development. *Journal of Early Childhood Teacher Education* 23: 215–226.

Clements, D.H., and J. Sarama. 2003. Strip mining for gold: Research and policy in educational technology — A response to "Fool's gold." *Educational Technology Review* 11 (1): 7–69.

Clements, D.H., and J. Sarama. 2008. Mathematics and technology: Supporting learning for students and teachers. In O.N. Saracho and B. Spodek, eds. *Contemporary perspectives on science and technology in early childhood education* (pp. 127–147). Charlotte, NC: Information Age Publishing.

Clements, D.H., and J. Sarama. 2009. *Learning and teaching early math: The learning trajectories approach.* New York: Routledge.

Sarama, J., and D.H. Clements. 2006. Mathematics, young students, and computers: Software, teaching strategies and professional development. *The Mathematics Educator* 9 (2): 112–134.

135. Clarke, A.C. 2000. Hazards of prophecy: The failure of imagination. In *Profiles of the future: An enquiry into the limits of the possible* (1962, rev. 1973), 19–26. Guernsey, Channel Islands: Guernsey Press.

136. References for the National Institute for Early Education Research (NIEER) and for this article are:

Barnett, W.S., A.H. Friedman, J.T. Hustedt, J. Stevenson-Boyd. 2009. An overview of prekindergarten policy in the United States. In R.C.

Pianta and C. Howes, eds. 2009. *The promise of pre-K.* Baltimore: Brookes Publishing.

Barnett, W.S., D.J. Epstein, A.H. Friedman, J. Stevenson Boyd, and J.T. Hustedt. 2008. The state of preschool 2008. *State preschool yearbook.* New Brunswick, NJ: Rutgers University, National Institute for Early Education Research.
National Early Childhood Accountability Task Force. 2007. *Taking stock: Assessing and improving early childhood learning and program quality.* Washington, DC: Author.

Kagan, S.L., K. Kauerz, and K. Tarrant. 2008. *The early childhood teaching workforce at the fulcrum: An agenda for reform.* New York: Columbia Teachers College Press.

LeMoine, S. 2008. *Workforce designs: A policy blueprint for state early childhood professional development systems.* Washington, DC: National Association for the Education of Young Children.

137. The data referred to in this article can be reviewed in information available on the Web sites of the National Institute for Early Education Research, http://nieer.org/, and the Partnership for America's Economic Success, http://www. partnershipforsuccess.org/index.php?id=01.

138. Levin, H., C. Belfield, P. Muennig, and C. Rouse. 2007. *The costs and benefits of an excellent education for all of America's children.* New York: Teachers College, Columbia University.

139. Walmsley, R. 2009. *World prison population,* 8th ed. London: International Centre for Prison Studies, Kings College London. http://www. kcl.ac.uk/depsta/law/research/icps/downloads/ wppl-8th_41.pdf. Accessed January, 15, 2010.

140. Marshall, A. 1982. *Principles of Economics,* 8th ed. Philadelphia: Porcupine Press. 597.

141. For addition information, please refer to:
Barnett, W.S., and L.N. Masse. 2007. Comparative benefit-cost analysis of the Abecedarian program and its policy implications. *Economics of Education Review* 26: 113–25.

Belfield, C.R., M. Nores, W.S. Barnett, and L. Schweinhart. 2006. The High/Scope Perry Preschool program: Cost-benefit analysis using data from the age-40 follow-up. *Journal of Human Resources* 41, no. 1: 162–90.

Dickens, W.T., and C. Baschnagel. 2009. *The fiscal effects of investing in high-quality pre-school programs.* Washington, DC: The Brookings Institution.

Karoly, L.A., and J.H. Bigelow. 2005. *The economics of investing in universal preschool education in California.* Santa Monica, CA: Rand.

Lynch, R. 2007. *Enriching children, enriching the nation: Public investments in high-quality prekindergarten.* Washington, DC: Economic Policy Institute.

Reynolds, A. J., J.A. Temple, D.L. Robertson, and E.A. Mann. 2002. Age 21 cost-benefit analysis of the Title 1 Chicago Child-Parent Centers. *Educational Evaluation and Policy Analysis* 24: 267–303.

Rolnick, A. J., and R. Grunewald. 2003, Early childhood development = economic investment. *fedgazette,* March.

142. Senge, P. 2006. *The fifth discipline: The art and practice of the learning organization.* London: Random House Business.

Also see Wenger, E., R. McDermott, and W. Synder. 2002. *Cultivating communities of practice.* Boston: Harvard Business School Press. Hord, S., 1997.

Professional learning communities: Communities of continuous inquiry and improvement. Washington, DC: U.S. Department of Education, Office of Educational Research and Improvement, Educational Resources Information Center.

Cooperrider, D., S. Piderit, and R. Fry, eds. 2007. *The handbook of transformative cooperation.* Palo Alto, CA: Stanford Business Books.

143. Kaplan, S. 2002. Building communities—strategies for collaborative learning. *Learning Circuits.* American Society for Training & Development. http://www.astd.org/LC/2002/0802_kaplan.htm. Accessed February 16, 20010.

144. Refer to the World Vision organization for discussion of whole system engagement through collaborative technology, http://www.ovationnet.com/WorldVisionCaseBookChapter.pdf. Accessed February 16, 2010.

145. Of the 192 countries that are members of the United Nations, 30 had reached the saturation point of cell-phone penetration by mid-2006;

within six months, 10 more had joined the group. And the penetration rate is increasing. By May 2009, cell-phone penetration had reached 50% in China and more than 30% in India. By 2005, Africa had become the first continent with more cell phones than land-lines, illustrating how wireless access will help developing countries without copper-wire infrastructures or even a stable electrical grid to leapfrog into a future with widespread Internet access. http://news.mongabay.com/2005/0712-rhett_butler.html. Accessed February 16, 2010.

146. Ginot, H. 1972. *Teacher and child: A book for parents and teachers.* New York: Macmillan. 15–16.

147. Dobbert, M. L., and B. Cooke. 1987. Primate biology and behavior: a stimulus to educational thought and policy. In G. Spindler, ed. 1987 *Education and cultural process: Anthropological approaches.* (pp. 97–116) New York: Waveland Press.

148. Comer, J. P. 2004. *Leave no child behind: Preparing today's youth for tomorrow's world.* New Haven: Yale University Press.

149. Cochran-Smith, M. 2005. Editorial: Teacher education and the outcomes trap. *Journal of Teacher Education* 56 (1): 411–417.

150. For more information about the Harlem Children's Zone, see www.hcz.org. Also see: Tough, P. 2008. *Whatever it takes: Geoffrey Canada's quest to change Harlem and America.* New York: Houghton Mifflin Harcourt.

Whitman, D. 2008. *Sweating the small stuff: Inner city schools and the new paternalism.* Washington, DC: Thomas B. Fordham Institute.

151. From the Pathways Mapping Initiative of the Center for the Study of Social Policy. http://www.cssp.org/major_initiatives/pathways.html. The 191-page Pathway to Children Ready for School and Succeeding at Third Grade can be downloaded at http://www.cssp.org/uploadFiles/3RD GRADE PATHWAY PDF 9-07.pdf.

152. *The American Heritage® Dictionary of the English Language,* Fourth Edition, © 2009 by Houghton Mifflin.

153. NAEYC Statement of commitment 2005.

154. http://en.wikipedia.org/wiki/Timeline_of_children's_rights_in_the_United_States

155. Many items in this timeline are drawn from

National Association for the Education of Young Children. (2001). *NAEYC at 75.* Washington DC: National Association for the Education of Young Children. 6–32.

156. http://en.wikipedia.org/wiki/African-American_Civil_Rights_Movement_(1955–1968)

157. http://en.wikipedia.org/wiki/Native_American_boarding_schools

158. http://en.wikipedia.org/wiki/Timeline_of_children's_rights_in_the_United_States

159. Pre-K Now. October 2009. *Votes count: Legislative action on pre-k fiscal year 2010.* Washington, DC: The Pew Center on the States.

Massachusetts Budget and Policy Center. *An unstable ladder: how the fiscal crisis is threatening education and work support programs for many women.* Boston: Massachusetts Budget and Policy Center.